Making Memory

Making Memory

Jewish and Christian Explorations in Monument, Narrative, and Liturgy

ALANA M. VINCENT

PICKWICK *Publications* · Eugene, Oregon

MAKING MEMORY
Jewish and Christian Explorations in Monument, Narrative, and Liturgy

Copyright © 2013 Alana M. Vincent. All rights reserved. Except for brief quotations in critical publications or reviews, no part of this book may be reproduced in any manner without prior written permission from the publisher. Write: Permissions, Wipf and Stock Publishers, 199 W. 8th Ave., Suite 3, Eugene, OR 97401.

Pickwick Publications
An Imprint of Wipf and Stock Publishers
199 W. 8th Ave., Suite 3
Eugene, OR 97401

www.wipfandstock.com

ISBN 13: 978-1-62032-049-5

Cataloguing-in-Publication data:

Vincent, Alana M.

Making memory : Jewish and Christian explorations in monument, narrative, and liturgy / Alana M. Vincent, with a foreword by David Jasper.

xiv + 194 pp. ; 23 cm. Includes bibliographical references and index.

ISBN 13: 978-1-62032-049-5

1. Memory. 2. War and society. 3. War memorials. 4. Holocaust, Jewish (1939–1945)—Influence. 4. Holocaust (Jewish theology). 5. Holocaust (Christian theology). 6. Sophocles. Antigone. 7. Montgomery, L. M. (Lucy Maud), 1874–1942. Anne of Green Gables. 8. Vimy Memorial (France). I. Jasper, David. II. Title.

BM645 V47 2013

Manufactured in the U.S.A.

The plan of Vimy Memorial which appears on p. 97 is copyright Commonwealth War Graves Commission and is used by permission.

The image on p. 112 is copyright Tim Davies (2007) and is used by permission of the artist.

All other images are copyright the author.

For Mark,
my sounding-board and fellow traveller.

The fault lines of exile and diaspora always run deep, and we are always from elsewhere, and from elsewhere before that.

—André Aciman, *False Papers* (New York: Picador, 2001).

Regret is not the end of the story; it is the middle of the story.

When Jean was done, she knew how careful she had to be. Not to erase, but to wash away.

—Anne Michaels, *The Winter Vault* (Toronto: McClelland & Stewart, 2009).

Contents

List of Illustrations viii
Foreword by David Jasper ix
Acknowledgments xi
Abbreviations xiii

Prelude   1

PART ONE: Remembering to Forget

1   Remembering Amalek   11

2   Antigone and Athenian War-dead: Body and Identity in the Greek tradition   32

PART TWO: Mourning the Absent

Introduction   47

3   *Anne of Green Gables* and the Transformation of Public Mourning   51

4   Making Memory Solid: Jane Urquhart and The Canadian National Vimy Memorial   82

Interlude   111

PART THREE: Absent Mourners

5   Worship in the Ruins   119

6   Outside the Sanctuary   141

Coda   171

Bibliography   173
Index   189

List of Illustrations

Figure 1   Front view, Canadian National Memorial at Vimy.

Figure 2   Figure of Canada, Canadian National Memorial at Vimy.

Figure 3   Torchbearer and Spirit of Sacrifice, Canadian National Memorial at Vimy.

Figure 4   Justice, plaster figure, ½ scale. War Museum, Ottawa, Ontario.

Figure 5   Faith (detail), plaster figure, ½ scale. War Museum, Ottawa, Ontario.

Figure 6   Hope (detail), plaster figure, ½ scale. War Museum, Ottawa, Ontario.

Figure 7   Peace, plaster figure, ½ scale. War Museum, Ottawa, Ontario.

Figure 8   Torchbearer, plaster figure, ½ scale. War Museum, Ottawa, Ontario.

Figure 9   Plan of Vimy Memorial. Image courtesy of Commonwealth War Graves Commission.

Figure 10   Tim Davies, European Drawings (2007). Used by permission of the artist.

Figure 11   Main staircase, The Jewish Museum, Berlin.

Figure 12   Menashe Kadishman, "Fallen Leaves", The Jewish Museum, Berlin.

Figure 13   Room of Names, Memorial to the Murdered Jews of Europe, Berlin.

Foreword

The twentieth century is now but a memory, existing in the minds, souls, and seared flesh of those who survived it and we who write and read the words that become our past. Theology—whether Jewish or Christian—is embedded in the past and the command to remember, or to forget. But remembering or forgetting are both unstable and unreliable. We remember and we forget but in part, as individuals and as communities. We remember things that we would prefer to forget, or seek to blot out those things which make life intolerable or are an offense. Alana Vincent's book returns us to the past in memorials of words and stone, to memories that remain close to us in individual bodies and their collective identities, and that are made meaningful in the ancient words of Scripture and sacred traditions. Her book begins in the memorials of war and the possibility of any theology after the Holocaust, linking the violent history of the twentieth century with the internal contradictions both to remember and to forget Amalek (Deut 25:17–19): to remember what Amalek did to the Israelites on their journey from Egypt, and then not to forget to "blot out the remembrance of Amalek from under heaven." We must remember to forget.

A central text in this discussion, and not from Scripture, is read in two versions: the *Antigone* of Sophocles and of Jean Anouilh, the latter written during the Second World War. Thus we move across the millennia of human history in the contesting over the dead body of Polynices, from the ancient history of Israel, to ancient Greece as early as the fifth century BCE, up to the history of our own times in Europe and the Western world, bound together in grief for those whose lives end violently and who abide in our memories, both individual and national. They are memorialized in stone, but even more often in words, and at the heart of this book lie the works of novelists and writers who remember through works of the imagination.

The violence of war and genocide tears into our narratives and our worldviews even as it haunts our memories. Unable to forget and finally unable to forgive, we strive to stabilize and anchor the memories which

Foreword

haunt us in forms and texts which spill over the boundaries of religious forms of consolation and theological utterance, and in its exploration of "liturgical moment" this book finds them in forms of memorial which do not seek to replace any formal liturgy, but are, rather, "moments and interactions in which the functional concerns of formal liturgy are attended to."

A book such as this cannot be easy to read or absorb as it gives attention to things of the deepest importance. It defies over-simple categories, and the danger of any attempt to settle things in their terms—profoundly religious, but beyond religion, deeply committed to ways of Jewish and Christian thinking and practice, but finally lodged in spaces of humanity that are both and neither. It draws us to give attention to public memorials which we too often see and reflect on too little, as well as the literary texts which seek to give expression to hauntings of the mind and spirit that are beyond words. The reader of this book should expect to be unsettled and moved, called to remember things that we would often prefer to forget when forgetting is impossible. In its varieties of texts it seeks the reconciliation of the promises of theology and faith with the disruptions and ruptures within the human chaos of history within which all of us are lodged as both its victims and it perpetrators. It reminds us of the crucial importance of literature and art as they unpick easy resolutions, yet continue to offer, in their utterances, the possibility of our continued existence in spite of the violence and in the face of death itself.

David Jasper
University of Glasgow

Acknowledgments

The production of this book—from its genesis as a doctoral thesis at the University of Glasgow, through several revisions, which finally resulted in the object you hold in your hands (or the text you behold on the screen of your e-reader)—has taken place over five years, in ten different countries, in conversation with a wide number of individuals, and with the support of several institutions. In particular, I would like to thank:

My colleagues at the University of Glasgow, especially David Jasper, Julie Clague, Meg MacDonald, Werner G. Jeanrond, Sarah Nicholson, and Heather Walton, and my former colleagues at the Swedish Theological Institute in Jerusalem: Jesper Svartvik, Håkan Bengtsson, and Gunnar Haaland.

Petra Carlsson, Mattias Martinson, and Lena Roos from the University of Uppsala, and Jayne Svenungsson from Stockholm School of Theology, who conspired together to ensure that my time as a visiting scholar in Sweden was both productive and comfortable, as well as Dorotoa Flipczak of the University of Łodz for arranging for me to meet Jane Urquhart—and to Jane Urquhart herself; for her helpful remarks on a very early piece of this project.

Laura Levitt, Pamela Anderson, David Klemm, Michael Mack, and Melissa Raphael, Priscilla Stuckey, and Dan Zins, for their input, encouragement, and support.

The Rothschild Foundation (Hanadiv) Europe and the Barbro Osher Pro Suecia Foundation for sponsoring the postdoctoral fellowships which enabled me to complete the final revisions on the manuscript.

Bob Anger of The Presbyterian Church in Canada Archives and Records Office, Toronto, the archives staff at Queen's University, Kingston, Ontario, the on-site staff of the Canadian National Monument at Vimy, and Gerrit Wegener of the Kaiser-Wilhelm-Gedächtniskirche, Berlin, for the research assistance they have provided.

Acknowledgments

The libraries and special collections at Emory University, the New York Public Library, the University of Waterloo School of Architecture, Wilfred Laurier University, the Canadian War Museum, and the National Archives of Canada, for providing me with reference material and a place to work while travelling.

The Commonwealth War Graves Commission and Tim Davies for permission to use images contained herein.

The members of a mysterious online discussion group: Kara Andersen, Michelle Brown Boucher, James J. Donahue, Jane Dryden, Alexandra Gerber, Max L. Goldman, Rebecca Futo Kennedy, Valéria M. Souza, and Erica Owens Yeager.

My postgraduate colleagues, who read, commented, edited, and encouraged many, many drafts of the papers that turned into chapters that turned into a thesis that turned into a book, especially Mark Godin, Elizabeth Anderson, Anna Fisk, Amanullah De Sondy, Rachel Kent, and Jennifer Reek.

And, finally, thanks especially to my family for their staunch support, even when they may not have been entirely certain what it was they were supporting, and to Alexandros Salazar, for his unwavering friendship and sarcasm.

Abbreviations

ANCIENT AND MEDIEVAL SOURCES

m. Meg.	Mishnah Megillah
m. Pesaḥ.	Mishnah Pesaḥim
Soph.Ant.	Antigone, by Sophocles
MT	Mishneh Torah

NOVELS

By L. M. Montgomery

AGG	*Anne of Green Gables*
AA	*Anne of Avonlea*
AI	*Anne of the Island*
AHD	*Anne's House of Dreams*
RV	*Rainbow Valley*
RI	*Rilla of Ingleside*
BQ	*The Blythes are Quoted*

By Other Authors

FP	*Fugitive Pieces*, by Anne Michaels
SC	*The Stone Carvers*, by Jane Urquhart
YSE	*Your Sad Eyes and Unforgettable Mouth*, by Edeet Ravel

Abbreviations

ORGANIZATIONS AND PLACES, AND RELATED ITEMS

PCC	The Presbyterian Church in Canada
A&P	Acts and Proceedings of the General Assembly of The Presbyterian Church in Canada (distinguished by year)
CoS	Church of Scotland
CBMC	Canadian Battlefields Memorial Commission
KWG	Kaiser-Wilhelm-Gedächtniskirche
MH	Memorial Hall

Prelude

This is a book about living with the past—not about memory itself *per se*, but about the process of constructing cultural memory, about the negotiation, implicit or explicit, between what is remembered, transmuted into narrative, handed on from generation to generation, and what is forgotten, unspoken, overlooked. My underlying assumption is that the understanding of the past generated by such a process plays an essential role in shaping attitudes and actions of individuals and societies in the present. This understanding ("memory") is at times difficult to distinguish from the process of its formation ("memorialization"); the former is often the only evidence that may be found of the latter. That the two concepts blur together in discourse heightens the need for clarity on this point. The process of memorialization is never complete; memory is not set in stone—it is constantly open to re-negotiation, and "reading backwards"—an insertion of more recent understanding and experience into discourse about the past. This is discussed more fully in chapter 1.[1]

This book is about identity. Memory and individual identity are closely linked; we are what we remember as much as we are anything else. This is apparent when philosophers of identity theorize scenarios such as the transplant of one person's memory into another's body—the term for such a scenario in science fiction is the "body swap," which is to say that we speak of Rachel inhabiting Leah's body, rather than Leah acquiring Rachel's

---

1. An example of reading backwards is brought forward by Nicola King, in the introduction to her book *Memory, Narrative, Identity*, when she describes a Holocaust survivor recounting his experience, constantly punctuated by the insertion of the claim "he didn't know that then"—understanding he acquired after the fact was so intimately bound up in his memory of what he did experience that he could not separate the two in his recounting. King writes that "[h]is memory of that moment seems to have been deeply affected by what he didn't know at the time of the event: what he also has to remember is the painful fact of his own ignorance" (1).

brain or personality; the *locus* of identity in such a scenario is with the consciousness, rather than the body.[2] At the same time, an amnesiac is a person who has "lost their memory," not an entirely new person; memory is not the sole criterion which determines identity. Nor is identity shaped just by personal experience, but also by the complex of stories—history, folk tales, other people's memories—which surround individuals and help them to locate themselves within their socio-cultural *milieu*. Ricoeur argues that "we never cease to reinterpret the narrative identity that constitutes us, in light of the narratives proposed to us by our culture."[3] In other words, such stories (which I will define in my first chapter as components of "cultural memory") do not simply inform people about past events, they provide models from which one might learn how to perform the "-ness" of group identity—Canadianness, Jewishness.[4]

This book is about imagination, which refers to both "the power or capacity to form internal images of objects or ideas not actually present to the senses, including remembered objects" and the activity of the mind exercising this capacity.[5] Sidra Ezrahi has written that "what is 'remembered' is of course also imagined, as mimesis takes on the authority and license of memory and memory becomes an article of faith. In its most radical form, memory and imagination describe a circularity that promotes an aesthetics of the whole."[6]

Memorials, the vehicles constructed to convey cultural memory from one generation to the next, depend upon imagination: they stem from the imagination of their creators, and act on the imagination of those who encounter them. This is true of each of the sub-types of memorial with which I am concerned here. Monuments invite the visitor into a physical space, but within that space one encounters images (and sometimes text) which prompt the construction of a mental picture of the events and lives represented therein.[7] Narrative invites the reader into a space that is not physical, but nonetheless real, as Ricoeur insists: "To speak of a world of the text is to stress the feature belonging to every literary work of opening before it a horizon of possible experience, a world in which it would be possible to

2. See Schechtman, *Selves*, 16–17.
3. Ricoeur, "Life in Quest," 32.
4. See also B. Anderson, *Imagined Communities*.
5. *Oxford English Dictionary*, 2nd ed., s.v. "imagination."
6. Ezrahi, *Booking Passage*, 9.
7. See especially my discussion in chapter 4.

live. [...] To appropriate a work through reading is to unfold the world horizon implicit in it."[8] This unfolding, like the reconstruction of events represented by a monument, takes place primarily in the reader's mind; it is a work of the imagination. The barrier between fiction and memory is more permeable than one might expect; both are constructions. This also holds true for the third category of memorial I consider, liturgy.

Liturgy, and especially Jewish liturgy, as I discuss more fully in my concluding chapter, has historically been considered to be a type of text which describes a public performance of worship.[9] Neither the text nor its performance is imaginary—and, indeed, some might take offence at such a characterization[10]—however, the space which they construct for participants is *imaginative*. The many variations on the Passover Seder, for example, are carefully constructed to guide participants through an imaginative reconstruction of the exodus, so that each participant might "regard him or herself as if he or she had come out of Egypt."[11] Likewise, the *Ne'ilah* service on Yom Kippur is dominated by the image of the worshippers standing at the gates of heaven, pleading for admittance; the worshippers, in fact, pray as though they are at those gates, they imagine themselves in that space just as the participants at Passover imagine themselves as slaves in Egypt.[12] The imaginative space of liturgy differs from that of narrative in that it is a shared space; liturgy is primarily a communal endeavor.[13] However, liturgical space functions in a similar fashion to narrative space, insofar as

---

8. Ricoeur, "Life in Quest," 26.

9. See Hoffman, *Beyond the Text*, 1–3.

10. For example, Stanley Hauerwas insists that "Attending liturgy is a Christian's duty because it's *true*. It's what makes life make any sense at all" (emphasis added) in "Christianity," 530.

11. *m. Pesaḥ* 10:5 (adjusted for gender neutrality). For a more robust discussion of the imaginative function of several variants on the Passover seder, see my article "Seder and Imagined Landscape."

12. See Hammer, *Entering the High Holy Days*, 167–74.

13. The difficulty with considering liturgy to be entirely communal is that this results in having to consider the recitation of the Amidah, for example, as liturgical when it takes place in the presence of a *minyan*, but not when it is recited privately. While context is certainly important, such a finely drawn distinction verges on nonsensical—a Catholic priest who says the Daily Office by himself is still engaged in a liturgical performance, and for the same reason that some solitary acts of Jewish worship ought to be considered liturgical: it connects him to the history and life of the community, even if the community itself is not physically present. This is yet another example of the imaginative dimension of liturgy.

it provides the community with an identity-generating narrative that may be interpreted and re-interpreted as circumstances and the needs of the community change.

The issues surrounding memorialization in the past century are, as even this brief prelude indicates, complex and diverse, and the form of this book is dictated by the complexity of its material. My structure is loosely inspired by Emmanuel Levinas's suggestion that Europe (by which I understand a civilization which also extends to former European colonies such as Canada, Australia, and the United States) "is the Bible and the Greeks," a culture formed in the interstices between two distinct modes of being in the world.[14] What follows is an attempt at disentangling the two strands, laying them side-by-side, and seeing how they pull on one another.

The Bible and the Greeks are, in this work, represented by the two ancient approaches to loss and catastrophe, which I probe in my first two chapters: Amalek and Antigone, memory and mourning. It is important to note at the outset that, in this scheme, Amalek emphatically does not represent vengeance, but rather the ambivalence of Deuteronomy 25:17–19, a people caught between the urge to blot out the traumatic past, and a pressing need to remember the history which has shaped them. My reading of this passage does not engage with the idea of the ban, חרם, which is a vector of analysis commonly applied by (Christian) biblical scholars.[15] In her study, *War in the Hebrew Bible*, Susan Niditch divides passages dealing with חרם into two types: those that treat the ban as a sacrificial system, in which "[i]mposition of the ban, so that dead enemies become an offering to God, is one way of making sense of the inevitable carnage of war,"[16] and those that treat the ban as a mechanism of God's justice, "rooting out [. . .] impure, sinful forces damaging the solid and pure relationship between Israel and God."[17] Niditch links this latter interpretation to the idea of the just war, which has been an important concept in twentieth-century

---

14. Levinas, *Time of the Nations*, 133.

15. See, for example, Childs, *Exodus*, 313; Fox, *Five Books of Moses*, 352, 966; Meyers, *Exodus*, 135; R. D. Nelson, *Deuteronomy*, 302; G. Ernest Wright's commentary on Deut. 25.19 in *The Interpreter's Bible*, Volume II, 482. The word חרם does not actually appear in either the Exodus or the Deuteronomy passages dealing with Amalek; such analysis of those passages must begin by assuming a similarity between the treatment of Amalek and nations which are explicitly subjected to the ban.

16. Niditch, *War in the Hebrew Bible*, 50.

17. Ibid., 56.

justifications of warfare.[18] While the passages from Deuteronomy and Exodus that I analyze do not make an appearance in this volume (and nor does the verb חרם make an appearance in either passage), Niditch does analyze 1 Samuel 15, which details a later interaction between the Israelites, led by King Saul, and the Amalekites, led by King Agag (from whom Haman, the villain of the book of Esther is said to descend) as an instance of the ban as a measure of God's justice.[19] It is worthwhile to quote Niditch's final analysis of this approach to warfare at some length:

> It is not easy for humans to kill others. To participate in mass killing in war is destructive of individual psyches and of the larger community's mental health. The ban in either trajectory is a means of making killing in war acceptable. [...] [T]he ban-as-God's-justice ideology actually motivates and encourages war, implying that wars of extermination are desirable in order to purify the body politic of one's own group, to eradicate evil beyond one's group, and to actualize divine judgment. In the ban as God's justice a sharp line is drawn between us and them, between clean and unclean, between those worthy of salvation and those deserving elimination. The enemy is thus not a mere human, an offering, necessary to win the assistance of God, but a monster, unclean, and diseased. The ban as God's justice thus allows people to accept the notion of killing other humans by dehumanizing them and the process of dehumanization can take place even within the group during times of stress, distrust, and anomie.[20]

While Niditch does not make reference to the work of Elaine Scarry at any point in her book, the parallels between what she writes here and Scarry's 1985 book, *The Body in Pain*, are striking. Scarry discusses, at some length, the psychological necessity to disguise and obscure the actual injuring of bodies, which, she argues, is the single inarguable fact of warfare.[21] The main means by which this disguise is perpetrated is linguistic rearrangement:

> the act of injuring, or the tissue that is to be injured, or the weapon that is to accomplish the injury is renamed [...] as prisoners subjected to medical experiments in Japanese camps were called "logs," and as the day during World War I on which thirty

18. Ibid., 57.
19. Ibid., 61–62.
20. Ibid., 77.
21. Scarry, *Body in Pain*, 63.

thousand Russians and thirteen thousand Germans died at Tannenberg came to be called the "Day of Harvesting."[22]

This inversion, in which people become inanimate ("logs," or crops to be harvested) and weapons take on a life of their own ("arms," parts of a body, as Scarry describes slightly later in the same paragraph as the passage quoted), acts just as the notion of holy war, the ban as justice, described by Niditch, in "allow[ing] people to accept the notion of killing other humans by dehumanizing them."

Scarry takes what may be rightly labeled a logically extreme view of the idea of the "just war"; by reducing war to two structural components (injury and competition), she is able to argue that, while there may be some justification for the existence of "a contest based on a reciprocal activity that would produce a nonreciprocal outcome abided by all," there is no necessity, and thus no justification of, or justice in, such a competition being based on the injuring of human bodies.[23] Niditch does not go nearly so far—which is to be expected, as her book is a descriptive study of war as it is portrayed in the Hebrew Bible, rather than an argument for or against war itself—but is, at times (such as in the passage quoted above) sharply critical of fictions (to use Scarry's terminology) that make the taking of human lives too easy by obscuring the basic humanness of the lives to be taken. If such fictions are reprehensible *during* times of conflict—and I agree with Scarry and Niditch that they are—then how much more problematic do they become afterwards, when the dehumanization of the enemy is no longer a response to the exigencies of war but rather an integral part of the narrative on which a society builds its identity?

In the following pages, I will examine a sample of memorial sites and texts through which the boundaries between living (individual) memory, cultural memory, and history are constantly being re-negotiated. None of these is neutral. Each one is a construction; each both presents a particular interpretation of the event(s) it represents and is itself subject to interpretation and re-interpretation.

In Part One, I address Amalek and Antigone, two ancient texts which continue to be read, interpreted, and used as touchstones in discourse concerning memorialization. Chapter 1 presents the liturgical space opened up by Parshat Zakhor, one of four short passages appended to the normal order of Torah readings in the month prior to Passover. This examination

22. Ibid., 66.
23. Ibid., 142.

Prelude

both illuminates the backwards-reading tendency of memorials, as the responses of various communities over different points in history demonstrate the way that each found in the text a model for their own situation,[24] but also provides a framework for a more widely-ranging discussion of what memory is and how it functions, on both an individual and communal level.

In chapter 2, I engage in a closer study of the way memorialization contributes to the formation of identity, both individual and cultural. Due to the strong parallels between the social situation of the Athenian Empire in the fifth century BCE and that of the British Empire in the early twentieth century CE, as well as to the great influence classical forms had on the accoutrements of memorialization in the First World War, I begin by briefly returning to ancient Greece, to examine what light the conflict over the burial of Polynices portrayed in Sophocles' *Antigone* may shed on the issue of how, and by whom, the meaning of history is negotiated.

This discussion provides the foundation for my investigation of the way the memory of the First World War was constructed in Canada. Throughout Part Two, I argue that the dead (or wounded, or missing) bodies of soldiers are the locus of such negotiations. I further argue that the dominant Christian theology of the time neither challenged nor was challenged by the events of the war; rather, commemorative activity freely borrowed images of sacrifice and atonement, and the churches incorporated the transformed images back into their regular vocabulary of worship. Focusing on Canada permits me to draw on a particular set of historical circumstances that, taken together, provide a useful interruption to more dominant (British and American) understandings of the war, thus underlining the element of selectivity at work in memorialization. My main vehicle for this discussion is a parallel reading of four novels from L. M. Montgomery's *Anne of Green Gables* series (the publication of which spanned the years 1908 to 1921) and the work of the Imperial War Graves Commission (now known as the Commonwealth War Graves Commission).

I conclude Part Two with a close examination of one particular Canadian monument to the First World War, the Walter Allward-designed Canadian National Vimy Memorial. "Reading" the monument alongside Jane Urquhart's fictional account of its creation in *The Stone Carvers* permits me to unpack the way the memory of the First World War has evolved from the time it was being constructed by Allward, Montgomery, and a

---

24. Cf. Walzer, *Exodus and Revolution*, 7.

host of other Canadian culture-makers, until the present day, when more nuanced historical readings are available to undermine the triumphant, nation-building myth of Canada's War. One of the great risks of constructing memorials that carry the past forward into the present is that the consciousness of the present can, then, also infect the past. Memorials are too dependent on their readers ever to be truly stable texts.

In Part Three, I begin by conducting a similar, though briefer, examination of the presentation of memorials to the Holocaust. I suggest that, where the First World War memorials were originally designed to serve an existing community of mourners, acting as substitutes for the bodies of dead soldiers, the Holocaust memorials, particularly those that take the form of museums, have been designed to *create* a community of mourners, guiding the visitor towards a sense of sympathy for and responsibility to the victims they commemorate.

Two churches bombed during the Second World War and rebuilt afterwards provide the framework for my consideration of the relationship between the history of the years 1933–1945 (the total span of Nazi rule in Germany) and religious practice since that time. Where the vocabulary of memorialization at work in the First World War was well in tune with the Christian theological language of the time, the memory of the Holocaust poses a direct challenge to Jewish theological understanding. It is the negotiation between theology and history, and the role that memorialization plays in this, that is my primary concern in this part. After a survey of several notable academic theologians, I focus primarily upon the relatively recent work of David Blumenthal and Melissa Raphael, both of whom, in different ways, are concerned particularly with the issue of encounter between God and humanity, and how the understanding of and approach to such an encounter is altered by understanding of the Holocaust. Thus, my focus returns to the issue of Jewish liturgy—not within a calendrical framework, as at the beginning of this book, but as a space of encounter. I conclude with a reading of two contemporary novels by Canadian Jewish women, both of which point towards the possibility of, but do not actually accomplish, a reconciliation between liturgical and quotidian existence, a renewal of connection between God and humanity, accomplished in part by a re-interpretation of existing memorials.

PART ONE

Remembering to Forget

ONE

Remembering Amalek

זכור את אשר־עשה לך עמלק בדרך בצאתכם ממצרים:
אשר קרך בדרך ויזנב בך כל־הנחשלים אחריך ואתה עיף ויגע ולא ירא אלהים:
והיה בהניח יהוה אלהיך | לך מכל־איביך מסביב בארץ אשר יהוה־אלהיך נתן לך נחלה לרשתה תמחה את־זכר עמלק מתחת השמים לא תשכח:

Remember what Amalek did on the road when you were brought forth from Egypt. Finding you on your journey, he struck at the stragglers, the feeblest of all that were faint and weary; he did not fear God. When the Lord your God grants you rest from the enemies that surround you, in the land that the Lord your God will give you to hold as your inheritance, you shall blot out the remembering of Amalek from under heaven. Do not forget.

—Parshat Zakhor: Deuteronomy 25:17–19[1]

At the end of every winter, in the month of Adar, the normal order of Torah readings is supplemented with four special readings which, taken together, lay the foundation for the observance of Pesach-Shavuot,[2]

---

1. All translations preceded by the original Hebrew are my own. All other translations are taken from the JPS Tanach, unless otherwise specified. Throughout this book, quotations from the Torah are cited first by parsha and then by their standard chapter and verse. Because the Jewish lectionary is fixed to a one year reading cycle, a parsha citation not only identifies a certain point in the text, but also a certain fixed point in time—thus, citing this as Parshat Zakhor, rather than Ki Seitzei, indicates that I am reading it in the context of the Sabbath immediately preceding Purim—and therefore in conversation with the Book of Esther—and only a few weeks after the parallel passage (Exod 17:14), part of Parshat Beshalach, would have been read out loud in the Synagogue, rather than near the end of the lectionary year, when passages from Deuteronomy are normally read.

2. I am here choosing to treat Pesach and Shavuot, linked by the counting of the omer, as the beginning and end points of a continuous festival commemorating the

PART ONE: Remembering to Forget

which begins in the following month of Nissan. The readings are, in order, Shekalim (Exod 30:11–16), Zakhor (cited above), Parah (Num 19:1), and HaChodesh (Exod 12:1–20).³ One may argue that these readings lay out four essential pillars of Judaism: charitable giving, remembrance, ritual purity, and observance of sanctified time.⁴ These four areas are firmly intertwined, and a discussion of any one will necessarily involve the other three. My primary concern, however, and the focus of my discussion is the second area: remembrance.

Parshat Zakhor, read on the Sabbath before Purim, is recorded as part of the law that God commands Moses to convey to the Israelites.⁵ It contains two positive commandments: to always remember the treachery of Amalek, and to blot out the memory of Amalek entirely.⁶ Instantly, then, we are confronted with a paradox: how is it possible to both remember and forget at the same time?

Rabbinic commentary mostly sidesteps this issue, as does contemporary Christian commentary, both seeming to read "blot out the memory of" as a poetic hyperbole meant to indicate total obliteration.⁷ The Harper

---

journey from Egypt to Sinai, rather than as two distinct festivals.

3. *m. Meg.* 3:4

4. Ronald Hendel identifies three marks of distinction between the Israelites and the surrounding tribes in the Hebrew Bible: "circumcision, food laws, and the observation of the Sabbath. The domains of these practices—the body, food, and time—are exemplary for showing the effective symbolism of rituals as markers of cultural boundaries"; see Hendel, *Remembering Abraham,* 19. My scheme differs from his in the inclusion of charitable giving, but more importantly in that it is drawn from and reflective of post-Biblical—indeed, post-Temple—liturgical practice.

5. Haman, the villain of the minor festival of Purim, is named "the Agagite" (Esth 3:1), which marks him as a descendent of Agag, and, by extension, of Amalek. There are two Agags identified in the Tanach: the first is the king of the Amalekites who employed Balaam to prophesy against the Israelites (Parshat Balak: Numbers 24:7); the second is killed by Saul in 1 Sam 15. A lengthy treatment of this connection can be found in Elliott Horowitz, *Reckless Rites,* 107–46.

6. MT, *Hilkhot melakhim,* 5:5 (Hershman, *Code of Maimonides,* 217). In the following discussion, I assume Amalek refers to the nation of Amalek, rather than the person Amalek; thus, the pronouns used are "it" and "their," rather than "he" and "his."

7. Jewish treatments of the passage are addressed later in this chapter. A brief survey of Christian commentary yields the following results: John W. Rogerson's commentary on Deut 25:19 in *Eerdmans Commentary on the Bible* ignores the difficulties of verse 19 entirely, focusing on Deut 25:17–19 as a whole and its place in the "narrative framework for the laws of ch. 12–25" (168), and S. R. Driver's *Critical and Exegetical Commentary on Deuteronomy* considers verse 19 "a striking and emphatic" passage entirely consistent with "the style and manner of Dt." (286); William D. Johnstone's commentary on the

Remembering Amalek

Collins Study Bible (NRSV) suggests the following cognate passages: Deut 9:14; 25:6; 29:20; 1 Sam 24:21 [sic]; Ps 9:5-6; 109:13. I can only assume that the reference in 1 Samuel is actually meant to be to 24:22, "So swear to me by the Lord that you will not destroy my descendants or wipe out my name from my father's house"; all the other passages noted similarly make reference to the blotting out of a name (שם) rather than memory

parallel passage, Exod 17:14, also in *Eerdmans Commentary*, is likewise more concerned with the passage's place in a larger narrative structure, noting the mirroring of pre- and post-Sinaitic events in Exodus and Numbers (89–90). Everett Fox's commentary in *The Five Books of Moses* notes the broad connection of these passages to the theme of holy war (352; 966), as does G. Ernest Wright's commentary on Deut 25:19 in Buttrick, *The Interpreter's Bible*, vol. 2, 482; Henry H. Shires and Pierson Parker, in the same volume of *The Interpreter's Bible*, note that the passage is decidedly un-Christian, and recommend that the dictates of Rom 12:20 be followed instead (482–83). J. Coert Rylaarsdam's commentary on Exod 17:14 in Volume 1 of *The Interpreter's Bible* does focus on the command to "blot out the name of Amalek," but is content with tracing the progression of the feud up through 1 and 2 Sam and 1 Chr (961); J. Edgar Park's commentary on the same passage, also in Volume 1 of *The Interpreter's Bible*, focuses on the command to write down "a memorial in a book" (961–62), as does both Rev. David Stalker's commentary on the same passage in Black and Rowley, *Peake's Commentary*, 225, and Carol Meyers's commentary in her *Exodus*, 135, although Meyers also notes the holy war connections. Again in *Peake's Commentary*, Rev. G. Henton Davies simply glosses Deut 25:17–19 as a simple command to remember (280). Peter C. Craigie's commentary on Deuteronomy offers an interesting interpretation of v. 19, "You shall not forget," proposing that it be read as a factual statement, rather than a positive commandment, because "in Israel's future history, the continuing aggressiveness of the Amalekites gave the Israelites little chance to forget, until at last the Amalekites seem to have ceased to be a nation, about the time of Hezekiah (1 Chr. 4:43)"; See Craigie, *Book of Deuteronomy*, 318.

Richard D. Nelson does note that "[t]he rhetoric of v. 19 is striking: wipe out all memory of them, but always remember!" However, Nelson does not go any further in addressing this as a difficult passage, focusing the remainder of his commentary, again, on the concept of holy war, justified by Amalek's "violation of universally accepted principles of war"; see Nelson, *Deuteronomy: A Commentary*, 302.

Brevard Childs's commentary on Exodus also concentrates on the theme of holy war, focusing primarily on the notion of perpetual enmity between Amalek and Israel; he finds this puzzling in light of the victory described in Exodus, but reads Deut 25:27 as recounting "a humiliating defeat of Israel by the hands of Amalek," in which Amalek committed "an act of barbarism and provided a motivation for Israel's continued hatred." See Childs, *Exodus: A Commentary*, 313.

William H. Propp's commentary on Exodus follows Childs's assertion that זכר and שם are interchangeable (see below), but makes an important point about the textual and oral modes of remembrance commanded in Exod 17:14: "That which is written is permanent in a sense; but, precisely because it is set down, it may easily be forgotten. In contrast, that which is taught orally, 'put into the ears,' remains in the forefront of consciousness (Calvin). Our passage thus adumbrates the Jewish tradition of Oral Torah (*m. 'Abot* 1:1)." See Propp, *Exodus 1–18*, 619.

(זכר), as in Deut 25:19. We could also add Exod 17:14, 32:33, Deut 32:26, and 2 Kgs 12:27 to the list of cognate passages; here, again, the direct object is always name, save for Exod 17:14, which is a very close parallel to Deut 25:19, and where the object is memory—but, again, the memory of Amalek. It seems clear that the standard interpretative key here is generally considered to be the verb (מחה), rather than its object, and, thus, Parshat Zakhor is read through comparison with passages dealing explicitly with family lineage and implicitly—since the family lineage under consideration is, in all of the cognate passages, that of an Israelite—covenant.[8] I would argue, however, that the change in direct object is too important to ignore; if memory is meant to connote family lineage, why not use the exact same word—name—as in all those other passages?

Brevard Childs argues that the noun form of the root זכר is properly translated as "name," rather than "memory," noting that it is frequently used in parallel to שם, and that the clearest distinction between the two words is that the former can be construed as a speech act, while the latter represents that which has been spoken. "Clearly there is a close relationship between cultic proclamation and memory [...] Yet again, it is important to see that *zēkher* is only secondarily related to memory. The emphasis lies with the act of proclaiming."[9] By this argument, then, the two positive commandments are to always remember what Amalek did, but to blot out the utterance of Amalek's name—which may appear to unravel the paradox, as, although Childs argues that the hiphil form of the verb is also an act of speech, the form that we see in Deut 25:17 is the qal, which even Childs agrees translates best as remember, an act of cognition.[10] However, Childs relies here on assertion, more than argument, to make his case; while he cites a number of passages in which the noun may be translated quite sensibly as

---

8. See Eslinger, "Drafting Techniques," 226. Rashi's commentary on this phrase also supports such an interpretation.

9. Brevard S. Childs, *Memory and Tradition*, 72. An interesting parallel with the Homeric tradition is the word κλέος, typically translated as "glory," which according to Gregory Nagy "should have meant simply 'that which is heard,'" but which came to indicate the transmission of great deeds through the recital of epic poetry. See Nagy, *Best of the Achaeans*, 16–17. An important distinction between κλέος and זכר is that, while both may take their roots from, and refer implicitly to, acts of recitation, the former is always positive, a property of heroes, while the latter is neutral, as can be discerned from the passage currently under discussion; a commandment to verbally convey the great deeds of Amalek would be jarring and nonsensical.

10. Childs, *Memory and Tradition*, 10–11. Hiphil verbs are very often rendered in English as causative, and qal verbs are usually rendered in English as perfect.

name, he does not produce a single passage in which that translation can be definitively shown to be superior, and several of his chosen passages become rather strained under his word choice.[11] Even if Childs is correct in his theory that memory was, to an ancient Israelite, an essentially active and vocalized, rather than purely cognitive, process, the majority of English translations contradict him,[12] which is to say that very few contemporary, English-speaking readers of the passage are likely to understand "memory" in the way that Childs suggests. Moreover, we are still left with another layer of paradox: this particular passage is read out loud in the synagogue twice in the year, once during the normal course of readings, as the end of Parshat Ki Seitzei, and once, the Shabbat before Purim, as Parshat Zakhor. The name of Amalek is uttered at the very moment of its prohibition; Amalek is commemorated in the very command that its memory be blotted out.[13]

And even if Childs is correct that שם and זכר are essentially interchangeable, it is still worthwhile to note that זכר is only used in reference to Amalek; Amalek is singled out for special treatment, even if only in the barest lexographical fashion. This is evident in commentaries upon Deut 25:19 and Exod 17:14 that focus on what Amalek did to deserve such a penalty. The Ramban maintains that Amalek's main sin was idolatry; their attack against the Israelites was actually a challenge to Hashem's divine authority.[14] This reading is echoed in the nineteenth century, by the German Orthodox

---

11. This is especially true of Pss 6:6 and 145:7, in which Childs must translate זכר as "praise" in order to arrive at a coherent reading. See Childs, *Memory and Tradition*, 71.

12. A brief comparison of translations currently in circulation should suffice to demonstrate this point. Of twenty-two translations sampled, eleven translate the word as "memory" (New Revised Standard Version, English Standard Version, New International Version, New American Standard Bible, New Living Translation, New Century Version, Holman Christian Standard Bible, New International Reader's Version, New International Version UK, New Jewish Publication Society Translation); a further eight translate it as "remembrance" (Amplified Bible, King James Version, New King James Version, 21st Century King James Version, American Standard Version, Young's Literal Translation, Darby, Interpreter's Bible); one transforms the noun into a verb (Contemporary English Version: "you must wipe out Amalek so completely that no one will remember they ever lived"), and only three render it as "name" (The Message, Today's New International Version, The Anchor Bible).

13. Lena Roos mentioned in a conversation that this tension between utterance and blotting out is enacted every year during Purim festivities, when the book of Esther is read out loud and noisemakers are employed to drown out the reader every time Haman's name is mentioned. However, no such measures are employed during the reading of passages concerning Amalek.

14. Nahmanides, *Commentary*, s.v. Exod 17:16.

PART ONE: Remembering to Forget

Rabbi Samson Raphael Hirsch, writing in the generation immediately following the Reform movement. Hirsch asserts that Amalek (and the command to remember Amalek) serves as an example to the people about to enter the Promised Land of the contrast between the faith in God demanded of Israel and the faith in military might—a thinly-veiled reference to the secularism promoted by the Reformers—represented by Amalek:[15]

> This most marked contrast was accordingly again pointed out to the people who were about to enter the Land of the Torah, there to faithfully carry out its dictates. The event itself—that first unprovoked attack by Amalek—with all the details of its contrast to what their mission in life was to be, was again brought to their minds, to be kept in perpetual recollection. [. . .] [H]ere Israel is exhorted to consider itself, and prove itself a co-working tool for this War of God against Amalek's leading mankind astray with the blinding glitter of military fame and glory in the palm awarded to victories of physical might.[16]

The retelling of the Amalek narrative in Ginzberg's *Legends of the Jews* places the emphasis on Amalek's deceitfulness: they lie in wait for the Israelites to cross the Red Sea, incite other nations to join in their attack, lure individual Israelites away from the camp to kill them.[17] The final proof of Amalek's treachery, by this account, comes well after their initial defeat by Joshua:[18]

> Concealing their weapons in their garments, the Amalekites appeared in Israel's camp as if they meant to condole with them for Aaron's death, and then unexpectedly attacked them. Not content with this, the Amalekites disguised themselves in Canaanite costume and spoke the speech of the latter, so that the Israelites might not be able to tell if they had before them Amalekites, as

---

15. I use "Israel" as it is used in Jewish liturgy, to denote the entirety of the religious community which traces its origins back to Jacob, who received the name in Parshat Vayishlach (Gen 32:29), because he "strove with God and with men and has overcome" (כי-שרית עם-אלהים ועם-אנשים ותוכל), rather than to denote citizens of the modern-day state. The implications of my chosen usage are theological, and the latter political.

16. Hirsch, *Pentateuch*, 524.

17. Ginzberg, *Legends of the Jews*, 37.

18. This is consistent with Peter Craigie's hypothesis that Deut 25:17–18 "probably have in mind a number of encounters with the Amalekites, of which that referred to in Exod 17 is the first." See Craigie, *Book of Deuteronomy*, 317.

their personal appearance seemed to show, or Canaanites, as their dress and speech indicated.[19]

Not only do the Amalekites initiate a surprise attack, in this account, they infiltrate the Israelite camp through deceit, both under the guise of offering condolences, and disguised as members of another tribe. Ginzberg's text emphasizes that the actions of Amalek are not due to a lack of fear in God; the reason given for assuming the speech and garments of Canaanites is that the Amalekites believed that God would, indeed, answer the prayers of the Israelites, and do so effectively, and thus, "[i]f we now appear as Canaanites, they will implore God to send them aid against the Canaanites, and we shall slay them."[20] The offense here is an attempt to subvert the bond between God and Israel, by deceiving Israel and directing their focus, and therefore their prayers, and therefore God's attention, away from their true needs. That the Amalekites believed such a trick would prove effective may arguably be construed as a lack of respect for the intelligence of the Israelites and their God, but this is a move beyond the boundaries of the text itself.

Other commentators point to some aspect of the attack as particularly violating universal standards of decency in warfare: either they attacked without cause, or without warning, or (as suggested in Deut 25:18) unfairly targeted those unable to defend themselves; a rather exhaustive summary of such commentaries appears in Avi Sagi's article on the subject and need not be rehearsed in further detail here.[21] Still others view the issue as not so much what Amalek may have done, but what Amalek represents; this is the mode of interpretation that has dominated twentieth and, thus far, twenty-first century Judaism, although its roots go back at least to Isaac Luria (d. 1572).[22]

Rabbi Kalonymos Kalmish Shapira, the Piaczena Rebbe, preached two sermons on Parshat Zakhor during his imprisonment in the Warsaw Ghetto. In his sermon on 23 March, 1940, Shapira bases his reading of Amalek on an alternative reading from Rashi, which translates אשר קרך as "who

19. Ginzberg, *Legends of the Jews*, 214.
20. Ibid., 215.
21. A number of these interpretations are detailed in Avi Sagi, "Punishment," 325.
22. Sagi further subdivides this mode of interpretation into three sub-modes: metaphysical, conceptual, and psychological; he traces the metaphysical mode back to Luria, the conceptual only back as far as Hirsch, and attributes the psychological mode to "the Hasidic tradition;" see Sagi, "Punishment," 330–36.

PART ONE: Remembering to Forget

chilled you" rather than "who encountered you," arguing that the encounter with Amalek cooled the Israelites' ardor for Torah.[23] He thus equates Amalek with worldly wisdom, which tempted and continues to tempt the Jewish people away from Torah, and suggests that "the text is saying: 'Now that you have seen and experienced all this, go and 'obliterate the memory of Amalek from beneath the heavens.'"[24] His sermon on 28 February 1942 is considerably longer and more complex, delving into the Kabbalistic underpinnings of his interpretation of the passage, but the message is essentially the same:

> The implication is that we have to obliterate the seeds Amalek has planted, because otherwise, after Amalek himself is destroyed, the seeds that he has planted will remain. Who knows how long the Sabbath that today so many Jews, constrained by Amalek's torments, are forced to desecrate, God have mercy, will remain so desecrated? After this war is over, people will not be as afraid of doing work on the Sabbath as they once were. [. . .] Those young people who are forced to abandon the Torah now, who are enduring so much pain and suffering they do not even know if they are alive: Will they put their whole heads and bodies back into the study of Torah, after the destruction of Amalek?[25]

For Shapira, Amalek is not a specific people, but a specific type of people (or, perhaps, people who engage in a specific type of behavior); the command to blot out the memory of Amalek remains unfulfilled so long as that sort of person and that sort of behavior continue to exist. Thus, it is no contradiction for the Israelites to be commanded at once to remember

---

23. Shapira, *Sacred Fire*, 55–57. Rashi offers three separate explanations of קרך: first, because קרך (encounter) is linguistically connected to מקרה (a sudden thing) that Amalek attacked by surprise; second, that because קרך is linguistically connected to קרי (pollution), Amalek polluted the Israelites through pederasty (see Horowitz, *Reckless Rites*, 114); third, because קרך is linguistically related to קור (cold), Amalek "chilled" the Israelites. Shapira's reading is somewhat different from the parable provided in the Rashi commentary, which compares Amalek's attack on the Israelites to a man who jumps into a pot of boiling water and is scalded, but nonetheless persuades others around him that the water is cool enough to bathe in (i.e., Amalek showed other nations that Israel was susceptible to attack). It is also notable that Rashi connects Deut 25:17, "Remember what Amalek did to you," directly to the previous verses concerning fair weights and measures, warning that unjust measures constitute a provocation to enemies—and thus placing some blame for Amalek's attack upon the Israelites themselves.

24. Shapira, *Sacred Fire*, 57.

25. Ibid., 300.

and to blot out the memory of Amalek; the blotting out is a struggle that continues to this very day.²⁶

Having dispensed with one apparent contradiction, however, we find ourselves immediately confronted with another: to whom is the command to remember actually given, and how can it possibly be fulfilled? To a Jewish reader, this question is hardly worth asking; the idea of memory stretching continuously from generation to generation is part of "the taken-for-granted, tacit background of beliefs, concepts, values, attitudes, and so forth"²⁷ that constitutes Jewish culture.²⁸ But it flies in the face of the concept of memory which has, at least until recently, been the basis for philosophical treatments of the subject in what, for the sake of simplicity, I refer to as the "Western" philosophical tradition, although I do so in full consciousness that this is, at best, an oversimplification and at worst a complete misnomer. Jewish thought, insofar as it constitutes a unified system of thought at all, is a "Western" system (in contrast to Chinese philosophy), simply not the dominant one, and there is, as evidenced by instances of Rashi borrowing from Plato's *Symposium* in his gloss on Parshat Bere'shit (Gen 1:27), a reasonable amount of overlap and borrowing between the two systems. The distinction I am drawing here (along with the collapsing of two vastly complex and diverse networks of thought into two unified systems) is, in other words, a useful fiction—but still a fiction, a narrative constructed in hindsight.

---

26. For further examples of this reading of Amalek, see Horowitz, *Reckless Rites*, 2–4.
27. Tanner, *Theories of Culture*, 30–1.
28. See, for example, Parshat Nitsavim, Deut 29:13–14: "I make this covenant, with its sanctions, not with you alone, but both with those who are standing here with us this day before the Lord our God and with those who are not with us here this day;" also the injunction in *m. Pesah.* 10:5: "In every generation one must see oneself as if one had personally experienced the exodus from Egypt." See also Plaskow, *Standing Again*, 25–28; Plaskow notes that Parshat Yitro (Exod 19:15) seems to specifically exclude women from the revelation at Sinai, and that its annual reading perpetually re-enacts that exclusion. See also Yerushalmi, *Zakhor*. Again, there is an interesting parallel with the Homeric tradition, with the verb μιμνήσκω, which Nagy suggests "means not so much that the Muses 'remind' the poet of what to tell, but, rather, that they have the power to put his mind or consciousness in touch with places and times other than his own in order to witness the deeds of heroes (and the doings of gods)" (*Best of the Achaeans*, 17). However, Nagy makes clear that this "witness" is not a direct transportation of the poet to the scene, but rather mediated through the witness of the Muses; they convey the κλέος which he is to recite to the poet, who then repeats it to the audience.

PART ONE: Remembering to Forget

MEMORY AND THE INDIVIDUAL

Michael Rossington and Anne Whitehead open their recently published volume, *Theories of Memory: A Reader*, with an historical overview of the evolution of concepts of memory.[29] They begin with Plato, working their way through Aristotle, Cicero, Yates, Locke, Hume, and Hegel, before finally arriving at the Late Modern era. It is notable that, while they do have a section devoted to "Jewish Memory Discourse," it is entirely separate from this initial overview; it does not fit into the narrative of intellectual history that the editors are attempting to present. A brief examination of the theorists who do fit into that narrative reveals the reason for the separation between the Western philosophical tradition and the Jewish concept of memory: all the theorists represented in Rossington and Whitehead's overview, up until late modernity, treat memory as an individual faculty. This distinction is made most clearly in Locke, when he writes:

> Had I the same consciousness that I saw the ark and Noah's flood, as that I saw an overflowing of the Thames last winter, or as that I write now, I could no more doubt that I who write this now, that saw the Thames overflowed last winter, and that viewed the flood at the general deluge, was the same self, place that self in what substance you please, than that I who write this am the same myself now whilst I write (whether I consist of all the same substance, material or immaterial, or no) that I was yesterday.[30]

Locke is here engaged with what Marya Schechtman has labeled "the reidentification problem"—the philosophical problem of whether a body moving through time and acquiring different experiences can be said to be the same entity at point *A* as at point *Z*.[31] This is the normative approach to the philosophy of identity.[32] Schechtman's analysis of earlier treatments of this problem concludes that reidentification puzzles are asking the wrong question, and she goes on to theorize identity in terms of character and

---

29. Rossington and Whitehead, *Theories of Memory*. This is the first major historical anthology dealing with memory studies to be published; I am reading it here as representative of the generally accepted approach to the intellectual history of the topic. See also the review of the volume by Rebecca Bramall in *Memory Studies* 1 (2008) 341–43.

30. Locke, *Human Understanding*, XVII:16 (185–86). Although Locke here uses the word *consciousness* instead of *memory*, later passages demonstrate that he uses the terms equivalently, if not interchangeably; memory is, to Locke, consciousness of the past.

31. Schechtman, *Selves*, 2.

32. See also Parfit, *Reasons*, still a highly influential treatment of the reidentification problem; and also Ricoeur's critique of Parfit in "Narrative Identity."

narrative—a much more intuitive approach for scholars, such as myself, already steeped in narrative. However, even Schechtman does not carry the narrative approach to identity forward past the boundaries of an individual's self-awareness; to the best of my knowledge, no philosopher of identity has made the leap between the internally oriented statement "My selfhood is defined by the continuity of my memory" and the externally oriented statement "My selfhood is defined by another's memory of me." While under most circumstances, the latter statement could very quickly be shown to be logically untenable (I do not cease the exercise of my selfhood because my mother happens to forget who I am), it becomes reasonable in situations where the "self" under consideration is deprived of agency—as, for example, a dead body would be (I am not interested in pursuing questions concerning the immortality of the soul). Thus, it is the latter statement that becomes most relevant to the issues of commemoration that will be taken up in the following chapters.

This, however, is not the passage that Rossington and Whitehead have chosen to excerpt for their anthology. Rather, they select an earlier chapter of the same book, "On Retention," which describes, rather mechanistically, the functional relationship between mind and memory. This decision on the part of the editors—and the absence of any excerpt from Descartes—obscures the linkage between memory and individual identity that I will place at the center of Part Two of this study. However, it cannot obscure, and may even serve to emphasize, that memory, from Ancient Greece to the Enlightenment, has been conceived of as a function restricted to an individual mind. Every excerpt in the first two sections of the *Reader* operates with the implicit assumption that memory functions as a link to knowledge or experience acquired in an individual's own past, and is concerned primarily with either describing (primarily in the case of the Enlightenment and Romantic philosophers) or improving (primarily in the case of the ancient and medieval thinkers) this function. Within such a framework, either commandment in Parshat Zakhor is logically incoherent; no person currently alive could be commanded to remember something which they did not themselves experience, nor could they be commanded to blot out a memory which cannot be reasonably said to exist.

This is not the case in the third, and final, portion of the historical section, which covers representative texts from late modernity: Marx, Nietzsche, Bergson, Freud, and Benjamin. While the excerpts from the last three theorists continue the pattern of reflection on memory as a

PART ONE: Remembering to Forget

marker of individual existence and experience, the excerpts from Marx and Nietzsche appear to approach the relationship between memory and history. Nietzsche uses the term *history* to signify events in the past, including an individual's own experienced past:

> A leaf flutters from the scroll of time, floats away—and suddenly floats back again and falls into the man's lap. Then the man says "I remember" and envies the animal, who at once forgets and for whom every moment really dies, sinks back into night and fog and is extinguished forever. Thus the animal lives *unhistorically*: for it is contained in the present, like a number without any awkward fraction left over; it does not know how to dissimulate, it conceals nothing and at every instant appears wholly as what it is; it can therefore never be anything but honest.[33]

In other words, Nietzsche here uses *history* and *memory* in a somewhat interchangeable fashion, being more concerned with the role the past plays in distinguishing human from animal consciousness (the latter existing only in an eternal now) than with distinctions between memory and history as potentially different types of past.

The excerpt from Marx's *The Eighteenth Brumaire of Louis Bonaparte* involves a similar conflation of *history* and *memory*, although that conflation appears in this case to be at least as much on the part of Rossington and Whitehead as on the part of Marx himself. Granted, only fifty-two years elapsed between Napoleon Bonaparte's original *coup d'état* and what Marx characterized as an echo event orchestrated by Louis Bonaparte; there were certainly people alive at the time Marx wrote who had a clear living memory of the time of Napoleon, even if Marx himself (born in 1818, some nineteen years after Napoleon's *coup*) was not among them. Nonetheless, Marx's critique is almost entirely historical; the word *memory* occurs only twice in the entire book, and the second time (in a later chapter than that excerpted by Rossington and Whitehead) it refers in an uncomplicated fashion to the function of an individual mind.[34] The first instance, from the passage excerpted for the *Reader*, is more interesting: "As long as the French were engaged in revolution they could not free themselves of the memory

---

33. Friedrich Nietzsche, "Uses of History," [1874], 102–3; reprinted in Rossington and Whitehead 102–8. While Rossington and Whitehead have selected a relatively short portion of the essay to excerpt, Nietzsche's conflation of *history* and *memory*—or, perhaps, cultural and personal history—is consistent throughout the larger essay.

34. See Karl Marx, *Eighteenth Brumaire*.

Remembering Amalek

of Napoleon."[35] Neither Marx nor the editors of the *Reader* note anything unusual in this usage, nor make any attempt to explain it; absent that sentence, the excerpt reads as a straightforward critique of a political misuse of history. This is, however, the first time in the *Reader* that memory does not clearly refer to an individual experience and, in fact, appears to describe a link to the experience of a collective past, the sort of memory that would be necessary to the fulfillment of the commandments in Parshat Zakhor.[36]

MEMORY AND THE SOCIAL COLLECTIVE

The conflation of memory and history in the above passages from Marx and Nietzsche may appear to have been mostly unselfconscious, the result of an innocence with regards to the past that seems to have been mostly lost by the dawn of the twenty-first century—though, in truth, it was already well eroded by the time either of them wrote. Bill Schwartz's entry on memory in *New Keywords: A Revised Vocabulary of Culture and Society* suggests that conscious division between "subjective" and "social memory" dates to the development of the discipline of historiography in the nineteenth century.[37] Schwartz supports this in part by citing a passage written by the historian Thomas Macaulay in 1849, prior to the passages from Marx or Nietzsche discussed above; even if neither of them were deeply familiar with the discourse of the emerging discipline, it left a mark on their language. However, even Schwartz places the movement of memory to "the center [sic] of

---

35. Rossington and Whitehead, *Theories of Memory*, 99.

36. The Oxford English Dictionary's entry on memory complicates this picture somewhat. The first instance of the word in English is recorded in 1225 CE, and refers specifically to a commemorative activity, rather than a mental faculty: "þe Memoires of þe halhen" (a margin note in *Ancrene Riwle*). This usage died out after the sixteenth century, re-emerging briefly in the middle and late nineteenth century (although use of terms such as "in memory of" or "to the memory of" remained in usage from the fourteenth century to the present day). The earliest recorded usage of memory as "the action of remembering" is c. 1250 CE, which is not terribly long after the *Ancrene Riwle* note, but the idea of memory as a mental faculty does not appear until 1380 CE, in Chaucer. Prior to the importation of the word memory from French to English, via the Normans, the Anglo-Saxon term for contemplation of the past (particularly the traces of the past that precedes living memory which are evident in the landscape) was dūstscēawung, which literally translates as "contemplation of the dust." See Mitchell and Robinson, *Old English*, 253.

37. Schwartz, "Memory," 214–17. See also Crane, "Writing the Individual," 1372–85.

23

modern consciousness" in the late nineteenth century, primarily crediting Freud with bringing it to prominence.[38]

While Freud's memory discourse was, for the most part, strongly centered on the individual mind, later works, such as *Moses and Monotheism*, expand the scope of his theories from the individual to a social collective.[39] In Freud, this shift is accomplished in the simplest way possible, by treating the collective metaphorically, as one very large individual, possessed of a single mind and will—a model which renders the commandments in Parshat Zakhor perfectly comprehensible, but is too high a level of abstraction to pass a test of realism; no collective operates in as neat or as unified a fashion as Freud imagines.[40] Other theorists, such as Maurice Halbwachs and Paul Connerton, have attempted to correct this, offering increasingly complex models meant to account for the collective as a collection of individuals, each with their own mind and motivations.

Halbwachs was a contemporary of Freud, and a follower of Durkheim.[41] A sociologist, rather than a psychologist, he had little interest in the function of individual minds, instead insisting that the consciousness of a social collective possesses "a self-sufficient reality. In spite of the fact that they are engendered by society, they are assumed to originate and develop independently of the forms of social life."[42] At the same time, Lewis Coser, who edited and translated a number of Halbwachs's works into English, insists that Halbwachs's collective memory is not "some mystical group mind," but rather a specific group context which provides a basis for the memories of individuals.[43] Coser is here citing a passage from Halbwachs's 1951

---

38. Schwartz, "Memory," 215.

39. Freud, *Moses and Monotheism*.

40. This is perhaps an oversimplification of Freud, though not by much. Patrick H. Hutton protests that Freud did not envision "a free-floating collective memory," but rather saw it as an issue of historical repetition (quite similar to that discussed by Marx) in which "the re-creation of similar conditions historically calls the same psychical predispositions to come into play. [...] The legend of Moses could be made to evoke a deeper content because it was only a place marker for the hidden "deep memory" of the original experience," although this "deep memory" and "original experience" still belong to a collective, rather than a collection of individuals. See Hutton, "Freud and Halbwachs," 152.

41. For a brief description of Durkheim's work, especially in relation to Halbwachs, see Coser, "Revival," 365–73.

42. Halbwachs, "Individual Psychology," 615. Note that this article was published only a year before Freud's *Moses and Monotheism*.

43. Coser, "Revival," 367.

work, *Les cadres sociaux de la mémoire*.⁴⁴ This, therefore, represents over a decade's worth of development and refinement in Halbwachs's thought from the publication of "Individual Psychology and Collective Psychology," and if a younger Halbwachs was a bit more focused on the importance of viewing the collective mind and collective memory as phenomena in their own right, the mature Halbwachs was careful to identify collective memory as a contextual system in which—and even because of which—individual memories function:⁴⁵

> it is in society that people normally acquire their memories. It is also in society that they recall, recognize, and localize their memories. If we enumerate the number of recollections during one day that we have evoked upon the occasion of our direct and indirect relations with other people, we will see that, most frequently, we appeal to our memory only in order to answer questions which others have asked us, or that we suppose they could have asked us. [. . .] Most of the time, when I remember, it is others who spur me on; their memory comes to the aid of mine and mine relies on theirs. There is nothing mysterious about recall of memories in these cases at least. There is no point in seeking where they are preserved in my brain or in some nook of my mind to which I alone have access: for they are recalled to me externally, and the groups of which I am a part at any time give me the means to reconstruct them [. . .]⁴⁶

Halbwachs's theory of collective memory remains one of the most, if not the single most, influential explanations of group memory.⁴⁷ However, it still does not provide a particularly satisfactory explanation of social memory enduring beyond a single generation, or two at the most—the sort of memory commanded in Parshat Zakhor. With the aid of Halbwachs, we can see that the command given to all of Israel is really meant to be fulfilled by all of Israel, acting in concert, rather than by each individual Israelite

---

44. Partially available in English as Halbwachs, *On Collective Memory*.

45. Halbwachs's earlier reification of collective memory is even more apparent in his 1939 article, "Individual Consciousness and Collective Mind," 812–22.

46. Halbwachs, *On Collective Memory*, 38.

47. See Castelli, *Martyrdom and Memory*, 11–24; Connerton, *How Societies Remember*, 36–40; Hervieu-Léger, *Religion as a Chain of Memory*, 125–30; Misztal, *Social Remembering*, 4, 7, 50–56; Olick, *Politics of Regret*, 5–7; Volf, *End of Memory*, 99. Castelli's summary of Halbwachs's critics (pp. 19–24) is especially useful; the main criticism she cites is the philosophical difficulty involved in applying the language of individual actions and attributes to a collective.

guarding the nooks of his or her mind, but we cannot quite extrapolate the continuity of that memory from the time the command was given down to the present day.

This gap in Halbwachs's explication was noted and largely corrected by Paul Connerton, in his 1989 book *How Societies Remember*.[48] Connerton argues that collective memory is performative; it is transmitted primarily through ritual and bodily practices. By this Connerton means primarily unconscious, non-deliberate habits and postures, but more deliberate rituals are also vehicles for memory transmission—particularly commemorative rituals tied to a fixed and recurring point in the yearly calendar, as in the annual recitation of Parshat Zakhor.[49] Connerton also places a particular emphasis on ritual speech, maintaining that

> The *performativeness* of ritual is partly a matter of utterance [. . .] Curses, blessings and oaths, together with other verbs frequently found in ritual language, as for instance "to ask" or "to pray" or "to give thanks," presuppose certain attitudes—of trust and veneration, of submission, contrition and gratitude—which come into effect at the moment when, by virtue of the enunciation of that sentence, the corresponding act takes place. Or better: that act takes place in and through the enunciation. Such verbs do not describe or indicate the existence of attitudes: they effectively bring those attitudes into existence by virtue of the illocutionary act.[50]

We have already noted that, paradoxically, Amalek is commemorated in the command to blot out its memory, though we neglected to point out that, more obviously, Parshat Zakhor also contains the self-fulfilling

---

48. It is also entirely possible that Halbwachs's theory remains preeminent not due to its innate perfection, but rather due to several decades during which there was little academic interest in social or collective memory (with the exception of the early critics mentioned by Castelli; see above, note 37); Halbwachs was not even translated into English until 1980, and a complete translation of *La topographie légendaire des évangiles en terre sainte: Etude de mémoire collective* has yet to appear. See Coser, "Revival," 365; Crane, "Writing the Individual," 1375–78; Hutton, "Recent Scholarship," 537; Lang, "Review," 596–600. See also Hirst and Manier, "Towards a psychology," 183–200, the introduction of which seems to imply that academic interest in collective memory has been constant and continually progressing—however, Hirst and Manier are psychologists, and as ill at ease with the literature of the humanities and social sciences as I am with the literature of psychology; they may be mistaking the large number of articles now in existence for evidence of a uniformly high level of interest in the subject since the time of Halbwachs.

49. Connerton, *How Societies Remember*, 45.

50. Ibid., 58. Emphasis in original.

commandment to remember; the very first word of the passage, "Remember," is a performative verb of the sort that Connerton describes.[51] This may appear to be arriving back at the conclusion reached through Childs's conflation of memory with utterance, albeit by a different route, but Connerton does not quite suggest that it constitutes memory on its own.[52] Rather, ritual utterance (such as a public reading of a set text at a fixed point in the liturgical calendar) forms part of the structure which supports the transmission of collective memory, which also includes family relations, oral tradition, clothing, unconscious gestures, movements, and postures—in short, Connerton argues that collective memory is encoded and transmitted in culture itself.[53] I will henceforth use the term "cultural memory" to refer to collective memory deliberately constructed and transmitted through artifacts, rituals, and texts.

MEMORY AND HISTORY

To characterize cultural memory as memory deliberately constructed and transmitted through texts, as I have done above, opens up another set of questions: what difference, if any, is there between cultural memory and history? Why is Parshat Zakhor, with its commandment to remember, the important passage, the passage that gets read out loud in the synagogue twice during the liturgical year? Why not its cognate passage (Exod 17:14), in which God commands Moses to write the fate of Amalek "as a remembrance in the record" (זכרון בספר) to be passed on to Joshua and the generations that followed?

What we saw in the passages from Marx and Nietzsche discussed at the end of the second section of this chapter was a subtle shift in the way that memory has been construed: at the time they wrote, "memory" was

---

51. Connerton himself holds that "In both the Old Testament and the prayer-book 'remembrance' becomes a technical term through which expression is given to the process by which practising Jews recall and recuperate in their present life the major formative events in the history of their community" (*How Societies Remember*, 46).

52. The distinction between "remember" as a performative verb and memory-as-utterance is subtle, but the performative verb is still referring to a process which takes place through the utterance, whereas in Childs's memory-as-utterance, the utterance *is* the process.

53. Connerton, *How Societies Remember*, 38–39; Connerton's admission of oral tradition, passed from grandparent to grandchild (rather than from parent to child) is based on his reading of Marc Bloch, who was a colleague of Halbwachs (see Castelli, *Martyrdom and Memory*, 19).

beginning to move from signifying an operation of an individual mind to signifying a mode of relationship between the present and the past. It is from this wider construal that twentieth-century theories of memory arose, striving to make distinctions between memory and history (as well as between different types of memory) that would have been unnecessary prior to this merging of terms. Halbwachs began to draw the line between the two in the second chapter of *The Collective Memory*.[54] He characterizes history as an external framework, devoid of personal connection: "Proper names, dates, formulas summarizing a long sequence of details, occasional anecdotes or quotations, are the epitaphs to those bygone events, as brief, general, and scant of meaning as most tombstone inscriptions. History indeed resembles a crowded cemetery, where room must constantly be made for new tombstones."[55] Paul Ricoeur writes that this passage in *The Collective Memory* marks a sharp division between "living memory" and the abstract anonymity of history:

> History is first learned by memorizing dates, facts, names, striking events, important persons, holidays to celebrate. [...] At this stage of discovery, itself remembered after the fact, history is perceived, mainly by the student, as "external" and dead. The negative mark placed on the facts mentioned consists in the student's not being able to witness them. It is the province of hearsay and of didactic reading. The feeling of externality is reinforced by the calendrical framework of the events taught: at this age one learns to read the calendar as one learns to read the clock.[56]

It is worth noting that while Connerton identified the repetition of rituals *within a calendrical framework* as one of the primary methods of collective (or cultural) memory transmission, Ricoeur sees the calendar as enforcing the externality of the past, moving it away from the realm of memory and into the realm of history. It is also worth noting that, for Ricoeur, as for Halbwachs, memory is "living" and history "dead"; this dichotomy is present, to greater or lesser extents, in most attempts to theorize the difference between history and cultural memory.

Thus, we have also Pierre Nora's assertion that "There are *lieux de mémoire*, sites of memory, because there are no longer *milieux de mémoire*,

---

54. Halbwachs, *The Collective Memory*, 50–87.
55. Ibid., 52.
56. Ricoeur, *Memory, History, Forgetting*, 394.

real environments of memory."[57] Nora identifies the cause of the "memory boom"[58] as "the acceleration of history," the increased speed at which the past is overtaken by "our hopelessly forgetful modern societies."[59] It does not take Nora long to arrive at the same point as Ricoeur:[60]

> Memory and history, far from being synonymous, appear now to be in fundamental opposition. Memory is life, borne by living societies founded in its name. It remains in permanent evolution, open to the dialectic of remembering and forgetting, unconscious of its successive deformations, vulnerable to manipulation and appropriation, susceptible to being long dormant and periodically revived. History, on the other hand, is the reconstruction, always problematic and incomplete, of what is no longer.[61]

The two commands in Parshat Zakhor now become quite clear: to keep the wrongdoings perpetrated by Amalek in living memory (the commandment is not "Remember Amalek," but "Remember *what Amalek did*"), but to let the Amalekites themselves fade from the immediacy of memory into the distant realm of history; to recite, but not relive, the details of the encounter.

This distinction (though not its relation to Parshat Zakhor) has also been made by the historian Yosef Hayim Yerushalmi, in his influential book *Zakhor: Jewish History and Jewish Memory*. "The biblical appeal to remember [. . .] has little to do with curiosity about the past," he writes. "Israel is told only that it must be a kingdom of priests and holy people; nowhere is it suggested that it become a nation of historians."[62] Rather than the distinction between living, immediate memory and dead, external history found in Ricoeur and Nora, however, Yerushalmi argues that memory is selective in nature. History is neutral, recording the past in its entirety; memory transmits only the fragments of past that it deems relevant—in the case of Jewish memory, only the moments of God's intervention into his-

---

57. Pierre Nora, "Memory and History," 7. This article is identical to the preface to *Les Lieux de Mémoire*, available in English as *Realms of Memory*.

58. This phrase is widely used to describe the surge of interest in memory, and especially collective memory, evident in the humanities since the 1980's. See Berliner, "Abuses of Memory," 197–211; David G. Rosenfeld, "A Flawed Prophecy," 508–20; Volf, "End of Memory," 39–40; Winter, *Remembering War*, 1.

59. Nora, *Realms of Memory*, 8.

60. Ricoeur actually wrote *Memory, History, and Forgetting* after Nora's *Realms of Memory* was published, and includes Nora in his analysis.

61. Nora, *Realms of Memory*, 8.

62. Yerushalmi, *Zakhor*, 10.

tory are worthy of passing into memory.[63] This distinction perhaps ignores the claim that history is itself not a set of events, but rather a set of texts, a narrative constructed after the events themselves have passed.[64] It does, however, highlight the constructed nature of cultural memory. This process of construction is my concern in the remainder of this book.

Rabbi Shapira's reading of Parshat Zakhor placed the deeds of Amalek firmly in the realm of living memory by relating those deeds to the situation in which Shapira and his congregation found themselves. The Jews hearing Shapira's sermon in the Warsaw Ghetto did not have to strive to recall the details of what Amalek did to them on their journey, after they left Egypt, as Ricouer imagined the young Maurice Halbwachs straining to recall the details of his history lessons; they knew perfectly well how the SS took advantage of their famine and weariness, cutting down those too weak to defend themselves.[65] Shapira's sermon built a connection between the two oppressions, enabling his listeners to reach back beyond their own personal memory to interpret their experiences within the narrative framework provided by the cultural memory transmitted through the regular recital of scripture. In turn, the personal memories of the members of the community buttressed the viability of the Amalek narrative as a cultural memory, a part of their own living (and lived) experience.

This, I suggest, is the primary function of a memorial: to move the past from the realm of history into the realm of memory, by forging an active connection to the lived experience of the individuals who encounter it. A memorial, as I understand it, should not be confused with Nora's *lieu de mémoire*, although many of the *lieux* that Nora describes could also, given the proper circumstances, function as memorials. However, Nora believes that *lieux de mémoire* are little more than archives, sorting facilities which

---

63. Yerushalmi, *Zakhor*, 10–11.

64. See, for example, de Certeau, *Writing of History*, 5-6: "It appears to me that in the West, for the last four centuries, 'the making of history' has referred to writing." See also Clark, *History, Theory, Text*, 19: "The historical fact must be recognized not as 'what really happened,' but as 'what the evidence obliges us to believe.'"

65. Compare with Emil Fackenheim's description of the search for a biblical parallel to Hitler: "Though foredoomed to failure—Hitler is without precedent—inevitably the search goes on, must go on. It fails with the Pharaohs, for these were pragmatic enemies only. [. . .] Failing with Pharaoh, the search then turns to Amalek, but this too fails, for this Biblical enemy attacks the weakest only because they are easiest to defeat. The enemy of our time has only one Biblical type that comes close to being his prototype, but this one is uncannily close: the Haman of Esther, who wants to kill all Jews because of the trifling slight of a single Jew." Fackenheim, *Jewish Bible*, 60–61.

help to shepherd the last vestiges of living memory into the storehouse of history; a memorial functions in the opposite direction. A memorial forges an emotional link between an individual and a past event which they themselves did not experience directly, enabling them to relate to the past *as if* they had personally encountered it, and through that relation renders the past an active part of that individual's living experience. This is a well-documented function of Jewish liturgy, but such functionality is not limited to Jewish tradition, nor to liturgy; architectural sites (the classic "memorial" form, although I hasten to point out that not every monument provides the emotional conduit necessary for it to be a memorial in the technical sense that I am proposing), literature, even film, music, and visual art can act as memorials.

This process is similar, though not quite identical to, Marianne Hirsch's concept of postmemory. Hirsch coined the term to describe the experience of the children of Holocaust survivors (such as the protagonists of the two novels I discuss in my concluding chapter), whose lives are shaped by a consciousness of events which they themselves were not alive to experience. Hirsch suggests that "postmemory is distinguished from memory by generational distance and from history by deep personal connection"—it is, in her formulation, like the wreckage that piles at the feet of Walter Benjamin's Angel of History, real and present detritus from an unseen catastrophe, around which the children of Holocaust survivors must navigate with care.[66] Postmemory functions in a very similar fashion to cultural memory, but on a familial, rather than societal, scale; the network of social performances which Halbwachs and Connerton suggest constitute social memory is denser and more immediate within the family sphere, and the emotive quality of the consciousness of the past thus transmitted is sharper. Hirsch is not entirely consistent in her deployment of the term, however; Laura Levitt in particular has critiqued Hirsch's suggestion that a site such as the Tower of Faces at the United States Holocaust Memorial Museum is capable of bringing visitors who lack a personal family connection to the Holocaust into the circle of postmemory.[67] This inconsistency is itself consistent with the slight blurring of boundaries between familial and societal loss experienced in wartime, a topic which I will address over the course of the next three chapters, before returning to a direct engagement with issues of Holocaust representation and postmemory in my final two chapters.

66. Hirsch, *Family Frames*, 22; Walter Benjamin, "Philosophy of History," 249.
67. Levitt, *American Jewish Loss*, 32–33.

TWO

Antigone and Athenian War-dead

Body and Identity in the Greek Tradition

Biblical texts are not the only ancient texts with a significant interpretative afterlife. Western culture has also had a lengthy relationship of re-reading with the literature of ancient Greece and Rome—this is the origin of the "Western philosophical tradition," which I contrasted with the Jewish tradition of biblical interpretation in chapter one. In this chapter, I will turn to a brief examination of Sophocles' *Antigone* and its history of interpretation as a window into the way that discourse over mourning and ownership of the dead has developed. This discussion will provide a framework for the readings of Canadian material that I will undertake in the second part of the book, and especially my reading of Jane Urquhart's *The Stone Carvers*.

George Steiner locates Jacques Barthélémy's 1788 work, *Le Voyage de jeune Anacharsis*, at the beginning point of *Antigone*'s entrance into modern Western cultural consciousness after a lengthy period of textual obscurity. "In chapter XI," he writes, "the hero is taken to see his first Attic tragedy. It is Sophocles' *Antigone* and the young Anacharsis is overwhelmed: 'Quel merveilleux assortiment d'illusions & de réalités! Je volois au secours des deux amants . . .'"[1] It is a rather peculiar sort of reading that would characterize Sophocles' tragedy as first and foremost about the love between Antigone and Haemon; however, Barthélémy was simply the beginning of a long tradition of readings which have inserted emotional motivations into the play at the cost of obscuring its more substantial discourse on the opposition between state and familial power.

Simon Goldhill argues that Greek tragedy as a whole is intimately bound up in the political concerns of the time and place in which it was first written and performed, as a contribution to the "continuing public debate

---

1. Steiner, *Antigones*, 7.

Antigone and Athenian War-dead

on internal political developments."[2] A number of readings of Sophocles' *Antigone* link it to a debate over public burial in Athens during the fifth century BCE, as the city was in transition from an oligarchy to a democracy. I will briefly review these historically contextualized contemporary readings before returning to my own reading of the character of Antigone, in both the Sophoclean tragedy and a twentieth-century re-interpretation of the Antigone myth penned by Jean Anouilh. It should be noted at the outset—and repeated frequently—that I am not at all interested in a reading of *Antigone* that casts her as a tragic heroine defending religious values against the encroachment of the state. Rather, I am interested in the competing claims of authority exercised over the body of Polynices, and the way they are presented and negotiated, without attributing value to one position over or against the other. As my later analysis of the competing claims of Antigone and Creon shows, Sophocles presents both positions as significantly flawed, in startlingly similar fashions.

HISTORICAL CONTEXT

The early fifth century BCE saw Athens transforming from a city-state (*polis*) into an empire.[3] Following a victory over the Persian army in the battle of Salamis (478 BCE), a number of Greek city-states banded together to form the Delian League; by 454 BCE, the League's treasury and governance were both firmly located in Athens.[4] Over the next several decades, Athens consolidated its position as the center of the Empire.[5] This transition wrought many changes in Athenian daily life; I am interested here particularly in the relocation of mourning and burial practices for dead soldiers from the private to the public sphere.

---

2. Goldhill, *Orestia*, 2. See also Goldhill, "Civic Ideology." While Goldhill's primary textual engagement is with Aeschlyus, rather than Sophocles, large portions of his argument are about ancient Athenian tragedy in general.

3. I am greatly indebted in this section to Rebecca Futo Kennedy, for the many informative conversations we have had about the development of the Athenian empire. Most of what I now understand about the history of the period was learned in the process of editing her book, *Athena's Justice*. For the significance of Athenian imperialism in *Antigone*, see Patterson, "Practice of Burial," 38.

4. Kennedy, *Athena's Justice*, 5.

5. Kennedy argues that this process of consolidation took place largely through the transference of legal authority from the other cities in the League to the Athenian courts (*Athena's Justice*, 22; 31–32), and also, importantly, through the spread of the cult of Athena from Athens to the rest of Greece (*Athena's Justice*, 7).

33

PART ONE: Remembering to Forget

Prior to the fifth century, it is unclear whether most Athenian war-dead were cremated, and their ashes brought back to Athens for private burial, or whether internment on the field of battle was more common. Thucydides mentions the soldiers who were killed at the Battle of Marathon as receiving the exceptional honor of battlefield burial.[6] However, this passage is commonly known as "Thucydides' Blunder," due to a wealth of evidence indicating that battlefield burial was far more common than that passage indicates.[7] Regardless of where soldiers were buried—in their native earth or the ground on which they fell—it is clear that both the internment of repatriated bodies and commemoration of un-repatriated soldiers were carried out by private families on public ground: the Acropolis was littered with military memorials erected by members of the aristocracy.[8] There is a wide gap between the public burial of war dead described by Thucydides (and his description of the ceremony is still regarded as authoritative, regardless of the puzzle of the Marathon burial) and any picture that has been drawn of Athenian war-burial and commemoration prior to 508 BCE, and the transition from one practice to another was no more seamless than the advent of democracy, with which it coincided. The tensions that arose in fifth century Athens over burial, commemoration, and above all ownership of the bodies of the dead played out on the tragic stage, particularly in Sophocles' *Antigone*.[9] These tensions echo into the present day, and a particularly strong parallel exists between the Athenian Empire in the mid-fifth century (BCE) and the British Empire in the early twentieth century (CE).[10]

Christoph Clairmont dates the genesis of public burial of war dead to the early fifth century BCE.[11] Prior to that, he suggests the textual evidence

---

6. Thucydides, *History*, 319 (Book 2, ch. 34, section 5). See also Clairmont, *Patrios Nomos*, 16; Tyrrell and Bennett, *Recapturing Sophocles' Antigone*, 7.

7. See, for example, Toher, "'Thucydides' Blunder,'" 497–501; see also Pritchett, *Greek State at War*, 94–95.

8. G. Anderson, *Athenian Experiment*, 107; Clairmont, *Patrios Nomos*, 16–21.

9. See Tyrrell and Bennett, *Recapturing Sophocles' Antigone*, 7–14. See also the essays collected in *Helios* 33S (2006).

10. Judith Butler traces the heritage of family/state tension through philosophical criticism of *Antigone* in Lacan, Irigary, and Hegel; however, her analysis focuses on Antigone as an agent against the state, and ignores the significance of the dead body as an object to be claimed by one group or another, lacking in voice, agency, or intrinsic identity of its own. See Butler, *Antigone's Claim*, 1–25. See also Griffith, "Introduction," 48–50.

11. Clairmont, *Patrios Nomos*, 2.

indicates that "individual families cared for the burial of the sons who died in warfare," although he admits that public honors for particularly exceptional individuals were not unheard of.[12] However, it would be incorrect to assume that the difficulty of repatriation or the honor associated with a public funeral made the removal of mourning and burial rites from the familial domain a simple matter. William Blake Tyrrell and Larry J. Bennett note that this removal signaled a sharp divide in Athenian society:

> The public funeral exacerbated the antagonism of the demos and the family over funeral celebrations by separating the dead from their families. Women had brought the dead into the world in the company of women, and they or other women of the family should have prepared the bodies for burial and mourned them. Bones and ashes brought home by family members could be tended in the house, but the public funeral replaced the body of the deceased and moved the place of grieving from the house with its familiar things and smells to the open sunny spaces of the men's agora. Although the public ritual allotted two days for the family to mourn the loss, twice that allowed for private funerals, such concessions paled before the splendor of the third day, when the civic values underlying the ceremony came to the fore.[13]

It is in this context that they suggest the confrontation between Antigone and Creon, staged by Sophocles circa 442–438 BCE, should be read, with Antigone representing the female, familial sphere usurped by the intrusion of Creon's male public law.[14] This thesis has been questioned by Cynthia Patterson, who notes that "[p]ublic burial 'in their native earth' was a notable honor and distinction; there is no evidence that men and women (as

---

12. Ibid., 2.

13. Tyrrell and Bennett, *Recapturing Sophocles'* Antigone, 9. See also Holst-Warhaft, *Dangerous Voices*, 121–23.

14. The earliest date given for the first performance of Sophocles' *Antigone* is 442–441 BCE; see Ferrario, "Replaying *Antigone*," 79; Griffith, "Introduction," 1–2; Patterson, "Practice of Burial," 34. Tyrrell and Bennett place the first performance at 438 BCE (*Recapturing Sophocles'* Antigone, 3–4): they make a convincing case for their dating, especially when they read the punishment inflicted on the corpse of Polynices as an echo of the punishment inflicted on the commanders of the Samian ships in the aftermath of the Samian war (440–439 BCE)—see *Recapturing Sophocles'* Antigone, 4–5. As the precise date is largely irrelevant to my discussion here, I have opted to maintain the range of possible dates. For the gender divide in *Antigone*, see Griffith, "Introduction," 51–54; Steiner, *Antigones*, 9–11, 236–42. For a discussion of the division between and overlap of public and private spheres of influence in the play, see Derderian, *Leaving Words to Remember*, 139–40.

PART ONE: Remembering to Forget

groups) disagreed on that point," and that only the intrusion of the state permitted burial of war-dead in Athens (as opposed to on the battlefield where they fell) at all.[15] I would suggest an interpretative middle ground between Tyrrell/Bennett and Patterson: while there may be no evidence to suggest that women, *as a group*, were unimpressed by the honor a public burial conveyed to their family members, neither is it unreasonable to suppose that women, *as individuals*, may not have been entirely happy to cede their authority over a previously private and familial ritual to the *polis*, no matter how much honor may have been involved. The error made by both Patterson and those she criticizes is to treat a group of people as though it possesses but one mind—the same difficulty which I pointed out as plaguing most theories of collective memory in chapter one.[16]

At the heart of the ambivalence surrounding the public funeral lies a question of memorialization and identity. A living body is complex, possessed of a personality and subjectivity, able to self-identify as a member of many different groups; a dead body loses the ability to self-narrate, and instead becomes an object to be claimed by one group or another.[17] The corpse of an Athenian soldier could not be buried both in the family tomb and in the common grave of the public ceremony; in death, one facet of identity would be emphasized, to the detriment of any others.[18] The honor

15. Patterson, "Practice of Burial," 26–27; 36.

16. Joan V. O'Brien points out that the "dialectical tension between individual and community" was peculiar to Athens at this "brief moment in Athenian history," in which the value placed on the individual was higher than at other times or in other Greek cities. O'Brien, *Guide to Sophocles'* Antigone, 34. See also Ferrario, "Replaying *Antigone*," 104–5.

It is also worth noting that, at approximately this same time, Pericles felt the need to include a warning regarding the proper conduct of female mourners in his funeral oration for the dead from the Peloponnesian War (Thucydides, *History*, 317–19; Book 2, ch. 34). The presence of such an exhortation would appear to indicate some nonconformity on the part of the Athenian women.

17. This transformation of body into object is similar to, but not the same as, the linguistic transformation described by Elaine Scarry, discussed in the prelude. The fundamental difference is that this transformation occurs after, and as a consequence of, death, whereas Scarry's transformation occurs prior to death, and, in her scheme, is what makes death (which is to say, the killing of one human being by another) possible.

18. Closterman, "Family Members and Citizens," discusses at length the ways in which burial practices cemented the identity of not only the person being buried but also their surviving family members. Closterman notes especially a pair of monuments to a soldier named Dexilos (d. 394 BCE) which appears to accomplish precisely what I have just said cannot be accomplished: Dexilos was buried in a public gravesite with other soldiers, and his family erected a monument in their family burial ground, thus memorializing him in both of the contexts at issue here. However, the fact remains that Dexilos's

of a public burial could obliterate, or threaten to obliterate, the private, familial identity of the soldier.[19] Indeed, since the public burial was a mass burial, with the war-dead of each tribe placed together in a common chest, and one funeral oration for all the war-dead of Athens, the individuality of the soldier was subordinated to their role as a member of the Athenian military.[20]

COMPETING CLAIMS

The conflict over the body of Polynices in Sophocles' *Antigone*, then, is a conflict between his civic identity and his familial role: between the meaning of his body to the state—as a traitor, an example, a locus of authority—and the meaning of his body in a more intimate context—as a brother, a link to the memory of a previously cohesive, now shattered family unit.[21] This conflict of meanings is evident even in two short passages from the text. The first comes at the end of Creon's first speech, delivered with only the chorus onstage; Antigone is not present to hear it, although she related the substance of the decree to Ismene in the previous scene:[22]

> Creon: Eteocles, who died fighting for this city, having excelled in battle, we shall hide in the tomb and we shall render to him all the

---

body was only buried in one grave; the other monument marked the absence, rather than the presence, of a body. It is, of course, possible for a corpse to be broken down into fragments and buried in different locations—this was, for example, common practice with saints' relics. However, I would argue that at that point the body ceases to be *a body*; moreover, there is, to the best of my knowledge, no evidence that this practice was ever utilised in ancient Athens, or in the British Commonwealth. The fragmentation of saints' bodies into relics is usually not the result of any ambiguity in their identities, but rather a way of making their already fixed identity available to a wider number of people.

19. Although the Athenian war-dead were placed in ten separate caskets, one for each tribe, and memorial stele in the Agora listed the dead by tribe, restoring some measure of ownership to the larger, extended family. See Loraux, *The Invention of Athens*, 19.

20. Loraux, *The Invention of Athens*, 55–56; Tyrrell and Bennett, *Recapturing Sophocles' Antigone*, 7; Ferrario, "Replaying *Antigone*," 85. See also Goldhill, "Civic Ideology," for a discussion of the role that public performances of tragedy (especially the ceremonies conducted prior to the play) played in subordinating the individual to the state.

21. Again, note that the crucial point here is that Polynices himself is unable to exercise any agency in determining what meaning will be ascribed to his body by outside forces. See Butler, *Antigone's Claim*, 2–5. Butler points out that these two apparently contradictory meanings ascribed to Polynices' body are actually mutually dependent; the state rests on structures of kinship, and kinship requires "the support and mediation of the state" (5).

22. Soph.*Ant.*, 7 (lines 21–39).

> rites that come to the noblest of the dead below. But his brother, I mean Polynices, who came back from exile meaning to burn to the ground and to enslave its people, as for him it is proclaimed to this city that none shall bury or lament, but they shall leave his body unburied for birds and dogs to devour and savage. That is my way of thinking, and never by my will shall bad men exceed good men in honor. No, whoever is loyal to the city in death and life alike shall from me have honor.[23]

Notable in this speech is Creon's strict adherence to a general civic principle ("never by my will shall bad men exceed good men in honor") without regard to the particular familial circumstances in which it is applied; Creon can remember that Polynices is Eteocles' brother, but either cannot or will not recognize that that relationship means that Polynices is also a member of Creon's own family—and that the proper burial of his body is thus Creon's own responsibility.[24] Creon's notion of family is entirely bounded by his notion of civic duty, and those who fall outside the latter (such as Polynices, and, later, Antigone) can have no claim on him in regards to the former. This rigidity of thought is also apparent in Antigone's last speech, delivered in front of the chorus and Creon, though not actually addressed to any living person.[25] A portion of this speech (lines 904–20; the section of the quote below beginning "Yet in the eyes of the wise") is regarded by some relatively recent scholars as an interpolation.[26] However, those lines

---

23. Soph.*Ant.*, 20–23 (lines 194–210).

24. See O'Brien, *Guide to Sophocles'* Antigone, 35; Rehm, *Marriage to Death*, 60; Tyrrell and Bennett, *Recapturing Sophocles'* Antigone, 46–49.

25. There is some debate as to whether Creon is present during this speech, or whether he exits and returns; see Griffith, "Commentary," 281; O'Brien, *Guide to Sophocles'* Antigone, 101; Steiner, *Antigones*, 279.

26. This may say a great deal more about modern reading habits than it does about the text itself; this bit of cold rationality runs counter to the image of Antigone as the distraught, devoted sister favored by emotively motivated interpretations of the play. Anouilh's re-imagining of Antigone, discussed below, is far more connected to this image than Sophocles' original. See Griffith, "Commentary," 277–79; O'Brien, *Guide to Sophocles'* Antigone, 102–3; Steiner, *Antigones*, 280–81. For an attempt at reading Antigone's motivations as equally emotional and duty-driven, see Held, "Antigone's Dual Motivation." George Steiner may shed some light on the modern tendency towards an overly emotional rendering of Antigone, when he traces the re-entry of the play into Western consciousness back to Abbé Jean-Jacques Barthélémy's 1788 work, *Le Voyage du jeune Anacharsis*: "In chapter XI, the hero is taken to see his first Attic tragedy. It is Sophocles' *Antigone* and the young Anacharsis is overwhelmed: 'Quel merveilleux assortiment d'illusions & de réalités! Je volois au secours des deux amants . . .'" It is a peculiar reading that would characterise the play as first and foremost about the love between Antigone

are firmly part of the textual tradition of the play, and, more importantly, illustrate the familial structure which undergirds Antigone's construction of Polynices' identity.

> Antigone: But when I come there, I am confident that I shall come dear to my father, dear to you, my mother, and dear to you, my own brother; since when you died it was I that with my own hands washed you and adorned you and poured libations on your graves; and now, Polynices, for burying your body I get this reward! Yet in the eyes of the wise I did well to honor you; for never, had children of whom I was the mother or had my husband perished and been moldering there, would I have taken on myself this task, in defiance of the citizens. In virtue of what law do I say this? If my husband had died, I could have had another, and a child by another man, if I had lost the first, but with my mother and my father in Hades below, I could never have another brother. Such was the law for whose sake I did you special honor, but to Creon I seemed to do wrong and to show shocking recklessness, O my own brother.[27]

Antigone values familial relationships based on blood ties (to mother, father, and brothers) over and above those formed by choice (to a hypothetical husband, or any children she may have produced with him), but, like Creon, favors some blood ties over others. Just as Creon forgets his relationship and responsibilities to the dead body of Polynices, Antigone willfully forgets her relationship to the living Ismene (and her more distant relationship to Creon himself).[28] Her family is defined by her contact with their bodies; they are those that she "with my own hands washed [. . .] and adorned."[29]

The actual face-to-face confrontation between Antigone and Creon is quite brief, and the dialogue nowhere near as philosophically satisfying as the speeches each makes when the other is absent. Creon and Antigone

---

and Haemon, but if this is, indeed, the vehicle by which the play came to popular attention, then the centrality of Antigone's love, transferred from Haemon to her brother, in later readings can better be understood. See Steiner, *Antigones*, 7.

27. Soph.*Ant.*, 86–89 (lines 897–915).

28. This is a case of Antigone exercising the exact same limited approach to kinship as does Creon; Ismene (and Creon) has transgressed the principles by which Antigone measures relationship and so no longer counts—see Soph.*Ant.*, 11–13, 53–55 (lines 70–96, 538–549); Butler, *Antigone's Claim*, 9–10; Steiner, *Antigones*, 265–66. For Antigone's similarity to Creon, see Butler, *Antigone's Claim*, 6; Patterson, "Practice of Burial," 38–39; Tyrrell and Bennett, *Recapturing Sophocles'* Antigone, 75.

29. Soph.*Ant.*, 86 (lines 900–901).

do not really enter into a conversation about the body of Polynices; they do not have sufficient common ground to converse. Their argument consists of each repeating and elaborating upon their basic assertion, neither able to enter into the other's worldview sufficiently to engage with and challenge their own assertion.[30] For both Creon and Antigone, one facet of Polynices' identity must override and obliterate the other: he is either a brother or an enemy; his body must be treated in the fashion appropriate for one or the other. It cannot be both.

What is markedly absent from all this debate over the appropriate role and placement of Polynices' body is any debate at all over Polynices himself. He exists for both Antigone and Creon almost entirely as a symbol of the principles, civic or familial, for which each of them argue. All of Antigone's speeches in defense of his right to burial concentrate on the strength of the familial bond. Not once does she mention that his behavior in life merits any particular treatment of his body in death—that he was, for example, a kind man, fond of dogs and small children. All of Creon's invective against him is focused on his symbolic role as an enemy of the *polis*, the leader of an attacking army, a set of claims which make little sense in the larger context of the drama. If Polynices was attempting to conquer Thebes in order to gain what he almost certainly saw as his rightful place on the throne (and let us not forget that he was the elder brother), how seriously can we take the idea of him defiling his own temples, selling his own household into slavery?[31] Creon never tells us, never offers any proof, that Polynices is exactly the sort of person who would do such things; rather, he seems to expect his listeners both on stage and in the audience to understand that the position of Polynices's body outside the walls of the city as complete substantiation of his claims—the body's location once again serving as proof of one identity, at the cost of other possible identities.[32]

---

30. See Griffith, "Introduction," 34–35.

31. Soph.*Ant.*, 21 (lines 199–202). See Griffith, "Introduction," 30–1, "Commentary," 161–62; Tyrrell and Bennett, *Recapturing Sophocles'* Antigone, 49; Steiner, *Antigones*, 215–21.

32. Of course, Polynices's willingness to bring foreigners to aid his capture of the city may have made it easier for Creon to paint him as a traitor. For commentary on this issue, see Griffith, "Commentary," 161; Holt, "Polis and Tragedy," 663. The body lying outside the city walls is different from the body lying outside the territory of the city, as that territory extended beyond the walls. Athenian law provided for denial of burial within the "native earth" of Athens; it is Creon's refusal to permit Polynices' body to be moved elsewhere for burial that is shocking to Athenian sentiment. See Griffith, "Introduction," 31; Holt, "Polis and Tragedy," 663–65; Patterson, "Practice of Burial," 33. Holt rejects the

ANOUILH'S *ANTIGONE*

Jean Anouilh's rendering of the tragedy, written and produced in Nazi-occupied France, both fills in and highlights the gaps in Sophocles' text.[33] This is an odd drama; its English debut included in the program a note from the translator, Lewis Galantière: "The reader will have to take my word for it that only the citizen of a German-occupied country [. . .] would be able to come away from the play feeling that Antigone's case is stronger than Creon's".[34] And yet, read with a strong consciousness that the play *is* meant to be about the French Resistance, that Creon's counsel that Antigone ought to live, and be happy, is the counsel of a totalitarian regime persuading its citizens to mind their own business and go about their daily activities uninterrupted, Anouilh's drama almost eclipses the *pathos* of the original. At the same time, however, we should remember that Sophocles' original Antigone, with her championing of aristocratic family values, was also a rather difficult character for the democratic Athenian audience to engage with; Anouilh's Antigone is, perhaps, true to the spirit of the problematic and unsympathetic original.

Antigone's defense of Polynices on the basis of their kinship is fatally undermined by Creon's attack against Polynices' worthiness *as a person*:

> CREON: Poor Antigone! With her night-club flower. Do you know what your brother was?
>
> ANTIGONE: Whatever he was, I know that you will say vile things about him.
>
> CREON: A cheap, idiotic bounder, that is what he was. A cruel, vicious little voluptuary. A little beast with just wit enough to drive a car faster and throw more money away than any of his pals. I was with your father one day when Polynices, having lost a lot of money gambling, asked him to settle the debt; and when your

---

suggestion that there is anything shocking about Creon's denial of burial, and maintains that he acts perfectly within what an Athenian audience would recognise as the law. His, however, is a minority opinion, and does not produce a particularly coherent reading of the play. However, see MacKay, "Antigone, Coriolanus, and Hegel," which argues that the controversy over the burial of Themistocles (c. 459 BCE) provides a useful context for the debate between Antigone and Creon.

33. For a point-by-point comparison between Anouilh's and Sophocles' versions of the drama, see Deutsch, "Anouilh's Antigone." See also the response to Deutsch's review by Schlesinger, "Anouilh's Antigone Again."

34. Cited in Berry, "Antigone and the French Resistance," 17.

PART ONE: Remembering to Forget

> father refused, the boy raised his hand against him and called him a vile name.
>
> ANTIGONE: That's a lie!
>
> CREON: He struck your father in the face with his fist. It was pitiful.[35]

Here, the argument could be made that the conflict is really one of (symbolic) familial affection against actual merit, as Creon's recollection of Polynices's actual character overwhelms Antigone's blind loyalty to a brother she last saw when she was twelve years old. However, Antigone's attempt at refutation here is not, as it is in Sophocles, an assertion of the familial bond transcending any flaws in character. Rather, she attempts to deny that the flaws are real: "That's a lie!" Presumably, then, in this version of the tale Polynices' merit or lack thereof in life still has some impact on the way his body ought to be treated in death. Otherwise, Anouilh's Antigone would have no need to refute Creon's claims. They would be, as they are to the Antigone of Sophocles, simply irrelevant.[36]

The continuation of Creon's speech, however, re-introduces an element of uncertainty regarding the state of Polynices's body:

> Funny, isn't it? Polynices lies rotting in the sun while Eteocles is given a hero's funeral and will be housed in a marble vault. Yet I have absolute proof that everything that Polynices did, Eteocles had plotted to do. They were a pair of blackguards--both engaged in selling out Thebes, and both engaged in selling out each other; and they died like the cheap gangsters they were, over a division of the spoils.
>
> But, as I told you a moment ago, I had to make a martyr of one of them. I sent out to the holocaust for their bodies; they were found clasped in one another's arms—for the first time in their lives, I imagine. Each had been spitted on the other's sword, and

---

35. Anouilh, "Antigone," trans. Galantière, 53–54.

36. The divide between Anouilh's and Sophocles' Antigone has much to do with the divide Lars Albinus has identified as existing between the ancient and modern concepts of ψυχή (psyche): "The modern meaning of psyche, or soul, is basically conceived in terms of *self* or *identity*. With regards to the concept of ψυχή, the opposite is actually stated in the beginning of the *Illiad*, where [. . .] the deceased is clearly identified with the 'corpse' (σῶμα) and not with the psyche, which flies off to the invisible realm of memory." In other words, for Sophocles, Polynices *is* his body, whereas to Anouilh, there is a distinction to be drawn between the body and the person. See Albinus, *House of Hades*, 43–44. See also Kurts and Boardman, *Greek Burial Customs*, 331.

the Argive cavalry had trampled them down. They were mashed to a pulp, Antigone. I had the prettier of the two carcases brought in, and gave it a State funeral; and I left the other to rot. I don't know which was which. And I assure you, I don't care.[37]

This passage shows also a sharp contrast between Anouilh's and Sophocles' Creon, the latter of which, "by differentiating between them [the brothers] [. . .] is blinded to the more compelling reality of their sameness as corpses."[38] Anouilh's Creon sees Eteocles and Polynices as interchangeable in both death and life; he uses this interchangeablility to blind *others* to their sameness, by creating a hero of one and a villain of the other. This now total ambiguity of the unburied body proves fatal to Antigone's position; she succumbs entirely to Creon's argument, and (briefly) resolves to let him cover up her disobedience so that she can live, marry Haemon, and be happy. Clearly, the issue of personal rather than symbolic identity matters more to Anouilh than it did to Sophocles; one would expect the latter's Antigone to respond here that the unburied body belongs to *a* brother, regardless of which *particular* brother it is.

In Anouilh's version, Antigone eventually chooses death, against all of Creon's arguments, as a protest against the banality of life, rather than out of deference to a higher authority or as a show of solidarity with her dead brother(s). The corpse of Polynices (or Eteocles) fades from the attention of both characters and audience—the revelation of the body's ambiguous personal identity is also a revelation of its unimportance, and the rest of the play focuses on the inexplicable and unavoidable mechanisms which compose Anouilh's vision of the tragic.[39] Not so for Sophocles, who insists that Creon must bury Polynices before attempting to un-bury Antigone, thus keeping the body, with all its symbolic weight (but no personality), at the center of the action right up until the end of the play. The burial and memorialization practices of the First World War, as we shall see, reflect the tensions that have been uncovered here: between body and personality, between familial and civic group membership. Although there have been attempts to restore the body to prominence, either in burial practice or in discourse about the costs of warfare (as in the work of Elaine Scarry), memorialization since 1914 has focused increasingly on a more nebulous

37. Anouilh, "Antigone," trans. Galantière, 55.
38. Tyrrell and Bennett, *Recapturing Sophocles'* Antigone, 49.
39. For a full discussion of Anouilh's tragic vision, see Heiney, "Jean Anouilh," and especially his discussion of Antigone on pp. 333–34.

PART ONE: Remembering to Forget

concept of identity—primarily through an emphasis on the names of individuals. The relationship between body and name remains ambivalent—sometimes it is a complementary substitution, flowers propped against a memorial plaque as they might be left on a grave; sometimes the two *loci* of identity appear to be in tension with one another. This will become especially clear in the final chapter of Part Two, "Making Memory Solid," which addresses First World War memorials from a contemporary perspective, and in which the main character, Klara Becker, plays an Antigone-like role, as she attempts to maintain familial control over the memory of her dead lover and the meaning of his death, while at the same time unraveling the puzzle of mourning without a body.

PART TWO

Mourning the Absent

Introduction

He would search out graves in fields and even in private gardens. Some were marked with wooden crosses roughly made by the dead men's comrades out of the inevitable army "soap boxes," but because of the haste in which they had been erected many bore inscriptions that were soon washed away. These he would replace with "well-made crosses with a painted inscription and a tarred base."

—Philip Longworth, *The Unending Vigil: A History of the Commonwealth War Graves Commission 1917–1984*, 3

He fell in love over and over again with the clay and then the plaster renditions of the young women he created, though never with the models themselves, who seemed too actual, too specifically human to be fully interesting. For the young men, once they had evolved into the perfection of plaster, he experienced huge compassion, knowing that he had caught them just as they were letting their individual personalities go, beginning to understand that they were part of a collective, moved by the lunatic actions of war.

—Jane Urquhart, *The Stone Carvers*, 350

PART TWO: Mourning the Absent

In October 1914, an officer of the British Red Cross by the name of Fabian Ware, accompanying a superior on an inspection tour, visited Béthune Cemetery in Northern France. There, he saw "a number of English graves all with plain but carefully made wooden crosses on them," but no sign that anybody had recorded their presence or made arrangements for their maintenance.[1] In conversation with his superior, Dr. Stewart, Ware committed his unit to locating and registering "all the British graves the Unit could find."[2] Over the next three years, the scope of his project grew. On 2 March 1915 Ware informed his superiors at the Red Cross that the War Office had recognized them as the "Graves Registration Commission," solely responsible "to deal with the question of the locality, marking, and registration of the graves of the British officers and men in France;" by May of that year Ware's unit gave up normal Red Cross ambulance work, and by September the Commission was absorbed into the British military command structure and separated from the Red Cross entirely.[3] The Graves Registration Commission's mandate eventually expanded beyond France, to include all areas in which British troops had been active, and in May 1917, the Imperial War Graves Commission was officially established by Royal Charter.[4]

In the wake of war's attempted obliteration of humanity, the blotting out of Amalek, comes a pressing desire—one might even say a necessity—to memorialize both individuals and the events which led to their deaths, to testify to the value and continuation of human life. It is this desire which Ware began to act upon, and the speed with which his enterprise grew is a testament to the strength with which the need was felt by others, as well. Much of what residents of Commonwealth nations now associate with war and remembrance is a direct result of the work of the Commission. The uniform character of the battlefield graveyards, the rows of identical gravestones, the Cross of Sacrifice and Stone of Remembrance, the monuments to those with no known graves—all of these elements were consciously established by the Commission in the years during and immediately following the Great War.

One of the great disruptions the war brought to the ordinary system of mourning and remembrance was the absence of a body, a fixed point

1. Longworth, *Unending Vigil*, 3.
2. Ibid., 3.
3. Ibid., 6, 10.
4. Ibid., 27.

Introduction

for grief to focus on. Not only were the numbers of the missing—both names lacking bodies and bodies lacking names—exceptionally high, but even when bodies were successfully found, identified, and buried, they were found, identified, and buried near the battlefield. This meant that, especially in the British Empire (and later on the Commonwealth) where a policy against the repatriation of bodies was developed early in the war, the body of the soldier was not available to the soldier's family as an object of consolation. Mourning thus became less a process of coming to terms with death, and more an exercise in coping with permanent and unalterable absence. This is attested to not only in novels, from L. M. Montgomery to Jane Urquhart, but also by the requests Fabian Ware's unit received for photographs of gravesites—according to an historical pamphlet published by the Commonwealth War Graves Commission, 12,000 of these requests had been fulfilled by 1917—as well by alterations in the liturgy of the Church of England and the young Presbyterian Church in Canada.

While the carnage of the First World War necessitated significant adjustments to the practice of memorialization, these adjustments took place within the socially dominant Christian theological framework. Although the war certainly contributed to social upheaval which left its mark on German theology, in Canada (and the rest of the British Commonwealth) the socially dominant Protestant Christian theology and national myth played a mutually reinforcing role.[5] This theologically-driven commemoration set the stage for the further transformation of memorialization which would come during and after the Second World War; that war heralded a far greater transformation of theological imagination, the effects of which are still being felt.

---

5. See, for example, Cremer, "Protestant Theology in Early Weimar Germany," 289–307.

THREE

Anne of Green Gables
And the Transformation of Public Mourning

What was true of poetry was also true of fiction, and the same qualities were expected of a good fictional account of the war; it too had to be "suffused with beauty of sentiment, [and] rich in noble ideas." Few novels approximated this ideal more closely than L. M. Montgomery's *Rilla of Ingleside* [...]

—Jonathan F. Vance, *Death So Noble*, 175

"People in the first war inherited their attitudes towards death from the Victorian period," writes Alan Wilkinson in his study, *The Church of England and the First World War*. "The Evangelical emphasis upon death as the moment of judgment, and the revival of Catholic rituals for dying and burial made the deathbed of crucial religious and moral importance; the pathos of the deathbed was believed to be morally purifying," not only for the dying person, but for the instruction of the survivors, as well.[1] Burial and mourning had elaborate rituals associated with them, and the gravesite of the deceased was central to these rituals.[2]

It is this context which renders coherent the efforts of Fabian Ware and the Imperial War Graves Commission to create "gardens of the dead," and may go some ways towards removing the charge of whitewashing leveled against the Commission by Jonathan Vance in his study *Death So Noble*,

---

1. Wilkinson, *Church of England*, 173. See also the discussion of "the Victorian cult of death" in Wheeler, *Death and the Future Life*, 25–68.

2. Wheeler, *Death and the Future Life*, 27; 47–68.

when he writes that "By turning soldiers' graveyards into gardens of the dead, the commission helped the relatives of the fallen to avoid the reality of death in battle. The ordered and charming cemeteries meant that visitors never had to confront the ugliness of their relative's death."³ However, Wilkinson's work (and a similar treatise on death in the Victorian era by Michael Wheeler) is specifically concerned with the Church of England; no similar study of the Canadian churches has been published, and the extent to which the social rituals Wilkinson and Wheeler describe translated to a long-established British colony such as Canada (from which Vance writes), with its own culture, social structure, and (not least) religious *milieu*, is a more open question.⁴

To understand the disruption the First World War brought to life and death in what was then a Dominion of the British Empire, it is thus necessary to understand what constituted a normal *Canadian* death prior to the outbreak of war. Literature from the period immediately preceding the war can provide some insight into this question, provided it is approached with full consciousness that it is literature, not ethnography; we may approach a realist novel with the expectation that what it describes is life-like, but must firmly maintain our awareness that it is not life itself. This is especially true when the author herself (or himself) deliberately attempts to blur such a distinction, as in the case of Lucy Maud Montgomery.⁵

DEATH AT *GREEN GABLES* BEFORE THE WAR

Montgomery's *Anne of Green Gables* series was published between 1908 (*Anne of Green Gables*) and 1939 (*Anne of Ingleside*), although it is set between the 1880's and 1919.⁶ The books begin and end as nostalgia pieces, in

---

3. Vance, *Death So Noble*, 65.

4. It is also worth remembering that Ware himself hailed from an urban, upper-class, English background, which may have had some influence on the approach to commemoration taken by the unit under his command. See <http://www.veterans-uk.info/remembrance/ware.html> (Accessed 3 July 2009).

5. Montgomery's 1917 autobiography, *Alpine Path*, explicitly draws links between her own life and her stories, and as will be discussed below, her novels borrow liberally from her journals; Irene Gammel has argued that Montgomery's life writing and self-presentation (not just her autobiography, but her journals and photographs) were "carefully crafted [. . .] as a literary and artistic artefact;" see Gammel, "Life Writing as Masquerade," 3.

6. I am accepting the dates for the setting of the novels given by Edwards and Litster, "End of Canadian Innocence," 31.

which Montgomery recounts stories and elements of an idealized girlhood on Prince Edward Island, or looks back from the shadow of the tensions which would give birth to the Second World War towards a simpler time before the First World War, as she does in *Anne of Windy Poplars* (1936) and *Anne of Ingleside*. But *Rainbow Valley*, published in 1919, is set only ten years earlier, and *Rilla of Ingleside*, set during the First World War, was published in 1921—it is, in fact, the earliest Canadian war novel still available in print, and precedes the general war book publishing boom by several years.[7] I will return to a close reading of *Rilla* later, in order to discuss the way that Montgomery's narratives recorded the shift in memorialization activities that occurred as a result of the First World War. I am first interested in Montgomery's earlier work, the novels written before the outbreak of war: *Anne of Green Gables*, *Anne of Avonlea* (1909), and *Anne of the Island* (1915), and what these might tell us of the "normal" process of death and grieving that the war disrupted. There are four notable death scenes in these three novels: Matthew Cuthbert (*Anne of Green Gables*), Thomas Lynde (*Anne of Avonlea*), and Ruby Gillis (*Anne of the Island*), as well as Gilbert Blythe's near death (*Anne of the Island*). With the exception of Ruby Gillis's death, each of these scenes takes part near the end of the novel in which it appears, and plays an important role in the progression of the plot

---

7. Kilian, *Great War and the Canadian Novel*, claims that of all the Canadian war novels published during and immediately after the war, *Rilla of Ingleside* is one of only two that remain in print (the other being J. C. Stead's *Grain*, first published in 1926). Janet S. K. Watson notes a few reviews in the *Times Literary Supplement* dated 1919 and 1920 which indicated some degree of weariness with war stories, but she suggests that memoirs and novels dated that early were the exception, rather than the rule, and the "war literature" the *Times* complained of being overexposed to was primarily trench poetry; Watson argues that the real boom in war stories began in 1927. See Watson, *Fighting Different Wars*, 185. While Watson's study is technically limited to "Britain," by which she seems to mean modern-day Great Britain, rather than the British Empire under whose banner Canada fought the war, and thus excludes Canadian literature, she includes authors such as the very American Hemingway in her survey of publication dates, and so seems in this particular instance to be surveying a more general trend in Anglophone literature. Samuel Hynes notes a handful of trench novels written by Englishmen beginning in 1915, which would appear to have contributed to the development of a standardized set of tropes for war novels from which Montgomery very likely drew, but again, he restricts his field of enquiry to English culture. See Hynes, *A War Imagined*, 43–45, 93–95, 129–35, 206–15, 263–65. Hynes also provides some evidence that the weariness exhibited in the *TLS* reviews noted by Watson may not have needed terribly long to develop, as "[B]y November 1914 there were enough bad war poems in print to inspire an anti-war-poem poem;" see Hynes, *A War Imagined*, 28–29.

PART TWO: Mourning the Absent

and the development of Anne's character; in each of these scenes, the physical presence of the deceased is crucial.

Matthew Cuthbert

Anne's guardian, the kindly Matthew Cuthbert, dies suddenly, of a heart attack, at the end of *Anne of Green Gables*. The most notable feature of this scene is its emphasis on the act of seeing: Matthew falls down in full view of Anne, his sister Marilla (with whom he has shared Anne's guardianship) and their neighbor, Mrs. Rachel Lynde, who is particularly instrumental in guiding Anne to see and recognize the signs of death written on Matthew's face. Anne presumably has ample opportunity to continue this process of looking and recognizing, as Matthew lies in his coffin in the parlor for two days, until he is carried out to be buried.[8] Matthew's burial is narrated with an emphasis on the familiarity of his surroundings; he is "carried [. . .] over his homestead threshold and away from the fields he had tilled and the orchards he had loved and the trees he had planted."[9] While "away" introduces an element of dissimilarity, and should signify the process of separation between the dead Matthew and the land on which he had lived, the weight of the sentence falls on repeated references to the connections between him and the land: "*his* homestead [. . .] the fields *he* had tilled [. . .] *he* had loved [. . .] *he* had planted" (emphases added). His grave is near the homestead; Anne visits it, tends it, and plants "a slip of the little white Scotch rosebush his mother brought out from Scotland long ago" on it—the rosebush forging a connection between Matthew's native land of Prince Edward Island and his ancestral land of Scotland.[10] Later books in the series make frequent reference to Anne's visits to tend the grave; such visits often mark or herald significant plot developments.[11]

Irene Gammel has argued that Matthew's death was a plot device which permitted Montgomery to accomplish several things: to bring the novel to a satisfactory moral conclusion—Anne is called upon to perform a gesture of self-sacrifice, giving up her college scholarship to stay with Marilla, whose failing eyesight would otherwise necessitate the sale of

---

8. AGG, 355–56.

9. AGG, 356.

10. AGG, 357. Commemorative gardening is an ongoing theme in the *Anne* series; see also the repeated references to Hester Gray's garden (often in parallel with references to Matthew's grave): AA, 96, 110, 114, 187, 203; AI, 287.

11. See AGG, 357; AA, 110, 203.

Green Gables—to insert literary echoes of "the typical Victorian sacrifice tale" popular at the time of writing, and thus increase the book's marketability; and, not least, to come to terms with "her own heroic sacrifice, which had gone unrecognized," which is to say her own decision to live with and care for her grandmother Macneill.[12] As alluded to previously, there is an undeniably close connection between Montgomery's novels and her life-writing—both her journals (passages from which frequently appear copied wholesale into her novels) and her autobiography; it is not surprising that a decision which shaped so much of her own life might find itself recorded in a novel, nor is it surprising that it would be cloaked in a pre-fabricated trope of popular fiction. It is, however, interesting for my purposes that this death is presented as, first and foremost, an opportunity for Anne's—and, not incidentally, also Marilla's—moral development, as it is Matthew's death which permits Marilla to finally confess affection towards Anne, breaking through the emotional reticence which has marked her character for the entirety of the novel.[13]

Thomas Lynde

Matthew's death is quite sudden; there is no proper deathbed scene of the type alluded to by Wilkinson, with final speeches and moral enlightenment. Montgomery waits until the second novel, *Anne of Avonlea*, to write a death scene of that sort. *Anne of Avonlea*'s ending is an inverse echo of *Anne of Green Gables*; Matthew's death at the end of *Anne of Green Gables* pushed Anne to make an heroic sacrifice, where near (though not exactly at) the end of *Anne of Avonlea*, the death of Rachel Lynde's husband, Thomas, frees Anne to pursue the college course she had previously given up, as Thomas Lynde's death leaves Rachel Lynde in a precarious financial position, the best solution to which is her moving into Green Gables with Marilla, taking over Anne's duties as companion and caretaker. Thomas Lynde "faded out of life" after a long, lingering illness,[14] which provides an opportunity for Rachel's own moral redemption:

> Rachel had been a little hard on her Thomas in health, when his slowness or meekness had provoked her; but when he became ill no voice could be lower, no hand more gently skillful, no vigil more uncomplaining.

12. Gammel, *Looking for Anne of Green Gables*, 186–88.
13. See AGG, 355. See also Drain, "Community and the Individual," 19.
14. Thomas Lynde's illness is first mentioned in AA, 170–71; he dies in AA, 197–98.

PART TWO: Mourning the Absent

> "You've been a good wife to me, Rachel," he once said simply, when she was sitting by him in the dusk, holding his thin, blanched old hand in her work-hardened one. "A good wife. I'm sorry I ain't leaving you better off; but the children will look after you. They're all smart, capable children, just like their mother. A good mother . . . a good woman."[15]

Throughout the books prior to this, Rachel Lynde has been characterized as having a forceful, difficult personality, and being somewhat lacking in human sympathy. She is the first character introduced in *Anne of Green Gables*, "one of those capable creatures who can manage their own concerns and those of other folks into the bargain," observing and ruminating on the comings and goings of the Green Gables family while "Thomas Lynde—a meek little man whom Avonlea people called 'Rachel Lynde's husband'—was sowing his late turnip seed on the hill field beyond the barn."[16] Mrs. Lynde's judgmental approach to all that she meets takes on an almost supernatural dimension, as readers are told that even the stream that passes by her door transforms from "an intricate, headlong brook," "with dark secrets of pool and cascade," and becomes, in her presence, "a quiet, well-conducted little stream, for not even a brook could run past Mrs. Rachel Lynde's door without due regard for decency and decorum; it probably was conscious that Mrs. Rachel was sitting at her window, keeping a sharp eye on everything that passed, from brooks and children up [. . .]"[17] Later commentaries on her character do not soften the sketch much; even Anne and Marilla privately confess that, while they admire some of her better qualities, they find Rachel Lynde exceedingly difficult to like.[18] While Rachel does have sympathetic moments—for example, conspiring with Matthew to produce a fashionable dress as a Christmas present for Anne—for the most part, she has served as a foil for the main characters, offering an outsider's commentary on their actions and decisions.[19] It is Thomas Lynde's dying that brings associations of softness ("low-voiced"), gentleness, and uncomplaining tenderness to her character, and it is his final benediction that removes Rachel from the ambivalent, mostly outsider, position she has

15. AA, 197–98.
16. AGG, 1.
17. AGG, 1.
18. See especially AGG, 81; AA, 199–200.
19. Even in the case of the dress, however, Rachel Lynde is acting *against* Marilla, and commenting upon Marilla's inadequacy with regards to childrearing. See especially AGG, 240–41.

occupied in the narrative, and permits her to move into the Green Gables circle, as a fully sympathetic character, a position she occupies for nearly the rest of the series, not disappearing from notice until *Rilla of Ingleside*. It is his deathbed benediction that transforms her into "a good woman"; the reader has not been able to identify her as such with any certainty before. I do not mean to imply that her character itself changes, or the way that Montgomery presents her; she remains as forceful and opinionated as ever, and later books contain just as many narrative jokes at her expense. But the loss of her husband transforms the reader's view of Rachel Lynde into a far more sympathetic one; *Anne of the Island* shows Rachel Lynde located as one of the two stable, welcoming figures whose love for Anne transforms Green Gables into a permanent home.[20]

Ruby Gillis

Two other death narratives remain to be examined before we turn to *Rilla of Ingleside*, both in *Anne of the Island*. The first is the passion of Ruby Gillis, Anne's schoolmate, who dies of what Rachel Lynde calls "galloping consumption."[21] Montgomery began writing *Anne of the Island* prior to the outbreak of war on 4 August 1914, but completed it in November of that year; Owen Dudley Edwards and Jennifer H. Lister suggest that Ruby may be Montgomery's "first war casualty."[22] While this may be technically accurate—and this is far from certain, as Montgomery's journals provide very little detail on the progress of her writing beyond the dates on which she began and ended each novel—it is also a rather hyperbolic claim, as the book was completed on 20 November 1914, early enough in the conflict that it is unlikely Montgomery would have yet felt the full force of the war's rearrangement of life and death—especially as casualty lists did not begin to make a regular appearance in the paper until spring of 1915.[23]

Like Rachel Lynde, Ruby is a generally unsympathetic character, whom the others confess to finding it difficult to like.[24] Ruby's great flaw is her flirtatious nature; she sets her own value by her ability to attract men.

20. AI, 67.
21. AI, 100.
22. Edwards and Litster, "End of Canadian Innocence," 33.
23. The completion of AI is noted in Montgomery's journal entry of 20 November 1914; see Montgomery, *Selected Journals*, 156. For the appearance of casualty lists in Canadian newspapers, see Brown and Loveridge, "Unrequited Faith," 59.
24. See, for example, AA, 206; AI, 48.

PART TWO: Mourning the Absent

Montgomery portrays Ruby as, at first, approaching death as blindly as she has lived her life; the narrative of her illness serves to magnify the flaws that have been part of her character throughout the series. Those around her see clear symptoms of her illness: "She was even handsomer than ever, but her blue eyes were too bright and lustrous, and the color of her cheeks was hectically brilliant; besides, she was very thin; the hands that held her hymn-book were almost transparent in their delicacy."[25] She, however, is willfully blind: "But just see my color. I don't look much like an invalid, I'm sure."[26] The other characters find visiting her a grim chore, as she refuses all attempts at comfort, continuing to speak heedlessly of dresses and concerts and courting.[27] But the process of dying transforms her: first, her character is reformed, in her final speech, and then her body is purified by death.

Ruby's final words in the novel are not, strictly speaking, a deathbed speech; she dies while all the other Avonlea young people are away at a party—a somewhat ironic end for the character who has previously cared for very little except parties—and her real last words go unrecorded in the novel.[28] Instead, Montgomery relates a conversation between Ruby and Anne the previous evening. This has some characteristics of a deathbed speech; Ruby looks ahead to what awaits her, and back upon how she has lived, and there is an element of moral instruction in the exchange. Ruby confesses to Anne that she is afraid to die, because "Heaven must be very beautiful, of course, the Bible says so—but, Anne, *it won't be what I've been used to.*"[29] Anne, in turn, reflects that this is "sad, tragic—and *true!* Heaven could not be what Ruby had been used to. There had been nothing in her gay, frivolous life, her shallow ideals and aspirations, to fit her for that great change, or make the life to come seem to her anything but alien and unreal and undesirable."[30] She attempts to rise to the challenge and support Ruby, although she finds herself unable to "tell comforting falsehoods" which might alleviate the burden of anxiety Ruby feels in abandoning the

---

25. AI, 100.

26. AI, 108.

27. AI, 129–30.

28. Although, to take Edwards and Litster's point to heart, her lonely death may reflect Montgomery's growing consciousness of thousands of young men dying far from friends and family.

29. AI, 131. Emphasis in original, in this and all other quotations from Montgomery unless otherwise noted.

30. AI, 131.

frivolous life which she has led and loved so dearly.³¹ The scene ends with Ruby promising to face death bravely, to "think over what [Anne] said, and try to believe it."³²

Anne leaves Ruby still struggling with the weight of eternity, and the next night, Ruby dies in her sleep, "and on her face was a smile—as if, after all, death had come as a kindly friend [. . .] instead of the grisly phantom she had dreaded," as if Anne's counsel to her on the previous night had been efficacious.³³ In death, Ruby's body is transformed:

> Ruby had always been beautiful; but her beauty had been of the earth, earthy; it had had a certain insolent quality to it, as if it flaunted itself in the beholder's eye; spirit had never shone through it, intellect had never refined it. But death had touched it and consecrated it, bringing out delicate modelings and purity of outline never seen before—doing what life and love and great sorrow and deep womanhood joys might have done for Ruby. Anne, looking down through a mist of tears, at her old playfellow, thought she saw the face God had meant Ruby to have and remembered it so always.³⁴

In death, Ruby can shed her "earthy," "insolent," "unrefined" flirtatiousness, and become the perfect creation God intended; dying is a process of moral purification for her, and moral instruction for those who witness it. The perfected body in the coffin is the final sign of this transformation.

Gilbert Blythe

The theme of dying as a process of moral transformation is echoed later, in the novel's penultimate chapter, "A Book of Revelation." Anne returns to Green Gables from a visit and is informed that her rejected suitor and longtime friend, Gilbert Blythe, is dying of typhoid fever.³⁵ This is consistent with the climactic structure of the previous two books, both of which depended on a death to resolve a major portion of their plot—in both cases, to move Anne on to the next stage in her life, first mature self-sacrifice, and then the delayed reward of that sacrifice, a fuller realization of her individual potential. In this case, a major plot-line of the novel has been courtship; Anne has

31. AI, 132.
32. AI, 133.
33. AI, 135.
34. AI, 135
35. AI, 283.

PART TWO: Mourning the Absent

rejected five proposals of marriage, including Gilbert's own. Gilbert's death cannot advance the plot in the way that Matthew's, or Thomas Lynde's, did. Anne has rejected all of her suitors on their own merits, so Gilbert's absence would not cause another contender for her hand to suddenly become more appealing, and while a remorseful woman dedicating her life to mourning for her spurned lover is a scenario that the younger Anne may have found deeply romantic, Montgomery herself is a pragmatist, and much of the moral development to which she has subjected Anne has been designed to move her away from precisely that sort of sentiment. Gilbert's actual death would accomplish nothing—and so, breaking the pattern of the previous books, he does not die, but instead recovers the morning after Anne is told of his illness. Nonetheless, his near-death provides the same opportunity for moral development in those who witness it—especially Anne—as Ruby Gillis's actual death did earlier. Faced with the possibility of his death, Anne is able to realize her love for him, and repent of her foolishness in rejecting his earlier proposal. She keeps a miserable vigil through the stormy night, emerging from her room at dawn:[36]

> Anne rose from her knees and crept downstairs. The freshness of the rain-wind blew against her white face as she went out into the yard, and cooled her dry, burning eyes. A merry rollicking whistle was lilting up the lane. A moment later Pacifique Buote came in sight.
>
> Anne's physical strength suddenly failed her. If she had not clutched at a low willow bough she would have fallen. Pacifique was George Fletcher's hired man, and George Fletcher lived next door to the Blythes. Mrs. Fletcher was Gilbert's aunt. Pacifique

---

36. An astute reader may note that most of Montgomery's death scenes take place at dawn or twilight—even if the death itself occurs at another time, as with Ruby Gillis and Thomas Lynde, information of it will be communicated at these times; even the dedication of RI partakes of this trope: "To the memory of Frederica Campbell MacFarlane, who went away from me when the dawn broke on January 25th, 1919." Vance notes that dawn (and, to a lesser extent, sunset) typically symbolises the resurrection, "the promise of a new beginning and of God's infinite good"; while Paul Fussell (who writes in a primarily modern British context, without accounting for social change in the Commonwealth) has argued that after the First World War this symbolism ceased to be used except in an ironic context, Vance maintains that in Canada "dawn continued to mean what it had meant in 1914" and earlier; this is clear in Montgomery's fiction from the death scene of Captain Jim in AHD, 287–88. By contrast, however, Montgomery's *Blue Castle* opens with a reference to "the lifeless, hopeless hour just preceding dawn" (1). See Vance, *Death So Noble*, 48–49; Fussell, *Great War and Modern Memory*, 61–64, esp. 63.

would know if—if—Pacifique would know what there was to be known.³⁷

Anne emerges from her night of prayer and introspection both into enhanced and more mature self-knowledge, and also directly into a tightly-woven web of kinship associations: Gilbert's uncle/next-door-neighbor's hired boy, passing by *en route* to visit his own ailing father, brings news that Gilbert's illness has abated. With any of these connections missing, Pacifique would have been unable to deliver the crucial intelligence. At the moment that Anne finds herself able to undertake what Montgomery presents as the final step into the world of adult responsibility—marriage—she also finds herself dependent upon the social and familial web of the village to provide her with the information necessary for that step. This completes a process of integration that has been ongoing since the first novel, and which, again, has been advanced by the climactic deaths in each book: Matthew's death led Anne to choose to assume familial responsibility for Marilla, and Thomas Lynde's death enabled Rachel Lynde to take over from Anne, adding an element of reciprocity to Anne's relationship with the people of Avonlea—Anne acquires the means to fulfill her individual ambition, but only by also acquiring a deeper dependence upon the community. The tangled web of inter-relation that Montgomery chooses to spell out at the moment of Pacifique's appearance serves to underline the dense structure of relationships into which Anne is about to choose (or has already chosen) to enter fully.

An Antebellum Conclusion

In all of the passages examined above, death is a community affair, in which interpersonal relationships are both affirmed and renegotiated. Every narrative contains an element of moral instruction—sometimes, as in the case of Ruby Gillis, for the dying person, but always for those who witness the death, including, perhaps especially, the reader; in the cases where they are available, the last words of a character are especially significant. In all but one of the narratives examined (excepting Gilbert Blythe's non-death), the body of the deceased has a central role; Thomas Lynde's does not, although this is well in keeping with his character, occasionally mentioned by others, but rarely appearing in person and even more rarely with any sense of agency. He is the only character whose funeral service is not described.

37. AI, 285.

PART TWO: Mourning the Absent

The death narrative of Matthew Cuthbert places an emphasis on burial in his "native earth," the land that he had farmed, loved, and taught Anne to love; although the other narratives do not mention the place of burial, it is reasonable to assume that this is because its proximity to the community is taken for granted, and only emphasized in the one instance because of particular resonances between land and character, rather than because the location is in any way unusual. The family's authority over the dead person's body and their memory is undisputed.

Thus, we have a fairly clear picture, though filtered through a literary and nostalgic lens, of what constituted "normal" death in Canada in the era immediately preceding the First World War; thus far, our picture harmonizes with what Wilkinson and Wheeler have to say of normal British death at that time, at least as far as the focus on body and gravesite is concerned. A similar literary examination of *Rilla of Ingleside* will reveal how and to what extent these characteristics were altered in the First World War, and the extent to which the language of Christian theology became entwined with wartime rhetoric.

RILLA OF INGLESIDE

Montgomery began writing *Rilla of Ingleside* on 14 August, 1919, some nine months after the Armistice.[38] Jonathan Vance notes that, at the time of its release, it was a critical favorite, "not for the author's finely drawn characters or deft handling of plot, but for a very specific reason: it captured the essence of small-town Canada during the war."[39] Vance goes on to note that, "[B]y praising the novel's verisimilitude, reviewers shifted *Rilla of Ingleside* from fiction to history: it became a 'true' record of Canada's war."[40] Vance credits the book's popularity to Montgomery's ability to tap into the pre-existing popular myth of the war and repackage it for popular consumption. However, he reads *Rilla of Ingleside* and its critical reception in the context of war writing from "the 1920s and 1930s," and fails to account for the early publication date of *Rilla* and the extent to which it may have been actively involved in shaping Canadian memory of the war.[41]

38. Montgomery, *Selected Journals*, 339.

39. Vance, *Death So Noble*, 176. Given Vance's other remarks about the book, it is safe to assume that "finely drawn characters" and "deft handling of plot" are meant to be read as sarcasm on Vance's part.

40. Vance, *Death So Noble*, 176.

41. Vance tells us that the book sold 27,000 copies in Canada between its publication

Nor does Vance care to credit Montgomery with any conscious historical accuracy; he attributes the promotion of the book as "a 'true' record of Canada's war" to reviewers, rather than the author herself. However, Montgomery herself strove to present a realistic picture of "Canada at war."[42] In writing *Rilla of Ingleside*, she drew heavily upon her own wartime journal entries; the novel contains an exacting record of newspaper reports and Montgomery's own reactions to them, filtered through her characters. The book opens with Susan Baker, the Blythes' housekeeper, reading "a big, black headline on the front page of the *Enterprise*, stating that some Archduke Ferdinand or other had been assassinated at a place bearing the weird name of Sarajevo, but Susan tarried not over uninteresting, immaterial stuff like that [. . .]"[43] Montgomery's journal entry of 5 August 1914, the day that England declared war on Germany, recounts that "Sometime in June I picked up a *Globe* and read that a Serbian had shot the Archduke of Austria and his duchess. The news was of little interest to me—as to most people on the continent."[44] Both the journal and *Rilla* go on to detail the enormous significance this seemingly distant and obscure headline would have for Canadian life and death. However, the book has been generally underappreciated, both as a novel and as an historical document. In the interest of providing a fuller picture of the vocabulary of war and commemoration in Canada between the years 1914 and 1921, I will devote some space to a discussion of themes from *Rilla of Ingleside* which parallel themes from the wider social discourse on the war, before returning to a closer examination of the way that Montgomery portrays death in the novel.

Rilla of Ingleside follows Anne and Gilbert Blythe's youngest daughter, Bertha Marilla Blythe, from the war's beginning in 1914, when she is fifteen years old, until 1919. The central drama of the novel, however, is not Rilla's coming of age in wartime, or even her courtship with Kenneth Ford, the son of the beautiful and enigmatic Leslie Moore, whose own courtship

---

and the outbreak of the Second World War (*Death So Noble*, 176), a rather high figure for the time. As the final novel in the internationally popular Anne of Green Gables series, RI has been read by several generations of girls at a sufficiently young age (9–13) that they are unlikely to have encountered discussion of the First World War at any length in their schooling.

42. Journal entry 5 March 1921: Montgomery, *Selected Journals*, 404.

43. RI, 1–2.

44. Montgomery, *Selected Journals*, 150. For more on the link between Montgomery's wartime journals and RI, see Epperly, *Fragrance of Sweet Grass*, 121–22, and for Susan as a mouthpiece for Montgomery, see Epperly, *Fragrance of Sweet Grass*, 125.

story was the main plot of *Anne's House of Dreams*.[45] Rather, it is Rilla's brother, Walter, with his struggle to overcome his fear of war's ugliness, his enlistment, and his eventual death, who provides the main force in the novel.

Walter is portrayed as very much his mother's son: sensitive, imaginative, a poet. Both Vance and Edwards and Lister have noted that, in this regard, Walter represents a type, "a Canadian version of Rupert Brooke."[46] Where Anne's literary talent wanes over the course of the series into a slightly eccentric hobby that does not threaten her true vocation as a wife and mother, Walter's gift is intimated to be something larger, approaching the true genius that Montgomery only ascribes to men within the *Anne* series.[47] At the beginning of the novel, he is recovering from typhoid fever, and his family has some concern over whether he will be well enough to attend college in the fall.[48] Both his precarious health and his poetic vision place him in a position perpetually between life and death, from which he speaks with a prophetic authority, relaying visions of the mysterious "Piper" who appears, beginning at the end of *Rainbow Valley* (1919), playing a wild tune which Walter predicts he and his playmates will be compelled to follow,

---

45. AHD was also written during the war, and Edwards and Litster argue that Leslie's story, especially, contains a dark realism that would have been foreign to Montgomery's pre-war writing, while Leslie herself, depicted with "blood-red poppies at her waist" is an early image of the self-sacrifice of Canadian women for the greater good, which Montgomery aimed to promote in her novels at this time—see "End of Canadian Innocence," 33, 43. Thus, the pairing of Rilla with Kenneth is the culmination and reward of two generations of selfless women, Leslie and Rilla; Leslie's story is very much a foreshadowing of the feminine sacrificial *ethos* which Montgomery lays out more explicitly in RI.

46. Vance, *Death So Noble*, 175; see also Edwards and Litster, "End of Canadian Innocence," 36.

47. The obvious exception to this is Mrs. Morgan, the author of Anne's favourite romance novels, who appears in AA, but the tone of the episodes surrounding her visit is ultimately comic, and the episodes themselves resurgences of the childish Anne's propensity for "getting into scrapes" and letting her romantic imagination run away with her (AA, 119–31, 153–57); there is an implication that Anne's judgment about Mrs. Morgan's literary value is similarly immature. This is in contrast to Paul Irving, Owen Ford, and Walter Blythe, to whose literary aspirations Anne (and, in the case of Walter, Rilla) plays helpmeet. My colleague, Elizabeth Anderson, points out that this restriction of genius to men is characteristic of the *Anne* series, rather than Montgomery's work as a whole; the *Emily* series—*Emily of New Moon*; *Emily Climbs*; *Emily's Quest*—follows a woman with authorial aspirations who does achieve success, and whose writing is presented as serious art.

48. RI, 6.

willingly or not.[49] This recurring vision is eventually transformed into a poem which, though never printed (or even quoted) in *Rilla of Ingleside*, becomes to the cast of that novel what John McCrae's poem, "In Flanders Fields" was (and, to a large extent, still is) to real-life Canadians.[50]

McCrae's poem is an important piece of literature, both in terms of its historical value and in the pervasive role it has played in remembrance rituals since the war, in Canada as well as abroad. Paul Fussell tells us that it was "[t]he most popular poem of the war" and "one reason the British Legion chose that [the poppy] symbol of [. . .] remembrance."[51] The poem was written in 1915, during a period when several public figures, including Woodrow Wilson (who is much maligned in *Rilla of Ingleside*), hoped to find a compromise capable of ending the war.[52] Fussell contends that the last stanza especially serves as "a propaganda argument [. . .] against a negotiated peace."[53]

Walter's poem is composed around the time of the Battle of Verdun, in 1916, a year later than "In Flanders Fields" and thus at a remove from the specific political context of McCrae's poem. However, Walter's poem still appears to be primarily an appeal to patriotic fidelity, and Montgomery presents it as a close analogue to McCrae's poem, depending on her readers' knowledge of that text to fill in details about "The Piper." Montgomery carefully identifies the author of "The Piper" as "[A] Canadian lad in the

---

49. The Piper vision, or reference to it, is repeated in RV, 55, 224–25, and RI, 20, 33, 124–25, 191.

50. John McCrae, "In Flanders Fields," first published in *Punch* 6 December 1915 (see Fussell, *Great War and Modern Memory*, 249).

The publication of BQ adds a level of complexity to the reading of "The Piper" as related to "In Flanders Fields." While the poem described in RI bears sufficiently close resemblance to McCrae's poem that it is reasonable to discuss the two as intertexts, BQ contains, on the very first page, a poem titled "The Piper" which bears very little resemblance to either "In Flanders Fields" or to the poem described in RI—it does not even contain the same number of stanzas (RI, 167, specifies three stanzas, the same number as "In Flanders Fields;" the poem in BQ has only two). An explanatory note from the author indicates that that poem was written "recently" (during the time she was working on the manuscript of BQ, which is set, in part, during the Second World War) in response to numerous requests from readers (BQ, 3).

51. Fussell, *Great War and Modern Memory*, 248–49; see also Hurst, "John McCrae's Wars," 76.

52. Montgomery's treatment of Wilson in particular and the U.S.A. in general was not pleasing to her American publishers; see her journal entry of 5 March 1921 (Montgomery, *Selected Journals*, 404).

53. Fussell, *Great War and Modern Memory*, 250.

PART TWO: Mourning the Absent

Flanders trenches," calling the title line of McCrae's poem to mind; both poems contain the same number of stanzas; the crowd which hears "The Piper" recited cheers and responds "We'll follow—we'll follow—we won't break faith," in clear reference to the third-last line of McCrae's poem.[54]

This very deliberate linking permits Montgomery to suggest that the quiet pastoralism which pervades both the opening stanzas of "In Flanders Fields" and Walter's letters home is also part of "The Piper," which is presented as the fulfillment of Walter's poetic gift. In so doing, Montgomery suggests that the lofty ideals of the great conflict must be mediated by reference to the smaller, more intimate, often familial details of everyday life. This point is made explicitly in Walter's last letter to Rilla, written the night before he is killed at Courcelette:

> I'm not afraid, Rilla-my-Rilla, and I am not sorry that I came. I'm *satisfied*. I'll never write the poems I once dreamed of writing—but I've helped to make Canada safe for the poets of the future—for the workers of the future—ay, and the dreamers, too—for if no man dreams, there will be nothing for the workers to fulfill—the future, not of Canada only but of the world. [. . .] It isn't only the fate of the little sea-born island I love that is in the balance—nor of Canada, nor of England. It's the fat of mankind. This is what we're fighting for.
>
> [. . .] And you will tell your children of the *Idea* we fought and died for—teach them it must be *lived* for as well as died for, else the price paid for it will have been given for nought. This will be part of *your* work, Rilla.[55]

When Walter dies, he does so with a clear sense of purpose. Both he and Montgomery present his death as a sacrifice, not just for "the fate of mankind," but also for "the fate of the little sea-born island," not just for the workers of the future, but the poets and dreamers. He fights and dies for a grand *Idea*, but understands the idea through its potential to be passed on to his sister's children, the "children of tomorrow" which feature in his penultimate vision of the Piper.[56]

---

54. RI, 167, 179, 230.

55. RI, 191–92.

56. RI, 124–25. Throughout the novel, Montgomery draws connections between the British/Canadian side of the war and the sanctity of childhood. See, for example, RI, 95, 98, and especially 106; see also Vance, *Death So Noble*, 157–59.

SACRIFICE

The theme of sacrifice, and predominantly self-sacrifice, dominates both *Rilla of Ingleside* and more general discourse surrounding the First World War, especially theological discourse. Walter's life and death epitomize a popular sacrificial narrative, in which one finds fulfillment by surrendering one's self to something greater. The notion of sacrifice as exchange is extremely important here: if Walter simply died, without dying *for* something, without receiving some sort of personal fulfillment, his death and life could not be analyzed as sacrificial narratives.[57] As we have seen, this has been a theme throughout Montgomery's *Anne of Green Gables* series—both because, as Irene Gammel has asserted, it was a popular literary theme at the time (even prior to the outbreak of war), and most likely because of the author's own religious convictions. The outbreak of war served to heighten the immediacy of this discourse, and political expedience may have contributed to its gaining a somewhat wider currency.

Where Anne's literary ambitions were a mark of a selfish individuality she had to surrender after Matthew's death in order to integrate herself into the local community, a first step towards her fulfillment as a wife and mother, Walter's literary gift stems from something beyond himself, and reaches fulfillment when he accomplishes his self-surrender. Both the Piper and "The Piper" come *through*, rather than from, Walter; he says of the poem: "it *came* to me [. . .] I didn't feel as if I were writing it—something else used me as an instrument."[58] Barely twenty-two pages elapse between Rilla learning of the poem Walter has written and her learning of his death, with no news of him appearing in the meantime.[59] There is, then, an implicit relationship between Walter's surrender to the force that brought forth his one great poem and his surrender to death; "The Piper" (the poem) and the Piper (Walter's visionary gift) appear to come from the same mysterious source. Where Walter's second-last letter brings news of his artistic achievement, his last letter details his final vision:

> One evening long ago [. . .] I saw the Piper coming down the Valley with a shadowy host behind him. The others thought I was

---

57. See especially McClymond, *Beyond Sacred Violence*; Maus, *The Gift*; Alles, "Exchange."

58. RI, 167.

59. The poem is introduced on 167; news of Walter's death comes at pages 187–88. "The Piper" is mentioned on 179, and Walter mentioned briefly on 185 as Rilla recalls the lighthouse dance, but he is otherwise absent from the narrative at this point.

> only pretending—but I *saw* him for just one moment. And Rilla, last night I saw him again. I was doing sentry-go and I saw him marching across No-man's-land from our trenches to the German trenches—the same tall shadowy form, piping weirdly—and behind him followed boys in khaki. Rilla, I tell you I *saw* him—it was no fancy—no illusion. I *heard* his music, and then—he was *gone*. But I *had* seen him—and I knew what it meant—I knew that I was among those who followed him.
>
> Rilla, the piper will pipe me "west" tomorrow. I feel sure of this. And Rilla, I'm not afraid. When you hear the news, remember that.[60]

This is not the first instance of Montgomery linking literary accomplishment with the notion of sacrifice; in her autobiography, she not only makes that link explicitly, but also makes an implicit connection between the self-sacrifice of the writer and the soldier, writing "The very day on which these words are written has come a letter to me from an English lad of nineteen, totally unknown to me, who writes that he is leaving for 'the front' and wants to tell me 'before he goes' how much my books and especially *Anne* have meant to him. It is in such letters that a writer finds meet reward for all sacrifice and labor."[61]

This linkage may appear somewhat odd at first blush, but it has its roots in theology with which Montgomery would likely have been familiar, such as Horace Bushnell's 1877 work, *The Vicarious Sacrifice*. Bushnell's book opened with an argument that Christ's substitutionary atonement involved his "bearing of our[sic] sins" just as a mother bears the "pains and sicknesses" of her child, or

> the patriot or citizen who truly loves his country [. . .] how does it wrench feeling, what a burden does it lay upon his concern [. . .] when that country, so dear to him, is being torn by faction. [. . .] Then you will see how many thousands of citizens, who never knew before what sacrifices it was in the power of their love to make for their country's welfare, rushing to the field and throwing their bodies and dear lives on the battle's edge to save it![62]

60. RI, 191.
61. Montgomery, *The Alpine Path* 75.
62. Bushnell, *The Vicarious Sacrifice*, 46–47. Bushnell is presumably writing here in response to the American Civil War, rather than the First World War, which points to an interesting dichotomy between Canadian and American experience entering into the First World War: the American Civil War was the last war fought in North America, and the last war fought by American troops prior to their entry into the First World War.

At least two sides of the sacrificial trifecta of Christ, mother, and soldier laid out by Bushnell are illustrated in *Rilla of Ingleside*; the analogy between feminine affection and military service is drawn out explicitly at several points (one of which is in the portion of Walter's last letter quoted above, in which he refers to Rilla's work as a continuation of his own), but the linkage between these and the sacrifice of Christ is left undeveloped in the novel. This is not the case in the more general public discourse surrounding the war, in which the analogous relation between the soldier and Christ is drawn out explicitly.[63]

Jonathan F. Vance has already detailed the myriad ways in which this analogy is presented in both discourse during the war and in monuments and memorials produced after the war. In brief, Vance contends that the equation between Christ and the soldier serves both a justificatory and a consolatory purpose. The justificatory purpose, as already mentioned, aligned Britain and the Allied nations with the side of God, transforming what may have otherwise been a rather obscure political conflict into a Holy War, in which Germans and their allies ceased to be viewed as human but instead represented the sin from which Christ died to cleanse the world.[64] The consolatory purpose did not simply align the soldier's sacrifice with that of Christ, but also the soldier's reward; the soldier, like Christ, willingly gave up his earthly life, but in so doing gained the rewards of resurrection and life eternal.[65] This latter treatment of the sacrificial theme grew quickly beyond a mere consolatory gesture and transformed war service into a religious and moral purification, participation in which was highly desir-

---

By contrast, Canadians (such as John McCrae) fought under the banner of the British Empire in the Boer War, at the turn of the century. Although the Boer War was geographically more distant, it was a more recent memory of conflict.

63. Especially notable in this regard is the myth of the crucified (Canadian) soldier, described in Evans, *Mother of Heroes*, 52–58.

64. Vance dedicates an entire chapter to Just War rhetoric in the First World War; see *Death So Noble*, 12–34. He also repeatedly returns to what might be more rightly characterized as Holy War rhetoric, although he does not identify it as such—see, for example, Vance, *Death So Noble*, 35, 44, 65. See also Evans, *Mother of Heroes*, 43–76.

65. Again, Vance dedicates an entire chapter to "Christ in Flanders;" see *Death So Noble*, 35–72. Evans cites a pamphlet put out by the Mothers' Union which instructs mothers whose children are killed in the war that they "would have 'a yet deeper cause for thankfulness that he is among the long roll of English heroes . . . [and] far better even than that—the welcome of the King of Kings will greet him—'Well done, good and faithful servant, enter thou into the joy of the Lord.'" Rickards and Moody, *First World War*, 20, quoted in Evans, *Mother of Heroes*, 85–86.

able. This is the attitude which prompted Montgomery's somewhat bizarre equation between her sacrifices as a writer and the soldier about to depart for the front.

The pages of *Rilla of Ingleside* are filled with arguments for women's place in the sacrificial endeavor; when Walter enlists, Rilla protests that "*Our* sacrifice is greater than *his*. [. . .] Our boys give only *themselves*. We give them."[66] This was, until August 1915, quite literally true, as until then Canadian men who wished to enlist required the written consent of their wife or their mother.[67] It was natural, then, that the language of sacrifice would extend to women who actually did sacrifice their loved ones to the war, both to encourage and to acknowledge their contribution, even after the requirement had been lifted.[68] In her study on motherhood and the First World War in Canada, Suzanne Evans notes that some of the earliest war recruiting in Canada and Great Britain relied on images of women and captions entreating men to fight in their defense.[69] This trope appears several times in *Rilla of Ingleside*; Ken Ford "carried the picture of [Rilla] in his heart to the horror of the battlefields of France," and Walter boards the train that will take him to war thinking that "[A]fter all it was not a hard thing to fight for a land that bore daughters like this."[70] Rilla and her mother consciously strive to embody the image of womanhood that encourages men to fight in defense of the homeland; "When our women fail in courage/shall our men be fearless still?" is an oft-repeated maxim in the book.[71]

The link between the soldier and Christ is clearest in attempts to derive moral meaning from the soldier's sacrificial death—in much the same way that moral development was derived from attendance at a deathbed prior

---

66. RI, 120. See also Epperly, *Fragrance of Sweet Grass*, 121–22, 125.

67. Evans, *Mother of Heroes*, 81–82.

68. Indeed, beginning December 1919, a special medal was struck for wives and mothers of men killed in service to the British Empire: the Memorial Cross. Eventually, an equivalent, and specifically Canadian, medal was struck for mothers only: the Silver Cross. See Evans, *Mother of Heroes*, 101–9.

69. Evans, *Mother of Heroes*, 78–81; more generally, 77–112. See especially Evans' discussion of the White Feather Campaign, in which women attempted to shame men into enlisting by presenting them with white feathers, meant to denote cowardice—Evans, *Mother of Heroes*, 82–84; see also Granatstein and Hitsman, *Broken Promises*, 39; also Morton, *Marching to Armageddon*, 27; Morton, *When Your Number's Up*, 50, 59. Montgomery's Walter is himself the recipient of a white feather prior to his enlistment; see RI, 81, 166.

70. RI, 134, 127.

71. RI, 40, 116; see also also 162, 221, and especially 247.

to the war. However, the latter seemed to require only attendance to be effective; as the war made witnessing death itself, or the moments leading up to it, impossible, survivors had to work harder to derive moral benefit from it. After Walter's death, Rilla writes in her journal that "my work is here at home. I know Walter wouldn't have wanted me to leave mother and in everything I try to 'keep faith' with him, even to the little details of daily life. Walter died for Canada—I must live for her. That is what he asked me to do."[72] Just as generations of Sunday School teachers enjoined children to give meaning to Christ's death by living their lives in accordance with the principles which his sacrifice represented, Rilla and her real-life analogues strive to render the sacrifice of their loved ones meaningful by identifying some principle that they can "live for" as their relatives "died for."[73]

Montgomery, however, also offers an implicit critique of an overly simplistic notion of sacrifice-as-exchange at the end of *Rilla of Ingleside*, when, as the war draws to a close, and Jem Blythe is numbered among the missing (he is in a German Prisoner of War camp, although the Ingleside family have no way of knowing this), Bruce Meredith, the son of the local Presbyterian minister, drowns his beloved pet kitten:[74]

> "Why did you do that?" Mrs. Meredith exclaimed.
> "To bring Jem back," sobbed Bruce. "I thought if I sacrificed Stripey God would send Jem back. So I drownded him—and, oh mother, it was *awful* hard—but surely God will send Jem back now, 'cause Stripey was the dearest thing I had [. . .]"
> Mrs. Meredith didn't know what to say to the poor child. She just could *not* tell him that perhaps his sacrifice wouldn't bring Jem back—that God didn't work that way.[75]

This passage stands in sharp contrast to earlier passages in which Mr. Meredith himself employed a sacrificial discourse.[76] Young Bruce is portrayed as taking his father's doctrine too literally, lacking an adult perspective that would enable him to discern between the (national) self-sacrifice his father calls for and the other-sacrifice in which he himself engages.

---

72. RI, 230.

73. See especially Vance, *Death So Noble*, 50–51, 72, 89, 126, 217, 219.

74. Montgomery tends to use the motif of a dead kitten to signify a corruption or betrayal of innocence. See also Montgomery, *Tangled Web*, 303–6.

75. RI, 261

76. E.g., RI, 50–51.

PART TWO: Mourning the Absent

MOURNING THE ABSENT

As we have seen, Montgomery's war writing tends to utilize language and imagery that was quite common to the more general Canadian (and, indeed, British) discourse regarding the war, in both the wartime and the post-war years. It should not be a surprise, then, that her images of death and mourning in *Rilla of Ingleside* also represent, or hint towards, a set of images and experiences more common to Canadians in general than specific to one (fictional) family on Prince Edward Island. While Walter's life is filled out with unusual details such as his poetic and prophetic gifts, his death is narrated sparingly, with very little detail to distinguish him from the hundreds of thousands of other young men who died in combat.

The striking elements which distinguish the narration of Walter's death from the deaths in previous novels are delay and distance.[77] Five days pass between Walter's death and his family hearing of it; a further unspecified length of time passes before Walter's last words are delivered to Rilla—along with a letter from his commanding officer, assuring the family that "he had been killed instantly by a bullet during a charge at Courcelette."[78] Vance notes that such letters were sent to comfort rather than inform; they were "more often than not used to hide from relatives the horror of the facts. After the war, this subterfuge was accepted as reality."[79] He goes on to note the common trope of the soldier dying with a smile on his face: "The beauty of the passing, manifest in a beatific smile, grew out of a sense of deep satisfaction of a job seen through to the end," the same sort of satisfaction expressed by Walter in his final letter to Rilla (discussed above).[80]

The events of Walter's death are exactly reversed from the events of Montgomery's pre-war death narratives. His final words do not precede his dying, but rather arrive a considerable time afterwards. His body is entirely absent, save for the brief mention of his "painless" passing in his commanding officer's letter, which Montgomery may have intended sincerely, but a contemporary reader conscious of the trope behind the letter cannot read as an honest representation of Walter's demise. There is no funeral, and no memorial service is recorded in the novel. Walter has no grave.

---

77. The other death which features these elements is that of Dick Moore in AHD, the other novel Montgomery wrote during the War, whose death in Cuba went unreported for thirteen years.
78. RI, 190.
79. Vance, *Death So Noble*, 99.
80. Ibid., 99.

Instead of the body and grave which were the focus of Montgomery's earlier death narratives, Walter is mourned through words. Rilla carries his last letter "unopened to Rainbow Valley and read it there, in the spot where she had had her last talk with him."[81] Where Anne's sight of Matthew's body opened her eyes to the reality of his death, Rilla's contact with Walter's final letter convinces her of his eternal life:

> For the first time since the blow had fallen Rilla *felt*—a different thing from tremendous hope and faith—that Walter, of the glorious gift and the splendid ideals, *still lived*, with just the same gift and just the same ideals. *That* could not be destroyed—*these* could suffer no eclipse. The personality that had expressed itself in that last letter, written on the eve of Courcelette, could not be snuffed out by a German bullet. It must carry on, though the earthly link with things of earth were broken.[82]

The repetition of "earthly/earth" in the final line here is reminiscent of the description of Ruby Gillis's body before it underwent the purification of death: "her beauty had been of the earth, earthy."[83] Walter has no body in which this purification may be observed; rather, it is his personality that is cleansed—primarily cleansed from fear, as detailed in the final letter that Rilla holds in her hands. The letter becomes a substitute for Walter's body, the site at which the morally instructive effects of his death may be observed. It also substitutes for his body as the site at which those who mourn him can make their final contact with him, as Montgomery did by kissing her dead mother's cheek. Rilla shares the letter with Una Meredith, a childhood friend who she strongly suspects was in love with Walter; moved by Una's silent grief ("her eyes were the eyes of a woman stricken to the heart, who yet must not cry out or ask for sympathy"), Rilla offers her the letter to keep, and "Una took the letter and when Rilla had gone she pressed it against her lonely lips."[84] It is worth noting that through all of this, Rilla and the rest of the Ingleside family do manage to maintain the role of gatekeeper to Walter's memory that is accorded to family members in Montgomery's earlier death narratives, although they must defend that role against outsiders who attempt to ascribe alternate meanings to Walter's death.[85]

81. RI, 190.
82. RI, 190. Compare with the sources quoted in Vance, *Death So Noble*, 44–47.
83. AI, 108.
84. RI, 193.
85. See especially RI, 189 and 194–95. Montgomery's patriotic Blythe family defend

PART TWO: Mourning the Absent

Anne planted a rosebush on Matthew's grave, and returned frequently, often at significant points in the narrative (and her life) to tend the bush and the grave. Rilla, instead, sits in church as the war draws to a close, "looking up at the memorial tablet on the wall above [the family] pew, 'sacred to the memory of Walter Cuthbert Blythe,'" and feels "filled anew with courage," and the certainty that "Walter could not have laid down his life for naught."[86] Rilla seeks consolation from the tablet much as she might have from a grave; the notable difference between the two is that Walter's body is in no way present at the tablet.

Walter's body is unavailable as an object of consolation not simply because of the difficulty involved in recovering it from France, but because in 1915 or 1916 the British government determined that no soldier's body should be repatriated, whether they be English, Canadian, or Australian; instead, the soldier was to be "buried on the spot where he falls."[87] At first, this practice was simply a practical response to the realities of combat; Fabian Ware's unit began its work of registering graves simply to have a record of where bodies were, so that when hostilities ceased they could be interred in a more permanent fashion—most likely in a common ossuary, as were Athenian soldiers in the fifth century BCE.[88] However, as the war progressed from a race to capture territory into the trench warfare that characterized the majority of action on the Western Front, "burials became concentrated rather than scattered," and Ware began to feel pressure to seek

---

Walter's memory from being used to undermine the state, whereas Antigone and Klara Becker from *The Stone Carvers*, discussed below, attempted to defend their loved ones' memories from being appropriated *by* the state; in all cases, however, the principle is that the family of the dead person must defend their right to ascribe meaning to that person's death.

86. RI, 235. It should go without saying that the sense in which Montgomery uses "memorial" here is to indicate a commemorative marker, rather than in the technical sense which I proposed in chapter 1.

87. MT - *Hilkhot melakhim*, 6:12 (Hershman, *Maimonides*, 223)—although it is highly unlikely that the British authorities were thinking of Maimonides when this decision was made. Samuel Hynes, who dates this decision to 1916, notes that "the spot where he falls" was a rough guideline only; "there were more than twelve hundred patches of soldiers' graves in France alone at the end of the war, and these were eventually consolidated." See Hynes, *A War Imagined*, 271. The 1916 date is also cited by Curl, *Celebration of Death*, 319. Philip Longworth suggests that the decision against repatriation originates in a March 1915 order issued by Marshall Joffre "banning exhumations during the period of the war," and that eventually this order took on more permanent force; see *Unending Vigil*, 14.

88. Longworth, *Unending Vigil*, 1–2, 11, 14.

a more permanent solution to the problem of burial.[89] He eventually negotiated a permanent grant of land from France for British cemeteries; the death of British soldiers bought the Empire the right to the land on which they fell.[90]

The negotiations over the land France grated for cemeteries reveals the importance accorded to gravesites. The French government originally proposed to provide both the land and the maintenance of the cemeteries; Ware objected to this "since, in providing for upkeep it might have prevented Britain from caring for the graves of her own soldiers."[91] The activity of tending a grave, as Anne did Matthew's, or as Antigone wished to do for Polynices, was understood to be significant enough that ensuring that those who did the tending were of an appropriate relation to the deceased (even if the relation was no stronger than "fellow citizen") entered into an international negotiation as a major concern. However, there does not appear to have been a similar drive to ensure that those whose particular relationship to the deceased (i.e., familial) would, by custom, entitle them to tend the grave were able to do so. In this regard, the military burial practices of the British Empire in the early twentieth century CE are a strong parallel to the military burial practices of the Athenian Empire in the mid-fifth century BCE. And just as in Athens, the public reaction was mixed. At least one body was disinterred and repatriated during the war, in spite of the general order to the contrary; Ware became concerned that this might set a precedent that "would increase the demand at home for repatriation."[92] Likewise, Vance recounts two separate instances of Canadians attempting to reclaim their relatives' remains after the war. In both cases, the bereaved relations (parents of the dead soldiers) eventually travelled to France to dig up their sons' graves in the hopes of personally transporting their remains back to Canada; both attempts failed.[93]

While public demand for repatriation may have been high enough to concern Ware, the majority of public concern was directed at the gravesites, rather than the bodies themselves. Providing photographs of

---

89. Ibid., 11.
90. Ibid., 11–12.
91. Ibid., 12.
92. Ibid., 14; the body was "of a British officer, a Lord Lieutenant, and a grandson of W. E. Gladstone;" it was "disinterred under fire at Poperinghe and sent home 'in obedience to pressure from a very high quarter.'"
93. Vance, *Death So Noble*, 62–63.

graves—images of names—became part of the Graves Registration Commission's regular work from March 1915 onwards.[94] By August of that year, demand was such that the Commission had developed a standard system for responding to such requests: letters of enquiry were answered with a photograph that showed four graves, one of which would be the grave of the soldier enquired about (photographing the graves in groups of four permitted a more efficient use of time and film than would photographing individual graves), and a card on which "were given certain particulars, including the best available indication as to the situation of the grave and, when it was in a cemetery, directions as to the nearest railway station which might be useful for those wishing to visit the country after the war."[95] The demand for these photographs indicated a concern for the care and upkeep of the graves, but also points towards the development of a system of substitutionary mourning.[96] Where a body and grave were unavailable, mourners compensated with artifacts (such as letters) and images of the grave.

CONCLUDING NOTE: PRAYER FOR THE DEAD

Mourners in the British Empire did not compensate for the inaccessibility of the body of the deceased soldier through material memorials alone. Alan Wilkinson informs us that "In 1914 public prayer for the dead was uncommon in the Church of England; by the end of the war it had become widespread."[97] As the elaborate Victorian system of public mourning steadily eroded, public prayer for the departed gained popularity.[98] While Montgomery omits mention of prayer from *Rilla of Ingleside*, a similar, though not identical, move is evident in the worship resources produced by The Presbyterian Church in Canada (to which Montgomery belonged) at the time; while there are still no prayers *for* the dead present in Canadian Presbyterian post-war liturgy, there is a marked increase in prayers which mention the dead and appeal to their memory as a moral exemplar.[99]

    94. Longworth, *Unending Vigil*, 15.
    95. Fabian Ware, "Introduction," vii, quoted in Longworth, *Unending Vigil*, 15.
    96. Concern for upkeep of graves led to the development of a horticultural program as early as 1915; see Longworth, *Unending Vigil*, 15–16, 20–21; Vance, *Death So Noble*, 61.
    97. Wilkinson, *Church of England*, 176.
    98. See Wilkinson, *Church of England*, 173.
    99. In both the case of the Church of England and The Presbyterian Church in Canada, however, caution should be exercised to avoid confusing the available documentary

In June 1914, prior to the outbreak of war, the Committee on Public Worship and Aids to Devotion reported that a volume which would eventually be printed as *The Book of Family Devotion* was "on the way to completion" and may be "ready for June or October."[100] Although the book was not actually published until 1919, due largely to the interruptions of the War, its form was mostly set before war was declared. It contains only one prayer that mentions the dead at all, "A Memorial of those who are at Rest," under the heading of "Occasional Prayers/Within the Family":

> O Thou Lord of all worlds, we bless thy Name for all those who have entered into their rest and reached the Promised Land where thou art seen face to face. Give us grace to follow in their footsteps, as they followed in the footsteps of thy holy Son. Encourage our wavering hearts by their example, and help us to see in them the memorials of thy redeeming grace and pledges of the heavenly might in which the weak are made strong. Keep alive in us the memory of those dear to ourselves whom thou hast called out of this world, and make it powerful to subdue within us every vile and unworthy thought. Grant that every remembrance which turns our hearts from things seen to things unseen may lead us also upwards to thee, till we, too, come to the eternal rest which thou hast prepared for thy people.[101]

By contrast, the 1922 *Book of Common Order*, the preparation of which began during the war, contains a prayer of thanksgiving or remembrance for the departed in every morning and evening service, as well as including three different prayers of Special Intercession under the heading "Commemoration of Those Faithful Unto Death for the Commonweal," and inserting mention of the dead into one of the prayers of General Intercession.[102] Although the dead are mentioned with a much greater fre-

---

evidence with the totality of liturgical practice—ministers may have composed *ex tempore* prayers of which there is no remaining record. See Yates, *Liturgical Space*, 139–40. The following discussion refers only to the official resources published by The Presbyterian Church in Canada, and makes no attempt to account for liturgical innovation on the part of individual ministers.

100. *A&P*, 40 [1914], 279.

101. PCC, *Book of Family Devotion*, 59.

102. The preparation of the book was recommended in the 1915 Report of Committee on Public Worship and Aids to Devotion, *A&P* 41 [1915] 279. The prayers mentioned may be found in PCC, *Book of Common Order*, 14 (First Morning Service), 21 (First Evening Service), 28 (Second Morning Service), 34–35 (Second Evening Service), 64 (General Intercession), 89–90 (Special Intercessions).

quency, the language of the prayers is mostly consistent with that of the single prayer in the 1919 *Book of Family Devotion*, with the focus falling on expressions of gratitude to God for the lives of the departed, and petitions that their memories may continue to set examples of faithful living to those who remain. However, several prayers are clearly influenced by the events of the war: a prayer in the First Morning Service, and the first two Special Intercessions for "Those Faithful Unto Death."

The "Thanksgiving for the faithful departed" in the First Morning Service is remarkable primarily for the militancy of its language:

> Blessed Lord, with whom do live the spirits of those departed in the faith, and who hast said unto us by Thy Spirit, Blessed are the dead which die in the Lord: enable us to be followers of them as they were followers of Christ; and so to run our race with patience, and to fight the good fight of faith, that, our course being finished and our warfare accomplished, we may join the innumerable company of the redeemed: through Jesus Christ our Lord, who ever liveth and reigneth with the Father and the Holy Ghost, world without end.[103]

The petition for aid to "fight the good fight of faith, that, our course being finished and our warfare accomplished, we may join the innumerable company of the redeemed" is strikingly similar to the just war rhetoric employed by preachers during the war—as well as an invocation of the specific memory of the soldiers who died in the war, rather than the more general population of the dead (those who died primarily of illness or old age).[104] The desire expressed to be "followers of them as they were followers of Christ" constructs an analogical relationship between "the dead which

---

It should be noted that, unlike what Wilkinson claims for the Church of England, the Church of Scotland's liturgy (on which The Presbyterian Church in Canada's liturgy was partially based) included a very brief prayer of remembrance in the "Short Form of Intercession especially for use when there is a celebration of Holy Communion." See CoS, *Book of Common Order*, 1884, lxxiv. This prayer appears, unchanged, in the twelfth edition of the same book, published 1929. No such prayers appear in the Free Church's *New Directory for Public Worship*. However, James Ferguson, in *Prayers for Common Worship*, treats "The Remembrance of the Blessed Departed" as a distinct moment in the order of prayers (following, as it does in the Canadian *Book of Common Order*, the general Intercessions); while Ferguson did not compile his volume at the behest of any church committee, this does indicate an eventual increase in the importance ascribed to such prayers of remembrance.

103. PCC, *Book of Common Order*, 14.
104. Vance, *Death So Noble*, 36–36.

die in the Lord" and Christ. This analogy is that of a moral exemplar, in which Christ's example of self-sacrifice leads others to emulate it, just as the "Memorial of those who are at Rest" in the 1919 *Book of Family Devotion* included a petition to "Give us grace to follow in their footsteps, as they followed in the footsteps of thy holy Son." In both cases, the example of the dead points the living towards the example of Christ, turning their hearts from things seen to things unseen and leading also upwards to God; the striking difference is that the 1922 *Book of Common Order* appeals specifically to a violent exemplar. It is, however, a bloodless violence; nowhere does the prayer indicate that "to fight the good fight of faith" or to "accomplish" warfare might involve inflicting actual physical damage upon another person's body, or suffering the infliction of physical damage upon one's own body—although, by 1922, the presence of veterans returned home with missing arms, legs, or eyes (to name but a few of the more immediately obvious physical injuries that marked veterans) may have been a sufficient reminder of the actualities of warfare that there would be no need to elaborate further.

The language of the first two Special Intercessions for "Commemoration of Those Faithful Unto Death for the Commonweal" is, theologically speaking, a far greater departure from earlier forms. The second of these makes recourse to the language of John 15, but subtly shifts the emphasis away from God's action through humanity (and especially the dead) and onto the actions of the dead:

> O Lord, who hast taught us that man hath no greater love than this, that he lay down his life for his friends: grant that their devotion may bear good fruit in us and in the generations coming after them, that we leave not their work unfinished, but in the might of such love likewise ever strive for a cleaner earth and a closer heaven.[105]

The role of God in this prayer is to guarantee the success of the mission begun by the dead: "grant that their devotion may bear good fruit in us [...] that we leave not their work unfinished," rather than to engage in any form of "work" directly or through the congregation (the line is not "that we leave not *Your* work unfinished," or even "that we leave not the work You began through them unfinished"). Likewise, the first of the three Special Intercessions under the heading offers praise to God "for all those through whom Thou hast blessed us in our earthly welfare," including "those who

---

105. PCC, *Book of Common Order*, 89–90.

gave themselves mightily in defense of freedom, mercy and good faith among the nations; especially for comrades and dear kindred whom we remember before Thee with undying affection; for those who in life and death have quickened our lives, and through whose sacrifice we live."[106]

This is a sharp shift from the idea of Christ and the dead—especially the war-dead—as co-workers of atonement, twin moral exemplars. Instead, the soldiers "who gave themselves mightily in defense of freedom, mercy, and good faith among the nations" are figured as offering a substitutionary atonement; it is they, rather than Christ, "through whose sacrifice we live."[107]

The conflation of the dead soldier with Christ was an understandable move during and immediately after the war, when the familiarity of the sacrificial discourse could help to reassure an unusually large number of mourners that, in spite of the widespread disruption of accepted and expected structures of grief, some portion of the world retained a semblance of normalcy. However, the sacrificial narrative became suspect as the years passed on and the majority of society moved from an expression of grief based primarily in denial and yearning to one mostly characterized by anger and disillusionment.[108] This shift is apparent even within Montgomery's work; the second half of the posthumously published volume *The Blythes are Quoted* is a collection of vignettes from after the First World War; it concludes with the following exchange between Anne and her grown son Jem:

> ANNE, *steadily*:- "I am thankful now, Jem, that Walter did not come back. He could never have lived with his memories . . . and if he had seen the futility of the sacrifice they made then mirrored in this ghastly holocaust . . ."
>
> Jem, *thinking of Jem, Jr., and young Walter*:- "I know . . . I know. Even I who am a tougher brand than Walter . . . but let us talk of something else. Who was it said, 'We forget because we must'? He was right."

---

106. PCC, *Book of Common Order*, 89.

107. This language remains in use in The Presbyterian Church in Canada, especially in Remembrance Day services—see the two sample liturgies available through the PCC's website: "A Liturgy for Remembrance Day" <http://www.presbyterian.ca/webfm_send/269> accessed 11 August 2009; "A Remembrance Day Service for November 11, 2007, Theme: The way to peace" <http://www.presbyterian.ca/webfm_send/899> accessed 11 August 2009.

108. BQ, 510.

The result of this is a marked contrast between what the First World War memorials were designed to convey and the way that contemporary visitors read them. This contrast will be explored in the final chapter of this section.

FOUR

Making Memory Solid

Jane Urquhart and The Canadian National Vimy Memorial[1]

The moon sank lower into a black cloud in the west, the Glen went out in an eclipse of sudden shadow—and thousands of miles away the Canadian boys in khaki—the living and the dead—were in possession of Vimy Ridge.

Vimy Ridge is a name written in crimson and gold on the Canadian annals of the Great War. "The British couldn't take it and the French couldn't take it," said a German prisoner to his captors, "but you Canadians are such fools that you don't know when a place can't be taken!"

So the "fools" took it—and paid the price.

—L. M. MONTGOMERY, *RILLA OF INGLESIDE*, 208

Montgomery's[1] fiction provides a useful window into the way that practices and understandings of death, mourning, and commemoration shifted from before the First World War to the period immediately following the war. However, the view from that window is necessarily limited: it the perspective of one woman, close to the events about which she writes. However influential *Rilla of Ingleside* has been in terms of carrying and constructing the memory of small-town Island life during the First World War, and in the minds of young girls (the intended audience of the

---

1. A much earlier—and shorter—version of this chapter appears under the same title in Filipczak, *Bringing Landscape Home in the Writings of Jane Urquhart*; while my reading of SC has not altered significantly, my understanding of the monument has benefitted from additional historical and archival research. I hope I may be forgiven for re-using the title, which I have found to be too apt an expression of the themes under examination to abandon.

Anne of Green Gables series) throughout the world, it does not tell much about the way that the memory of the war has changed over the decades since its end, nor does it tell us much about the ways in which the dominant narrative of the war (of which *Rilla* is very much a part) has been contested or undermined.

Montgomery, for example, recognizes that "Vimy Ridge is a name written in crimson and gold on the Canadian annals of the Great War," but was in no position to predict the mythology of nation-building that sprang up surrounding the Battle of Vimy Ridge in the years following the war. The assault on Vimy Ridge the morning of 9 April 1917 marked the first time the Canadian Corps fought together as a unit, and therefore, according to a pamphlet put out by the Canadian Battlefield Memorials Commission, marked "the first appearance of [A] young nation in arms."[2] The post-war years were dominated by the need to demonstrate that the war had been fought—and won—for a purpose; Vance notes that, on the whole, "Historians have been only too happy to aid and abet this process by articulating a vision of the war as a nation-building experience of signal importance," and the battle of Vimy Ridge has been widely figured as the root of that nation-building experience.[3]

Vance suggests that Vimy's place at the center of the Canadian nation-building myth is as much a result of the post-war monument-building activity as the decisions made by the CBMC were reflective of the historical and military significance of the Battle of Vimy Ridge. The original commemorative scheme put forth by the CBMC called for identical monuments at the eight battlefields (including Courcelette, where Walter Blythe was killed) put into that Commission's charge by the Imperial War Graves Commission.[4] A general competition for the design of all the monuments, announced in December 1920, yielded two entries which "were of too high a standard to be rejected and were too original to be repeated eight times."[5] One of these was an entry by the Ontario sculptor Walter Allward.

Allward described his design in a letter to André Ventre, the Chief Architect of the French Historic Monument Commission, as follows:

2. CBMC, *Canadian Battlefield Memorials*, 80–81; quoted in Vance, *Death So Noble*, 67.

3. Vance, *Death So Noble*, 9–10. See also the essays collected in Hayes et al., *Vimy Ridge*, especially the editors' "Afterthoughts," 313–17. See also Berton, *Marching as to War*, 178; Marteinson, *We Stand on Guard*, 154.

4. Vance, *Death So Noble*, 66; Brandon, *Art or Memorial*, 8–9.

5. Vance, *Death So Noble*, 67.

PART TWO: Mourning the Absent

> I am enclosing a description of the Memorial which accompanied my model in the competition.
> [...] The long walls are intended to suggest a line of defense, and also to be in harmony with the long and clean cut line of the Ridge.
> The two Pylons were an endeavor to create an outline against the sky, that would not be easily confused with towers or other landmarks, also, the pylons and walls suggest the upper part of a Cross. In the afternoon when a shaft of sunlight will break through the space between the pylons, and, illuminating part of the sculptures, will suggest a cathedral effect.
> [...] From my youth I have admired the qualities in the work of your great sculptors, and in making my design for Vimy, I endeavored to erect a memorial which might be acceptable to your people, fully appreciating their high regard for Art, and consequently the necessity for something artistic spiritual and broadly human in its expression.[6]

This letter suggests that Allward's original design was drafted with Vimy Ridge in mind, contrary to Vance's recounting of the Commission's competition and deliberations; the copy of Allward's original competition submission available on the Veterans Affairs Canada website shows a design not substantially different from the monument that now stands, although the entry does note that it is "intended for Vimy Ridge or any site on high ground or a slight grade—base of pylons can be altered to suit perfectly level sites."[7]

The papers stored in the Allward Archive at Queen's University in Kingston, Ontario include a large number of sketches, showing what appear to be iterative re-workings of the concept for the Vimy memorial, varying the number of pylons and their spatial relationship to one another, shifting their orientation from horizontal to vertical, and altering the location of the figure groups on and around them. As Allward was not in the

---

6. Letter from Allward to Ventre, dated 12 April 1926, from the Walter S. Allward Archive, Queen's University, Kingston, ON. I have taken the liberty of correcting obvious typing errors.

7. <http://www.vac-acc.gc.ca/images/vimy90/galleries/04_monument/01_competition/compete20_lg.jpg> Accessed 20 January 2010. The alterations from the proposal are very slight: in the final structure, the area of the platform behind the pylons is enlarged to permit visitors to approach from behind the monument, and all the figures are carved out of marble, rather than cast in bronze as originally proposed. Other entries in the competition may be seen at <http://www.vac-acc.gc.ca/remembers/sub.cfm?source=memorials/ww1mem/vimy/sg/04_monument/01_competition>.

habit of dating or labeling his sketches, it is impossible to determine which of these are preliminary and which represent him reworking the visual elements of the Vimy memorial at a later date, either for his own amusement or as a beginning point for other projects.[8] The sketches do, however, speak to certain formal and symbolic preoccupations which governed Allward's creative life.

Allward's letter to Ventre maintained that his goal in constructing the two pylons was "to create an outline against the sky, that would not be easily confused with towers or other landmarks," but his sketches tell a slightly different story. He arranges and rearranges clusters of rectangular pylons in forms that are reminiscent of the skyline of a medieval cathedral city. In the final monument, this effect is less obvious, but still evident in the stepped shaping at the tops of the pylons.

Allward's praise of French artistry in his letter to Ventre is no empty platitude; both his sculptural work and his figure drawings reflect a strong awareness of the conventions of French academic art, in sharp contrast to the modernism that was making its mark on the art world at the time.[9] His employment of classical idiom made him an extremely popular designer of public monuments, and lent a comforting veneer of familiarity to projects

---

8. There is, for example, a strong resemblance between the Vimy sketches and a set of sketches for an unrealized monument to Sir Fredrick Banting, and a similarly unconstructed monument to the Second World War. The Banting monument is more horizontal in orientation, but there is at least one sketch with an arrangement of horizontal elements similar to sketches positively identified as Banting sketches by the Queen's archivist, and with lettering on the front suggesting it is meant to be a monument to the Great War. The lack of dates on the sketches is not the only difficult puzzle in the Allward archive; his son, Hugh, records in a letter to E. A. Gardner dated 19 November 1968 that "On return from England, probably with a sense of frustration or even fury, I believe Dad in all or in part edited and destroyed correspondence relating to the Memorial." The correspondence which survives sheds some light on the creation of the memorial, but, like the sketches, or Montgomery's journals, should be approached with caution, and by no means as a complete record. A majority of the letters from Allward, for example, survive without signature, indicating that they are quite probably drafts and may differ slightly from what was actually sent. The reliability of Hugh Allward's allegation is itself undermined, as he goes on to say that his father "had no office in London only the Studio and hence his letters were written longhand," a remark which is belied by a fair number of typewritten letters with letterhead from Allward's studio at 16 Maida Vale, London.

9. Evans, *Mother of Heroes*, 124; see also Vance, *Death So Noble*, 102–10. Modernism was rendered especially unpopular by the war; the art critics of Britain and Canada "linked modern painting to German *Kultur*, then, after the October Revolution, to Bolshevism," Tippett, *Art at the Service of War*, 6. See also Hynes, *War Imagined*, 273–75.

PART TWO: Mourning the Absent

which may otherwise have been too complex, costly, or avant-garde.[10] The Vimy memorial project was all three. Its construction took sixteen years, and its final cost severely over-ran the original budget.[11] The twin pylons are reminiscent of the classic cenotaph form, but their proximity causes them to resemble, especially from a distance, a cenotaph cleft down the middle—a fractured monument.[12]

Figure 1: Front view, Canadian National Memorial at Vimy

Allward's design was, as indicated in his letter to Ventre, intended to convey the ideas of sacrifice (the horizontal and vertical elements of the monument representing "the upper part of a cross," the entire monument suggesting a cathedral, and the "Spirit of Sacrifice" stretched out cruciform on the altar between the two pylons) and unity (the twin pylons representing the continuing allegiance and goodwill between Canada and France). The form of the monument, however, the large cleft running down the center of the "united" pylons, undermines these ideas, just as the years since

10. See Brandon, *Art or Memorial*, 11–12.
11. Vance, *Death So Noble*, 68–69.
12. Brandon also notes the similarity of the Vimy memorial's structure to more traditional monument forms, and further notes that "the most traditional memorial in Canada was a column—for example, that to Generals Wolfe and Montcalm in Quebec City" (*Art or Memorial*, 11).

the monument's design and construction have brought a change in popular understanding of the war. The disillusionment that Watson charted through English literature can be readily read into the imagery of the monument; walking through the site brings the visitor into contact with not only the high ideals which characterized the discourse of the war, as recorded by Montgomery, but also the transformation those ideals have undergone in the decades since.

It is somewhat telling that the unity that Allward and the CBMC were most concerned with expressing at the Vimy monument was between France and Canada, rather than between the French and English populations within Canada. Nowhere in the correspondence archived at Queen's is there any expression of concern that the monument be hospitable or comprehensible to French Canadian soldiers or their families.[13] Rather, the memorial, and the committee behind it, relies on the assumption of a united Canada. Vance writes that "on a domestic level, historians have had to admit that the Great War was as divisive as it was unifying. Four years of battle, both in the trenches and at home, did not create a single nationalism, but instead strengthened the two nationalisms of French and English Canada; both societies gained a greater appreciation of their separate identities from the experience of war."[14]

The division between French and English Canada was apparent from the earliest stages of the war. The first wave of 36,267 volunteers to sail for England with the Canadian Expeditionary Force, beginning 29 September 1914, included only 1,245 French Canadians.[15] Admittedly, only 9,635 of the others were English speakers born in Canada; the rest were immigrants, primarily from the British Isles. While provincial borders are not a sure guarantee of ethnicity, it is still notable that the percentage of the adult male population that enlisted from Quebec—the main center of French Canadian population—was not terribly different from the percentage that

---

13. By contrast, there are a number of letters concerned with the monument's reception in France. In addition to the above cited letter to Ventre (in which Allward indicates that "because of the sympathy which existed between the French, and the Canadian soldiers, and the people, I have taken the liberty of introducing the Fleur-de-lis on a corner of the second wall"), there is a letter from Walter Allward to Colonel Osborne, 1st May 1927; Osborne to Allward 6th December 1928; Allward to Osborne 16th December 1928.

14. Vance, *Death So Noble*, 10.

15. Granatstein and Hitsman, *Broken Promises*, 23.

PART TWO: Mourning the Absent

enlisted from Ontario (0.7, compared to 0.9).[16] However, as the war wore on, the numbers of volunteers from Quebec dropped sharply in relation to the other provinces; by the end of the war, only 9 percent of the adult male population of Quebec had served, compared to 18 percent from the Maritimes (including Prince Edward Island), which had the next lowest rate of military service.[17] By 1917, the proponents of the Military Service Act were able to put forth a compelling argument that the Act would, by introducing conscription, "at last, force French Canadians to assume their share of the military burden."[18] The battle of Vimy Ridge itself was fought by a volunteer army, but a mere thirty-eight days afterwards, the threat of conscription caused riots in Montréal.[19] The deeply divisive Parliamentary election of 1917 was fought mostly over the issue of conscription, and the eventual victors, Robert Borden and his Union Government, "deliberately set out

---

16. Nearly half (15,232) of the first contingent of the CEF were English, with an additional 7,979 volunteers of Scots, Irish, and Welsh origin—see Granastein and Hitsman, *Broken Promises*, 23. Percentages of adult male population to enlist taken from Brown and Loveridge, "Unrequited Faith," 78, Chart F. Brown and Loveridge base their percentages on the population figures from the 1913 *Canada Year Book*, which measured male population 15–44 years old in 1911; the lower end of that spectrum would have been old enough to be eligible for military service by the time war broke out in 1914.

17. See Brown and Loveridge, "Unrequited Faith," 78, Chart F. Only 2.4 percent of the adult male population of Quebec volunteered during the militia recruiting conducted 1914–1915, compared to 3.6 percent of the adult male population from the Maritime Provinces, which had the next lowest volunteer rate (and, in fact, had the lowest rate of volunteers—0.4 percent—in the initial wave). In the period from 1915–1917, only 1.6 percent of the adult male population of Quebec volunteered, compared to 6 percent from the Maritimes. Granatstein and Hitsman argue that the roots of volunteerism or lack thereof go back to the local militias of the 1700s, and that *Québécois* antipathy to service in the military of the British Empire was a long established cultural phenomenon. See *Broken Promises*, 5–19.

Incidentally, these figures (as well as other literature on military volunteerism and conscription at the time) suggest that Montgomery's Blythe family, who, without prior militia affiliation or close ties (within two generations) to the British Isles, sent all of their sons into the military by the end of the war, were somewhat unusual for Prince Edward Island.

18. Brown and Loveridge, "Unrequited Faith," 64; see also Granatstein and Hitsman, *Broken Promises*, 44–46. Granatstein and Hitsman note that animosity between French and English Canada was particularly high at the war's beginning, and thus divisive political maneuvers would have been particularly effective in that political climate; in 1911, Wilfred Laurier "had been driven from office [as Prime Minister] on the grounds that he, as a *Québécois*, was disloyal to Empire" (*Broken Promises*, 27). See also Morton, *Marching to Armageddon*, 28.

19. Hayes et al., *Vimy Ridge*, 316.

Making Memory Solid

to create an English-Canadian nationalism, separate from and opposed to both French Canada and naturalized Canadians."[20] The schism between the pylons, though originally meant to represent the mutual accord between Canada and France, also appears, however unintentionally, to represent the schism in relations between French and English Canada that was deepened by the war, and especially by the conscription crisis, an impression deepened by the placement of all French language inscriptions on the east side of the monument, and English inscriptions on the west.

Figure 2: Figure of Mother Canada, Canadian National Memorial at Vimy

The ambivalence of the monument extends beyond the two pylons, however. The figures on and around the pylons also tell, perhaps, more than the story that Allward originally intended. As a visitor approaches the monument from the back, they pass between two reclining figures, one male and one female "mourner." The female holds an open book in her lap, although the pages appear blank (the plaster model of the figure on display at the Military Communications and Electronics Museum in Kingston, Ontario, shows a Greek cross on what is, from the figure's vantage point, the top left-hand corner of the page, but either this detail was not included in the final

---

20. Granatstein and Hitsman, *Broken Promises*, 78. In turn, the harsh rhetoric directed against Quebec led to an upsurging of *Québécois* nationalism; a motion "That this house is of the opinion that the province of Quebec would be disposed to accept the breaking of the Confederation Pact of 1867" was introduced to the Quebec legislature in January 1918 (*Broken Promises*, 82).

PART TWO: Mourning the Absent

carving or it has weathered away at the monument itself).[21] The Angel of Knowledge, a highly androgynous figure holding a closed book under one arm, looks down from the west pylon; opposite, above the male mourner, the Angel of Truth adorns the east pylon, clutching an olive branch in her right hand. Walking around to the front of the platform from which the pylons rise, the visitor sees the lone, bent figure of Canada in stark outline against the sky (figure 2); turning to face the pylons, there is only a short staircase between the visitor and the figures of the Torchbearer and the Spirit of Sacrifice (figure 3).[22] There are other figures clustered on the top of the pylons. At the top of the eastern pylon is the allegorical figure of Justice, almost hidden behind the large, unbroken sword held in the figure's arms (figure 4); below that figure are Faith and Hope, both with their gaze, and left hands, uplifted; Faith's arm stretches fully above her head, while Hope's is bent at the elbow, the hand level with her shoulder. Faith's right hand clutches a small cross to her heart (figure 5), while Hope's right hand rests by her side, on a larger cross inscribed in the marble behind her (figure 6). On the western pylon, Peace holds a triumphant olive branch above her head, echoing the pose of the torchbearer (figures 7 and 8) below. She is supported by Honour, holding yet another book, open to reveal blank pages, and Charity, with a basket full of poppies.

21. Brandon writes that "[A]n article published just before the memorial's unveiling claims that the mourning figure at the back holding an open book is reading the 'roll of death'" (*Art or Memorial*, 14), though she ventures no explanation of the other books on the monument.

22. Evans reads the figure of Canada, especially, as an example of classical iconography, with her half-bared breast reminiscent of Greek literature, in which it represented the bond of nourishment between mother and son (she also reads the bared chest of Charity in this way, although she fails to account for the similarly exposed breast(s) of Hope, Honour, Truth, or Peace in her scheme); her cowl resembles a mourning veil, and also refers to "many depictions of Mary," and her gesture, "reminiscent of Rodin's *The Thinker*," lends her an air of contemplation. More interestingly, Evans notes the proximity between Canada and the Spirit of Sacrifice as highlighting "the sacrificial element of her character." See Evans, *Mother of Heroes*, 124–26. Brandon reads the figure of Canada solely as a Mater Dolorosa figure, although she acknowledges the Greco-Roman influences in other figures—as well as the influence of Rodin; see *Art or Memorial*, 12–13. The resemblance between Allward's figures and those of Rodin is also noted by Robert Shipley, who contrasts the neo-classical style of figure evident on the Vimy memorial, with the "naturalistic" style of figure evident on Allward's earlier Toronto Boer War Memorial; see Shipley, *To Mark Our Place*, 134.

Figure 3: Torchbearer and Spirit of Sacrifice, Canadian National Memorial at Vimy

Figure 4: Justice (plaster, ½ scale). War Museum, Ottawa, Ontario.]

Figure 5: Faith (plaster, ½ scale). War Museum, Ottawa, Ontario. Note the pencil marks, which were used to translate the design from the plaster to the full-scale marble carving.

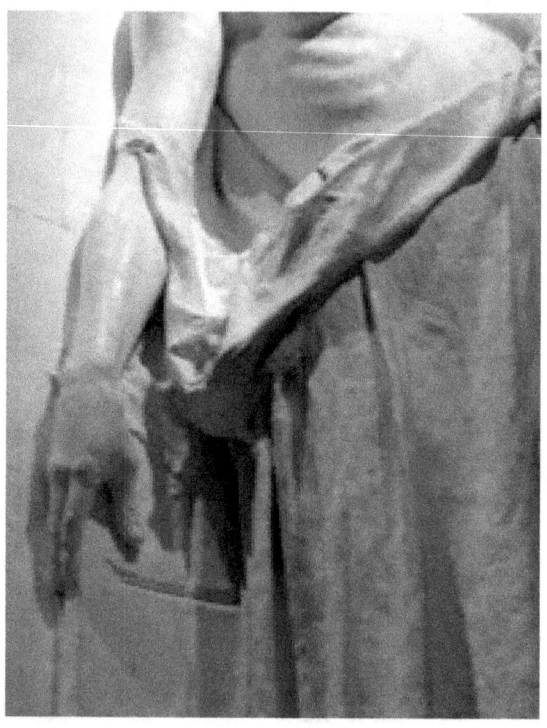

Figure 6: Hope (detail of plaster ½ scale model). War Museum, Ottawa, Ontario.

Figure 7: Peace (plaster, ½ scale). War Museum, Ottawa, Ontario.

Figure 8: Torchbearer (plaster, ½ scale). War Museum, Ottawa, Ontario.

Making Memory Solid

The visitor has to proceed along the upper rampart and down a flight of steps before being able to view the monument in its entirety, from the front. From this vantage point, four more important elements come into view. From the upper rampart, the barrels of two cannons, draped in laurel garlands, point out towards the plain—and the viewer. The rear of these cannons is also visible from the upper rampart, but their place in the overall design of the monument is not clear until they are viewed from the front. Two large figure groups stand at either end of the base of the rampart. To the south is the Breaking of the Sword group: two heroic male figures gaze off towards the center point of the monument, while behind them, a smaller and less well-clothed man strains to bend a sword over a rock. To the north is the Sympathy of Canadians for the Helpless: one heroic male figure stands tall, gazing out over the plane, with a supporting arm around a smaller male figure, half kneeling, with gaze directed up, though not quite at the central figure; to the other side, a seated male holds a bowl over the head of a huddled, naked female figure. At the center of the wall, underneath the gaze of the figure of Canada on the wall above, is a stone sarcophagus, symbolic of all the Canadians who died in the war.

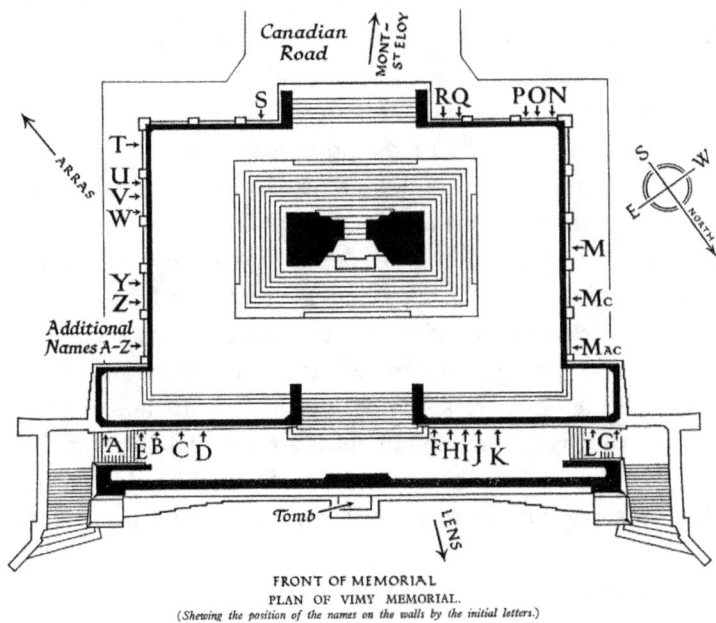

Figure 9: Image courtesy of Commonwealth War Graves Commission.

PART TWO: Mourning the Absent

The pervasiveness of carved poppies around the site, as well as the centrality of the Torchbearer figure, call to mind the last stanza of John McCrae's poem, "In Flanders Fields." On the surface, Allward's design appears to support the inherent rightness of McCrae's argument, showing Peace triumphant, yet inescapably supported by both the scenes of sacrifice and mourning that adorn the base of the monument and by the other allegorical figures that adorn the pylons. One might also note that there is no allegorical figure of Mercy to be found anywhere on the monument. Jonathan F. Vance has presented an extremely convincing, historically contextualized reading of the Allward corpus as representative of the militant triumph of civilization over the forces of barbarism, of pacifism as a privilege that could only be won at the point of a sword.[23] However, the monument also undermines this allegorical argument. The carved vegetation—even the poppies—appears wilted. The books held by three of the figures hold out the promise of knowledge, or understanding, but what they offer is a blank page, or a permanently sealed binding.[24] A certain weariness and strain seems to settle around the shoulders of even the most heroically posed figures. The figure of Canada mourning her dead seems startlingly old to be placed on a memorial to "the first appearance of [a] young nation in arms."[25]

The triumph here seems muted, the hope held out a distant one—as, indeed, Vance maintains Allward intended. Peace is not shown immediately triumphant, but rather supreme long after the memory of the current struggle has faded from view. But the belief in a war to end all wars is fainter, now, than it was in the 1920s and 1930s, when Allward created the monument; the signs of decay built into the design speak of abandonment, of precisely the broken faith that McCrae's poem warned of, rather than the eschatological lying of lions with lambs that a simpler reading of the monument would suggest. The hope expressed at the end of the First World War is tarnished by a contemporary viewer's awareness of the horrors of the Second World War, begun a scant three years after the monument's completion, and of all the other wars that have been fought since then, with no end any longer in sight. The monument is a memorial; it brings forth the idealism that characterized the discourse of the First World War out from the realm of history and into the visitor's own immediate, lived experience,

---

23. See Vance, *Death So Noble*, 27; 32–33.

24. This could also be read as an invitation to the viewer to create their own text from the disparate elements of the memorial.

25. CBMC, *Canadian Battlefield Memorials*, 80–81.

but it does not do so without also bringing forth some of the cynicism and awareness of failure that the intervening decades have attached to those ideals.

The double-image produced by the memorial, of both high ideals and the failure of those ideals, is nowhere so haunting as when the viewer's gaze is directed at the 11,285 names which adorn every vertical wall around the outside of the monument's base save for the very front. These are the Canadian soldiers who went missing from the battlefields of France—whose bodies were either never found, or else found but never identified, but buried under headstones bearing the inscription "A Soldier of the Great War Known Unto God". The names were the last element of the monument to be decided upon, and much of the correspondence in the archive at Queen's involves a debate over how they ought to be incorporated into the overall design.[26] Allward himself originally favored carving them into the floor-stones, after the fashion of gravestones in European cathedrals, although he was overruled by the rest of the committee. In the final design, the list of the missing begins on the southeast corner of the wall immediately behind the front rampart, and continues in horizontal lines, counterclockwise, around the outside of the base of the structure. The layout of the names is unusual; most local monuments, and the Menin Gate at Ypres, where the names of Canadian missing from Belgium are inscribed, list names in vertical columns. By carving names across, rather than down, each wall, Allward achieved a far more uniform, textural effect; the names bleed into and become part of the structure itself—just as the bodies of the missing soldiers became part of the landscape.[27]

---

26. As noted above, the functions of the Vimy memorial evolved over time. Jacqueline Hucker has argued that the finished monument has three distinct functions: (1) marking the site of the battle of Vimy ridge, (2) to be "this country's principal monument in Europe honouring the valour of all Canadians who fought in the First World War," and (3) to "serve as testament to those Canadians who lost their lives in France and whose bodies were never identified." She notes that it was designed with function (2) in mind, its location was determined by function (1) (not until 1922, according to Brandon, *Art or Memorial*, 9), and function (3) was decided upon only after the design and location were finalised. See Hucker, "After the Agony," 284.

27. This way of laying out the names was inspired by the "Soldiers' Tower" built in the early 1920s at the University of Toronto; see letter from Colonel H. C. Osborne to Allward, 18 October 1926. The decision was, however, as much practical as it was aesthetic; carving the names horizontally permitted more names to fit into a space that was not originally designed to accommodate them, as attested by an undated letter from Allward to Osborne (to which the 18 October letter appears to be a reply).

PART TWO: Mourning the Absent

The bodies of missing soldiers did not fade into the landscape simply as a consequence of their lack of burial; the landscaping of the memorial park surrounding the Vimy monument continually suggests battered bodies in the negative space of the shell craters that have not been ploughed level as the rest of the surrounding countryside—and the land immediately surrounding the monument itself—has. The land is as wrinkled as a mountain range seen from the air, as puckered as the skin of a burn victim. The velvety texture of the grass and the sensuous play of light across the curves of the earth draw attention to the fact that this is the land after ninety years of wind and rain have had time to soften the edges of the craters; the connection to what the land must have looked like during the war, and what artillery that could do this to the landscape must have done to the bodies of the soldiers there, is immediate and visceral. It is thus easy to read these names as a reproach, rather than a roll of honor.[28] It is difficult to find a comfortable balance between the collective identity represented by the monument and the individual identities represented by each name. It is at this point that a return to fiction once again becomes helpful—not, as was the case with Montgomery's work, for its historical value, but as a way of imaginatively reconstructing the balance between individual and collective, of grappling once again with the tension between civic and familial identity, body and name, that formed the subtext of *Antigone*.

THE STONE CARVERS

Jane Urquhart's novel, *The Stone Carvers*, is a family drama that begins in Shoneval, a fictional small town in southern Ontario (based loosely on the real town of Formosa), but reaches its climax at the site of the construction of the Vimy memorial.[29] The book enforces, to some extent, popular myths of the war, such as the memory of an all-volunteer army. All three of the Canadian soldiers described in its pages enlisted well before the passing of the Military Service Act; Tilman Becker, one of the main characters, lost his leg at the battle of Vimy Ridge. However, the high ideals that are given such a prominent place in Allward's monument have little place in the novel's narrative. Eamon O'Sullivan, the lost lover of Tilman's sister, Klara, enlists in spite of protestations from her and from his family (his

---

28. This division over the meaning given to memories of the war is not unusual. For a discussion of this in relation to SC, discussed below, see Branach-Kallas, "Carving the Names," 69.

29. Jane Urquhart, interview.

Irish father threatens to disown him if he goes to fight for the English king) because he wants to learn how to fly an aeroplane.[30] The stories of the other two—Tilman and his friend Giorgio—are far less concerned with reasons than they are with consequences, the toll that the decision to enlist has on the men and their families.

However, Urquhart also subverts these myths. Nobody else in the village that Tilman, Klara, and Eamon come from served in the war; they all received agricultural exemptions.[31] The novel implies that this may have as much to do with political ambivalence, or the desire to remain well outside of European conflicts, in a village settled by mostly German immigrants, as it does with the actual need for farm workers in the area, though this never moves beyond implication, as very few villagers from outside Klara and Tilman's family appear in the book. There is no honor or glory won on the battlefield, least of all at Vimy Ridge, where Tilman loses his leg and Eamon his life. The soldiers' sacrifices do not partake of Christ's resurrection or immortality; as the story opens, Klara's demands for a village war memorial are dismissed by her neighbors as the permissible eccentricity of an unhappy spinster.[32] Later on, Tilman tells of his rather inglorious life as a disabled, unemployed veteran, carving prosthetic limbs for other disabled veterans until even that work vanishes and he is forced to return to the childhood home he ran away from years before.[33]

In presenting stories that defy, in one way or another, the popular myth of the war, the novel helps to bridge the gap between the idealized image of the faceless, nameless citizen-soldiers of "In Flanders Fields" and the particular, embodied lives represented by the names on the Allward

---

30. SC, 137–38. Eamon's desire for flight is an echo of that which guides Anne and Gilbert Blythe's youngest son, Shirley, to enlist near the end of the war in *Rilla of Ingleside*. However, Montgomery's character successfully navigates the many hurdles on the way to enlistment in the Flying Corps (for a discussion of which see Morton, *Marching to Armageddon* 30–31); Urquhart's, whether due to the difference in timing (Shirley enlists near the end of the war, Eamon at the beginning), socio-economic status (Shirley is the son of a country physician, and his family is well-to-do enough to afford live-in domestic help and send to every child so inclined to college; Eamon's parents are Irish immigrants, farmers, and markedly less well-off than their neighbors), or the historical situation and disposition of the author behind the character, dies having "never got anywhere near an aeroplane" (SC, 162). This is one of many instances in which Urquhart takes an aspect of the popular myth of the war and subtly undermines it.

31. SC, 253.

32. SC, 29.

33. SC, 231–35; Branach-Kallas, "Carving the Names," 71.

PART TWO: Mourning the Absent

monument.³⁴ The tension between the two is brought into sharp focus towards the end of the novel, as Klara, having disguised herself as a man in order to travel to France where both she and her brother obtained employment in Walter Allward's work crew, seeks to use the monument as a means of release from the grip Eamon's memory has held on her life:

> No matter how much it is cherished, an absent face that is a fixed point of reference becomes tyrannical, and tyranny eventually demands revolt, escape. Klara had fled from the memory of Eamon's face over and over, his bright eyes and perfect skin, now almost two decades younger and more perfect than her own. She had [. . .] by a fierce act of will [. . .] almost succeeded in turning him into a faceless ghost, until all that was left was the vaguely human, dark shape of his absence. [. . .]
>
> Now she would have to remember the bones under the skin, the scar on his left temple, the beautiful, full mouth, his upturned glance and radiant expression when searching the sky for a kite, an aeroplane. Each detail. [. . .] He had been only a boy, the inquisitive child he had been had never left his face. He must hold the torch aloft, yes, but because this figure would become Eamon and would be looking up toward his beloved ether, his expression must be one of astonishment and joy at finding himself, at last, forever reaching toward the sky. [. . .] She stood on the ladder, eyes squeezed shut, scraping these images from the deepest recesses of her memory as if using a sculpting tool on the inner curve of her skull. Then she began.³⁵

Klara's imposition of her personal memory onto the monument is disruptive to its function as a nationally unifying memorial; later on in this same scene, Urquhart's fictional rendition of Walter Allward enters, and, upon discovery of her carving, accuses her of vandalism.³⁶ The universal, Allward implies, cannot be reached through the particular. The memory of a single, specific face not only cannot encompass the memory of all lost faces, it actually works against the ability of any future mourner to project their own particular, absent face onto the monument.³⁷

    34. SC is by no means the only Canadian postwar novel to challenge the myth of the war, although its connection to the Vimy memorial renders it particularly interesting in the current context. For other Canadian novels with a similar approach—especially to the postwar years—see Boyden, *Three Day Road*; Hodgkins, *Broken Ground*.
    35. SC, 332–33.
    36. SC, 336.
    37. It is interesting that Urquhart chose the figure with the least visible face of any on the monument onto which to project her own narrative.

It can be argued, however, that an instance of particularity is necessary to offset the attempt at universal expression which, otherwise, becomes too distant, too impersonal; there must be room to remember the soldier as a brother, a son, a husband, rather than simply as a faceless servant of the Empire. Urquhart's fictional Allward comes to this realization himself, at the conclusion of the scene: "The face was becoming a portrait, he could see that, but beyond that the expression had about it the trustfulness of someone who did not know he would ever be missing, lost from the earth. This woman had brought a personal retrospection to his monument, and had by doing so allowed life to enter it."[38] While the introduction of the particular breathes life into Allward's monument, it is only the first step towards easing Klara's own grief. Interjecting her memory of Eamon's physical presence into the monument does not abrogate the actuality of his body's absence. It neither satisfies her yearning nor enables her to find release from the crippling burden of memory that she carries. It does, however, permit Klara to begin to distinguish her own physicality from Eamon's, and to experience her own bodily existence and her sexuality without his mediation. After Eamon's death, we are told, "[h]er body, once awakened, had gone back to sleep, folding in on itself, the skin recognizing only the change of external temperature, or the touch of cloth. [. . .] Anything else she had simply willed away, refused to remember or even dream."[39] The combined event of the carving and Klara's discovery free her mind from the tyranny of Eamon's remembered face and her body from the restrictions she has imposed on it, first in her life as a respectable spinster, and then in the masculine disguise she adopted to facilitate her journey to the monument.

There are problems with this reading, of course. Klara does not actually reclaim her gender identity willingly, but has it re-imposed on her by the men around her. It is not Klara's choice to abandon her disguise after Allward discovers both her carving and her gender. Klara resists the suggestion that her living quarters be moved out of the men's dormitory, wishing instead to remain with her brother. The worksite supervisor has to insist that she move into the office, "[n]ow that you're a woman."[40] The gender confusion Klara undergoes in this passage is like that of a young girl, re-learning the boundaries between male and female, re-discovering the limitations her body places on her even as she is freed from the limita-

---

38. SC, 340.
39. SC, 344.
40. SC, 342.

tions her disguise has placed on her body. However, it is only the renewal of these boundaries that permits Klara to breach the divide between male and female again, by embarking upon another love affair.

It is noteworthy that two of the characters discussed in this book, Klara and Antigone, transgress (or are perceived as transgressing) gender boundaries in their pursuit of proper commemoration for their loved ones.[41] In Klara's case, the transgression is both more overt—her appropriation of masculine dress and mannerisms—and more subtle—her appropriation of Allward's creative prerogative. It is not just Klara's carving that blurs gender boundaries—although she acquired the skill as a side-effect of her grandfather's mostly frustrated attempts to teach Tillman, an early (and small) appropriation of what was meant to be her brother's birthright—but the *success* of her carving, her ability to transform the monument into something richer than Allward intended, which renders her threatening and thus necessitates her firm removal to a more securely female realm.[42] Allward's reflection on Klara's carving emphasizes her gender, as if to emphasize the contrast between her gender and her actions: "This *woman* had brought a personal retrospection to his monument, and had by doing so allowed life to enter it" (emphasis added). However, in the same sentence that contrasts femininity with creative achievement, Klara the childless spinster is endowed with the safely feminine characteristic of life-giving.

This is, however, an ironic statement; Klara's carving may have breathed life into Allward's monument, but it failed to breathe life into Eamon. Klara has the skill to create and alter many different bodies, from the Abbess she carves out of limewood under her grandfather's instruction, to her own gender transformations, but she cannot create the body she most desires. Upon first hearing of Eamon's death, Klara gropes for some physical artifact

---

41. Creon is quite concerned not only at Antigone's gender transgression, but at the degree to which her masculinity undermines his own: "Indeed, now I am no man, but she is a man, if she is to enjoy such power with impunity" (Soph.*Ant.*, 47; ln. 484–85); "But while I live a woman shall not rule!" (Soph.*Ant.*, 51; ln. 525); "If we must perish, it is better to do so by the hand of a man, and then we cannot be called inferior to women" (Soph.*Ant.*, 65; ln. 679–80).

42. As if to underline the gender transgressions inherent in Klara's carving, Urquhart links Klara's first experience of carving with her grandfather's story of the Infant of Prague: "Klara was delighted by the idea of a boy doll, holy or otherwise, wearing dresses, and she set to work immediately carving the body from an abandoned porch pillar [...]" (SC, 96–97). The gender play around the act of carving in SC both relies upon and undermines the gendered idea of creative genius put forth in the *Anne of Green Gables* series.

to serve as a substitute for his body. Her first, failed, attempt at a symbolic substitution to aid her mourning is the re-creation of the red waistcoat she made for him at the beginning of their courtship.[43] We are told that "[s]he believed that once she began to pull the scarlet thread through the wool, once she was involved in the act of reconstruction, some of her anguish would abate."[44] She sews the waistcoat as she might have sewn Eamon's pall, and in so doing calls up an echo of the prediction Eamon himself made about the use to which the original waistcoat would be put.[45] Unlike a pall, however, the recreated waistcoat has no ritual purpose; it is not laid in the ground with Eamon's body (it cannot be), but remains in Klara's keeping. It does not, and cannot, grant Klara any release from her grief, its presence instead serving to reinforce the stark fact of Eamon's absence, its outline pointing to the shape of, but not giving form to, the body that fails to fill it. Klara carries that absence, the resultant anguish, and her exacting attempt to reproduce Eamon's physicality, across the ocean with her, just as insistently as she carries the recreated waistcoat.[46] Her carving at the monument is, then, a second attempt at bringing to the absent body enough solidity that she can bury it, and fulfill the mourning ritual that the War interrupted.[47]

The failure of Klara's portrait carving to erase her grief is, in a larger sense, a failure of the pre-existing paradigm of loss and grief to accommodate the experiences of the wartime generation. Mourning rituals focused on the body and gravesite deepen, rather than mitigate, the sense of loss

43. SC, 161, 163.
44. SC, 164.
45. SC, 80–81.
46. SC, 258–59.
47. The obvious question here is why Klara's grief is continually seeking a better substitute for Eamon, where Rilla is capable of fulfilling her mourning with little more than a letter and a commemorative plaque on the family pew. It is not a simple difference of religion—while Rilla is Presbyterian and Klara Catholic, both are quite devout and should be equally capable of being comforted by the promise of eternal life (though it may be a difference in religion on the part of the authors, Urquhart's reticence in regards to her own religious belief prevents this from being anything other than speculation); it may be a difference in the circumstances surrounding Walter's and Eamon's deaths, as Klara's quarrel with Eamon remains unresolved, and she has no final letter by which to be comforted. However, especially in light of the gender transgressions discussed above, I would suggest that another answer to this question is simply that Rilla represents the paradigmatic "good woman," who never strays from her prescribed role, where Klara, like Antigone, represents the "bad woman," incapable of being satisfied by the limited role and rituals she is socially permitted. See Sourvinou-Inwood, "Assumptions and Creation," 140.

PART TWO: Mourning the Absent

felt when the body and gravesite are inaccessible or non-existent, just as the second waistcoat Klara sews heightens, rather than diminishes, her awareness of Eamon's absence—not simply his absence from her present life, which she has lived with for several years, but also, and perhaps even more, his absence from her future life: the elimination of any possibility of his return or of a reconciliation between them. The emotional void of this double absence is too great to be contained by and disposed of through physical representation. However detailed and memory-laden such representation may be—the waistcoat recalling the awkward hesitancy of early courtship, the upturned face of the Torchbearer recalling the reasons behind their quarrel and parting—it cannot contain the full depth and breadth of the absent loved one's being.

Representation is necessarily finite. It is a collapsing, a flattening, of the real into the symbolic—this is one of the reasons frequently cited for the prohibition against images in Judaism (and Islam).[48] Some forms of representation do this more than others. Klara's carving, for example, is a highly detailed physical representation; it may even be an exact reproduction of her memory of Eamon's face. But a representation of a memory of the real thing is not the thing itself, and much less so the person; it is at least one flattening too many. Klara's attempts at mourning through representation are ineffective because representation itself is fundamentally ineffective for this purpose. What Klara (and, I would argue, the rest of her generation) requires is, instead, abstraction. A carving of Eamon's face quickly becomes simply a carving of a face, a single representative of the collective generation of doomed youth in whose honor the carving was created, because Eamon's essence is no longer corporeal. Rather, the corporeality of his essence has been transfigured, and is no longer borne by flesh, or capable of being represented by stone, but can most effectively be contained and approached as word. Eamon's own face may be lost forever, and a representation of that face may fade from particularity into anonymity, but Eamon O'Sullivan remains Eamon O'Sullivan. The uniqueness of his being is, finally, represented by his name, by a particular arrangement of a series of abstract symbols representing sounds (letters), rather than by a realistic representation of his physical, fleshly, characteristics.

Klara's refusal to speak his name, to give physical form, however ephemeral, to the idea represented by the symbols, attests to her instinctive appreciation of this fact. So long as Eamon remains unspoken, Klara

---

48. For a more in-depth discussion, see Jacobs, *Judaism and Theology*, 10.

remains the guardian not just of his memory but of his essence; her intimacy with him is thus considerably greater than it ever could be with Giorgio, and much more bound up in the structure of her own self-identity: "[s]he felt that to release the syllables [of his name] into the air all these years later would be a kind of amputation, a violent removal of a part of the self."[49] The release of this bond, and the culmination of Klara's mourning, form the dual climax of the book.

After being revealed as a woman, Klara embarks on an affair with her brother's friend, Giorgio, who is employed at the monument primarily to carve the names of the missing onto its side. Her physical contact with another person enables her understanding of Eamon's death to move beyond the mostly physical level at which she had experienced his absence for much of the book. The consummation of their relationship undermines Klara's previous understanding of the war and its costs. In the tunnel system that lies beneath the land on which the monument is being built, "like extended tangled roots reaching up to the monument above, feeding its construction by their very existence," she begins to learn to release her insistence on the absolute uniqueness of Eamon and his fate.[50] Just as the intimacy she shares with Giorgio in these tunnels demonstrates that Eamon was not the only possible mediator for her sexuality, the carvings that she and Giorgio discover on the tunnel walls demonstrate to the reader that Eamon's fate, however tragic, was shared by many: "'I carved the letters of this boy's name yesterday,' [Giorgio] whispered, pointing to the second inscription. He shook his head. 'And the other . . . the other was found under the rocks when they cleared the entrance to Grange Tunnel. He was scratched from my list.'"[51]

The face of the torchbearer became a portrait; the portrait, in turn, fades and takes its place amongst the other allegorical figures that adorn the monument. A certain amount of distance has been imposed between the living and the memories of the dead. Klara, however, continues to cling to her position as the guardian of Eamon's particular memory, supported in this by the silence that she relied upon to insulate her since he went away to the war.[52] Her insistence on maintaining this silence, even against Giorgio's direct questioning, shields her not only from the pain of fully acknowledg-

49. SC, 360–61.
50. SC, 356.
51. SC, 356.
52. SC, 160, 163.

ing Eamon's loss, but also from the vulnerability of fully entering into a new relationship.[53] She can admit Giorgio to the knowledge of her own body, but not to the knowledge of her past; she can display Eamon's face for all the world to see, but she cannot bring herself to speak his name in another person's hearing.

The first of the book's two climaxes comes when Klara does finally speak Eamon's name out loud, and this in itself occurs in two parts: first, her unwitnessed whisper into the dark and, eight pages later, the performance of the speech act in front of Giorgio. It is worthwhile to note that both of these utterances mark a break in the narrative, which picks up afterwards from a different point of view. It is also worthwhile to note that, while the first whisper is presented from Klara's viewpoint, the second vocalization is seen through Giorgio's eyes; we readers are given only clues as to how and why Klara chooses to speak. The two speech acts are nearly identical: "'Eamon,' she [whispered/said]. 'Eamon O'Sullivan.'"[54] In the first instance, however, the narrative break occurs immediately after the utterance; in the second, Klara continues to speak: "'Poor boy. [. . .] He was so young.' She paused. 'And so much time has passed.'"[55]

The causal link between the passage of time and Klara's ability to speak is implicit, but deceptive. While it is true that Eamon has been gone for many years, no more than a few weeks have passed since Klara and Giorgio quarreled over her initial refusal release Eamon's name, and in so doing release her hold on his memory (and his memory's hold on her). What has changed is not time itself, but Klara's recognition of time. Her journey across the ocean, her carving of the portrait, her experiences with Giorgio, her encounter with the reality of other lives lost, all of these have worked to convince Klara of the distance between her self-identity and her role as the guardian of Eamon's memory-identity, to make it possible for her to release the syllables of his name into the air, where she can not protect or control them, without committing a violent removal of a part of her self. The days or weeks (the exact amount of time that elapses is unclear) between the two speech acts can be read as the time it takes for Klara to recognize what has,

---

53. SC, 360.

54. SC, 362, 370.

55. SC, 370. This last sentence is also an echo of an earlier statement by Tilman (SC, 366).

in fact, already happened, and reconcile herself to this new kind of loss, which is also a gain.[56/]

Klara's release is not yet complete, however: a second act of naming must occur, the final climax of the book. Nicola King has suggested that a final release occurs when a memory is transformed into text.[57] This certainly appears to hold true in the case of Klara's second naming of (and second attempt to carve) Eamon. Where a representation of his physical characteristics proved unsatisfactory, the abstract shapes of letters are capable of bringing his essence into a form physical enough for Klara to relinquish her hold on his memory: "Klara knew this would be the last time she touched Eamon, that when they finished carving his name all the confusion and regret of his absence would unravel, just as surely as if she had embraced him with forgiving arms."[58]

In carving Eamon's name on the memorial, Klara not only brings him into sufficient solidity to effect a reconciliation with his memory, she also places him irrevocably in the care of the national collective, a sharp contrast to her earlier attempts to guard and maintain his identity as an individual, or a member of her family unit. To Antigone, the individual personality of a body faded in the face of its overwhelming symbolic significance. In the Vimy memorial, and other monuments to the First World War, the body itself fades from view, to be replaced by a name which both asserts and obscures individual identity; even in the Imperial War Graves cemeteries, where the normalcy of graves and bodies is preserved, the uniformity of the tombstones overrides the differences in their inscriptions. The carved names do not simply represent the missing; in their ability to contain the complexities and nuances of unique lives, they, at least functionally, have become the bodies of the missing. The arrangement of these names on the Vimy memorial achieves something similar to Klara's experiences in the tunnel, undermining any perceived uniqueness in the manner of each death, even as each carved name embodies the individuality of the life it represents.

---

56. A more detailed reading of Klara's inner transformation can be found in Branach-Kallas "Exploring the Dark Tunnels of Memory," especially pp 64–65.

57. King, *Memory, Narrative, Identity*, 175.

58 . SC, 376.

Interlude

Blotting Out Amalek

When the Second World War broke out in 1939, less than three years after he had returned to Canada, Allward reacted with panic and rage. He deluged the Department of National Defence with telegrams begging for reports and demanding that the memorial be sandbagged against aerial bombardment. As the weeks passed and he received no replies, he retreated into an inner landscape of great bleakness, pacing the house in the middle of the night, imagining the worst [...]

With sharp coloured pencils he began a series of small, secretive drawings, each one more violent, more angry than the last. Tangled bodies littered torn landscapes, burning clots of brimstone rained down from a savage sky. And, in the background, tiny, almost insignificant in the drama, the wreckage of the monument [...]

The drawings seemed to feed his belief in catastrophe, his certainty that there was absolutely nothing on earth not subject to vicious attack. In his imagination, and on the rice paper he used, the allegorical figures of his sculptures stepped away from their fixed positions to engage in appalling dramas. Always with the ruins of the memorial smoking in the distance, he drew embracing lovers impaled by a single sword, cairns composed of lifeless bodies, a naked man straddling the torn, prone torso of a woman from whose chest he had snatched her bleeding heart. Allward knew, even before he had completed this particular drawing, that it was his own heart the man held aloft, a trophy steaming in his desperate hands.

He had spent fifteen years of his life obsessed by perfection and permanence. [...] He had believed that he was making memory solid, indestructible, that its perfect stone would stand against the sky forever. With this certainty threatened, his world collapsed.

—Jane Urquhart, *The Stone Carvers*, 380–81

Figure 10: Tim Davies, European Drawings (2007). Used by permission of the artist.

Blotting Out Amalek

Urquhart ends *The Stone Carvers* not with the completion of the Vimy memorial, but with images of its destruction. Working from sketches filed in the Allward Archive as "War Cartoons," she imagines how he became obsessed with the catastrophic scenarios that his own imagination spun out, making drawing after drawing of the monument reduced, or in the process of being reduced, to rubble. The fear of destruction that Urquhart attributes to Allward alone was, in actuality, echoed by the general Canadian public; both the Montreal *Daily Star* and the Toronto *Globe and Mail* published lurid, though ultimately erroneous, accounts of the memorial's destruction at the hands of German bombers.[1] Both the British and Canadian military attempted to obtain intelligence regarding the memorial's condition throughout the German occupation of France, hoping to either boost morale with news of its continued endurance, or else derive propaganda value from its wreckage.[2]

"The calculated barbarism that has characterized post-1939 conflicts has made us loath to admit that there can be anything positive about war," writes Vance. "Even Canada's social memory of the Second World War, as just a war as the modern world has seen, is dominated by overtones of negativity. Notions of individual heroism, self-sacrifice, and fighting in a good cause have been pushed to the background by a dominant memory that has come to emphasize mismanagement, injustice, failure, and cupidity."[3] In spite of this, the Second World War did not itself bring a great challenge to commemoration. In Canada and Great Britain, most localities that had constructed monuments to the First World War simply added another inscription to extend the monuments' reach over the Second, as well. The great upheaval of the Second World War was not entirely felt until the war's end, when details about activity within German-occupied territories began to become fully and irrefutably known. The great challenge to the accepted order of the world brought by the years 1939–45 was not the mass death of soldiers in war, but the mass death of civilians: the Holocaust. While death in the First World War could be folded into a religiously supported Just War narrative, death in the Holocaust defied—and continues to defy—attempts at theological response.

What the sketches Urquhart describes really depict is not the destruction of the memorial itself, nor of the monument-making culture that

1. Durflinger, "Safeguarding Sanctity," see especially 293–98.
2. Ibid., 296–97.
3. Vance, *Death So Noble*, 10–11.

produced it, but of the dominance of that culture, of the high ideals—and idealism—that the memorial enshrines. Although there is nothing to identify the figures in the war cartoons as the figures from the monument, the link Urquhart draws between the two, having Allward sketch "the allegorical figures of his sculptures stepped away from their fixed positions to engage in appalling dramas," accentuates the degree to which the Second World War undermined belief in the grand principles the figures represent. Urquhart's fictional Allward, in despair over the loss of those principles precipitated by the outbreak of another war, engages in an imaginative, visual deconstruction of his own monument, an attempt to blot out the memory he had so carefully constructed.

A similar attempt to blot out the memory of the past—not just the constructed monuments, but the ideas they represent—can be seen in the Welsh artist Tim Davies's recent series, *European Drawings*. The individual drawings in the series are presented without titles, but are displayed as a long row of identically mounted and framed images of presumably famous landmarks, united as much by their anonymity as by the uniformity of the graphite on their surface. As the viewer walks along the row, one or two familiar sites may come into view: here the London cenotaph, there a familiar face from along the Somme. But then the viewer moves on, the angle of the light shifts, and the surface becomes mirror-like, completely obscuring the image beneath it.

These are not drawings as one normally thinks of drawings. The pencil lines do not conspire to construct any sort of recognizable image. The most readily available visual point of reference is actually the paper beneath the drawn surface, a digital print which has then been furiously scratched out by thick, dark pencil lines. It is not unreasonable to say that the drawing, in fact, works *against* the image. But this is not an act of deconstruction; there is no attentive disassembling of component parts; the pencil lines betray no care for the way either the photograph or the monument which it depicts is composed. Instead, it reads as a deliberately failed attempt at obliteration— I say deliberately failed because the acts of selecting the photograph, of enlarging and printing it, of framing it and placing it on a gallery wall to be viewed, draw to the image the same attention that the graphite overdrawing seems meant to deflect or frustrate.

One wonders what exactly is being obliterated—the image itself, or the monument to which it refers. Or is the hand holding the pencil attempting to reach even further back, beyond the image, beyond the monument, to erase history itself? This last is impossible, and the mind behind the hand must surely know it to be so. However, it is precisely that reach for the impossible that Davies has portrayed. The drawings are a protest against the neatness and finality indicated by the memorial structures themselves. A press release from the Collins Gallery, Glasgow (where I first saw these images) quotes Davies saying that he used the drawings as attempt "to get my head around the concept of loss and futility."[4]

The idea of futility is enforced by the second, smaller set of "drawings" in the series. Rather than building up a drawn surface in front of them, Davies has pierced the images from behind, with the pattern of pin-pricks focused most heavily around the figurative element of whichever monument is portrayed. The pin-pricks are like shrapnel wounds. Inside each one is a tiny drop of red, as though the image of the memorial has taken on, or been given, some of the characteristics of the wounded flesh to which it attests. The injury of the absent injured body is brought back into view, even while its absence is underscored by the substitution of an image of a memorial figure for a body, or even an image of a body. The second set of drawings enforces the futility of the exercise undertaken by the first: what has been done cannot be undone; history cannot be blotted out; some losses are, in the end, irretrievable.

4. Collins Gallery, "Tim Davies."

PART THREE

Absent Mourners

FIVE

Worship in the Ruins

On a quiet street of what was formerly East Berlin, not terribly far from Checkpoint Charlie, a crowd shuffles through the door of an old courthouse.[1] A few at a time, they pass through a narrowly-guarded gate, down a steep and twisting flight of stairs, into a sloping corridor with tiled floors, dully reflecting the glare of the institutional fluorescent lights overhead. The angles at which this corridor is cut across by two other, nearly identical, passageways are more reminiscent of a funhouse than a hospital. These intersections seem to provide the visitors a multitude of potential destinations, though all are dead ends—even the recommended route up another long, steep flight of stairs is only the beginning of a long digressive path that will eventually deposit the visitor right back in the subterranean maze.

The journey, in this case, is as important as the destination. We are far away from Canada, but we will pause here for awhile, to let distance and a change of context inform our reflections, returning to "home territory" in the concluding chapter. Following the stairs up into the permanent exhibition space of the Daniel Libeskind-designed Jewish Museum Berlin propels visitors through a chronological recounting of the entire two thousand year history of German Jewry, from the earliest settlers, through the flourishing of Medieval Ashkenaz, to the Enlightenment and the Jewish Reform movement, the First World War, and beyond. This approach is a deliberate strategy on the part of the museum's curatorial team to present the German Jewish experience in terms that extend beyond "Auschwitz and guilt."[2] The overarching meta-narrative of the historical presentation is one of "continuous struggle"; in this respect, the Holocaust is integrated into the narrative, rather than being figured as an interruption, or a terminus.[3] The gallery presentation is complex and nuanced, drawing out individual

1. Schneider, "Jewish Museum Berlin," 21.
2. Museum director W. Michael Blumenthal, quoted in Pieren, "Being Jewish," 79.
3. Pieren, "Being Jewish," 82.

PART THREE: Absent Mourners

narratives as counterpoints to the anti-Semitic stereotypes that characterize common historical images of the German Jew, emphasizing instead the close integration between Jewish and German cultural identities.[4]

Figure 11: Main staircase, The Jewish Museum, Berlin

4. Pieren, "Being Jewish," 81.

All of this combines to enhance the sense of loss felt by the visitor when they return to the underground corridors and choose between the remaining destinations—three dead ends. They may walk up the sloping corridor to the outdoor Garden of Exile, with its dizzying, disorientingly tilted pillars, symbolically abandoning the rich cultural heritage they have only just learnt to appreciate. This is the path of escape; the other two options each lead to one of the "Voids" for which the building is famous, both of which house representations of the Holocaust.

The first of these, the "Memory Void," houses a work by Menashe Kadishman, entitled "Fallen Leaves"—a floor littered with thousands of pieces of iron, in various states of rust, cut to resemble human faces; it resembles the infamous piles of shoes on display at Auschwitz.[5] A plaque near the entrance to the void invites visitors to walk across the floor, over the faces; few even attempt it, and most of those manage only one or two hesitant steps before retreating. This space feels like the climax of the entire journey: the wall of the tower is perforated by openings on all the building's other floors, and so the room has drifted in and out of visibility as visitors have made their way through the exhibit, with each subsequent encounter bringing the room closer, rendering its contents more visible. This room, however, is but the final preparation for the last void. Down a different corridor, an attendant waits to usher visitors through a heavy door into another concrete tower. Unlike the "Memory Void," this one is nearly windowless (indirect light leeches in from somewhere near the top of the room) and completely unadorned. Libeskind has referred to this space as a "voided void"; it is the ultimate blank wall on which to project memories of all the experiences that preceded it. The effectiveness of the space as a memorial specific to the Holocaust depends upon the presence of Kadishman's work in the Memory Void, and upon the visitor's encounter with it; without that final, visceral encounter with human figures piled up like detritus, the voided void would risk becoming an overly stylized image of loss, much like the Mémorial de la Déportation in Paris. In the latter, a visitor appreciates the symbolism of descent and entry into an enclosed space; here in Berlin, they experience the sense of hopelessness and captivity that the Parisian memorial alludes to.

---

5. Schneider, "Jewish Museum Berlin," 26.

Figure 12: Menashe Kadishman, "Fallen Leaves," Jewish Museum Berlin.

Worship in the Ruins

The integration of a museum component to memorial sites is a particular feature of Holocaust memorials. Auschwitz has been transformed into a museum, as has Dachau; even the most cursory internet search for "Holocaust Memorial Museum" reveals, in addition to Yad Vashem in Jerusalem, the Holocaust Memorial Centre in Montreal, and the United States Holocaust Museum in Washington D.C., countless similar sites scattered throughout North and South America, Europe, and Australia. Not two kilometers away from Libeskind's site stands The Memorial to the Murdered Jews of Europe, a field of concrete stellae designed by Peter Eisenman (remarkably similar to the pillars which sprout up from the Garden of Exile), which rises over a hidden, subterranean museum complex.[6] The heart of this museum is the Room of Names, a dark room, empty save for a few benches in the middle, upon the walls of which are projected, one at a time, the names of Holocaust victims, along with their dates of birth and death, if known. As each name is projected, a brief biography—sometimes little more than place of birth and date of deportation—is read in German and English. Just as Libeskind's voided void depends upon the visitor carrying the experience of the museum into the space with them, the impact of the Room of Names depends not just on the preceding two rooms of the museum, but on the thousands of concrete stellae that the visitor had to walk through before descending into the museum at all.[7] Sitting in the Room of Names for any length of time, or reading the family histories housed in the room that precedes it, impresses upon the visitor the absolute, terrifying unremarkability of the lives commended to communal memory: they are as indistinguishable as the concrete grid above.

The prevalence of museum-memorials points to the crucial distinction between memorialization of the First World War and of the Holocaust, both in Canada and the rest of the world. The former arose in response to the disruption of communal mourning rituals caused by the absence of a body or gravesite; they support, through a series of substitutionary gestures, the continued expression of normalized narratives of loss and grief. The latter arises, profoundly, in the absence of not only body and gravesite, but in the absence of the normal community of mourners. The Memorial to the Murdered Jews of Europe documents entire families and villages wiped out; a sizeable portion of the individuals commemorated in the Room of

---

6. See Eisenman, "Memorial to the Murdered Jews," 10–13.

7. For an account of the contents of each room in the museum, see Stiftung Denkmal für die ermordeten Juden Europas, "Design Concept."

PART THREE: Absent Mourners

Names had no surviving relatives. The memorial museums first create a sense of attachment to the dead as members of one's own community—whether that community is defined by shared religion, shared nationality, or shared humanity—in order to give the visitor a reason to mourn, only later providing space in which that mourning might occur. This is Jewish liturgical space, both in the sense of λειτουργία, the public duty owed by one segment of the Jewish community (the living) to another (the dead), and in the sense that these memorials fulfill the same function as do more recognizable, textual forms of Jewish liturgy, providing a space of encounter between present-day individuals and their collective past.⁸

Figure 13: Room of Names, Memorial to the Murdered Jews of Europe

The museum-memorial form is ubiquitous in memorials to the Holocaust as well as more general memorials to the Second World War. Just under four kilometers west of the Memorial to the Murdered Jews of Europe—a rather pleasant stroll through the Tiergarten—the ruined tower

---

8. Of course, as Laura Levitt has pointed out, the Holocaust is the direct inheritance of only a relatively small number of European Jews; it has, however, grown in cultural significance, to become a defining historical event in Jewish collective identity. See Levitt, *American Jewish Loss*.

Worship in the Ruins

of the Kaiser-Wilhelm-Gedächtniskirche rises above the Kurfürstendamm, a fitting memorial to Germany's complex religious-political past. Like the Memorial to the Murdered Jews of Europe, it also contains its own museum, meant to guide visitors in the proper interpretation of the site.

The church was originally built in the last decade of the nineteenth century as a monument to Kaiser Wilhelm I by his grandson, Kaiser Wilhelm II.[9] In its first incarnation, under the architectural direction of Franz Schechter, it "took a neo-Romanesque style, rich in reference to Germanic medieval empires"; it served as "church, museum, and monument," richly decorated with lavish mosaic floors and ceilings depicting scenes from the Bible and from the life of Wilhelm I.[10] These—the ones which remain—are largely reminiscent of the mosaics in Byzantine Imperial churches, such as those at San Vitale, in Ravenna, locating the Kaiser-Wilhelm-Gedächtniskirche firmly in a long tradition of imperial church architecture and decoration.[11]

After the end of the monarchy in 1918, the building's popularity declined, and it came to be viewed largely as "an obstruction to traffic," a lonely island in the midst of a busy theatre district, a discarded relic of the imperial past afloat on the sea of modernity.[12] However, the building survived the interwar years, and remained a landmark of note, as well as a reasonably prestigious congregation. Dietrich Bonhoeffer preached several important sermons from the church in the early 1930s;[13] later, the church's regular pastor, Gerhard Jacobi, became an influential figure in the Confessing Church's resistance against the Nazi regime.[14] The church was

---

9. Retallack, *Imperial Germany*, 118.

10. Ibid.; see also Koshar, *From Monuments to Traces*, 112.

11. For the relation between the design of the Kaiser-Wilhelm-Gedächtniskirche (hereafter KWG) and Kaiser Wilhelm II's sense of the German Empire's place in history, see Eksteins, *Rites of Spring*, 89. See also Cecil, *Wilhelm II*, 44; Mayer, *Persistence of the Old Regime*, 225.

12. Much of the information on the site's history is taken from the rather thorough museum housed in the old church tower. See also Fulbrook and Swales, *Representing the German Nation*, 68–69; Pächter, *Weimar études*, 95–96. Also see Hake, *Topographies of class*, 27, 137. Hake suggests the post-WWI distaste for the church was also linked to anti-imperial sentiment.

13. See Bethge and Barnett, *Dietrich Bonhoeffer*, 236, 282; Kelly and Nelson, *The Cost of Moral Leadership*, 35; Langston, *Exodus through the centuries*, 247; Nelson, "Life of Dietrich Bonhoeffer," 22–49, 32, 45.

14. According to Victoria Barnett, the KWG was never officially a Confessing Church parish; rather, Jacobi carried on a Confessing Church ministry privately, while remaining

PART THREE: Absent Mourners

not, however, an unambiguous symbol of resistance; it was also used as the centerpiece of a 1928 essay by Joseph Goebbels, who was later to become Hitler's propaganda minister, which decried the theatres and cabarets that had sprung up in the area around the church, contrasting sacred German history with the contemporary commercial corruption that he linked unambiguously to Jewish business interests.[15]

Even today, the church sits in the middle of a busy commercial center; at night, the rotating Mercedes-Benz logo on top of the Europa-Center building is far more visible than the small gold cross on top of the campanile, and patrons spill out of nearby bars to congregate on the Breitscheidplatz around it. By day, it is apparent that the central tower structure was not meant to be square, but is, in fact, a remnant of a much larger building, and what appeared to be windows at ground level are actually arches that lead from the central portion under the tower off into naves and transepts that no longer exist. The old church was destroyed in the Second World War, first by a series of air raids and then by street fighting; by the end of the war, the wrecked central tower was all that remained standing.[16] Its continued presence is an accident of history and of urban planning: although the parish passed a resolution to rebuild the church in 1947, no steps were taken towards the selection of an architect for the project until 1956.[17] In the intervening years, much of the rubble that characterized Berlin at the end of the war had been cleared away, leaving the tower as a rare remnant of the wrecked cityscape, and one capable of attracting a certain degree of affection.[18] Public pressure prevented the tower from being demolished completely, and it was instead incorporated into the complex of new buildings that were designed by Egon Eiermann and constructed entirely of glass, set in the modular cement latticing that is his signature material. There is some

---

officially affiliated to the "German Christian" movement, until 1939, when he succumbed to pressure to join the military. See Barnett, *For the Soul of the People*, 168–69; Hockenos, *Church Divided*, 132.

15. Koshar, *From Monuments to Traces*, 112–13. See also Ward, *Weimar Surfaces*, 181, 183

16. Kaiser-Wilhelm-Gedächtniskirche, Memorial Hall, permanent exhibit (visited 5 August 2008). Hereafter referred to as KWG (MH).

17. Kabierske, "Kaiser Wilhelm Memorial Church," 173. Much like Allward and the Vimy memorial, Eiermann submitted the winning design to a competition, and further adjustments were made later on; see Kabierske, "Kaiser Wilhelm Memorial Church," 173–74.

18. Ladd, *Ghosts of Berlin*, 176–77. See also Diefendorf, *In the Wake of War*, 75; Sieverts, *Cities Without Cities*, 27.

indication that Eiermann was opposed to the ruin's continuing presence on the site, but the visual and symbolic tension achieved by the commingling of old and new imbues the church complex as it currently exists with a richness that would have been impossible to achieve by other means.[19]

This is an odd place for a Jewish theologian to begin a reflection on the memory of the Holocaust. However, the contrast between this church and the open-air cathedral of Allward's Vimy memorial provides a useful bridge between theological reflection on the First World War and on the Holocaust. The church, to the extent that it is presented as a memorial at all (and while it cannot avoid its landmark status, nor the steady stream of tourists that results, the majority of the informational materials at the site focus firmly on its role as a church with an active congregation), is a memorial to what Germans—and, in particular, members of the Confessing Church—endured during the Second World War; the little it has to say about the Holocaust focuses almost exclusively on baptized Jews who were members of the congregation.[20] This is unsurprising when the church is considered within the larger context of Christian theological reactions to the Holocaust.

CHRISTIAN GESTURES TOWARDS A POST-HOLOCAUST THEOLOGY

It is difficult to argue that the years 1933–45 (the total span of Nazi rule in Germany) have much to do with Christian theology, at least in the way that the shattered tower of the Kaiser-Wilhelm-Gedächtniskirche would suggest. Looking from the outside of the tradition, it would appear that the events of the Holocaust, when they enter into the worldview of Christian theologians at all, have tended to be figured as confirmation of the Christian message of salvation. For example, there is Jürgen Moltmann's famous reading of Eli Wiesel, in *The Crucified God*. Wiesel recounts an incident at Buna (one of Auschwitz's sub-camps) in which three men are hanged; two die quickly but one, a young boy, remains alive and struggling for some time: "'Where is God? Where is he?' someone asked behind me. As the youth still hung in

---

19. Eiermann's dislike of the ruined tower has passed down anecdotally through the congregation of the KWG, and was related to me in rather forceful terms by Mr. Wegener; it is also alluded to in Kabierske, "Kaiser Wilhelm Memorial Church," 173, Sieverts, *Cities Without Cities*, 27, and, more obliquely, in the multiple references to the public outcry that was necessary to keep the tower intact—see above, note 12.

20. In KWG (MH).

PART THREE: Absent Mourners

torment in the noose after a long time, I heard the man call again, 'Where is God now?' And I heard a voice in myself answer: 'Where is he? He is here. He is hanging there on the gallows.'"[21] To this, Moltmann adds the following commentary: "Any other answer would be blasphemy. There cannot be any other Christian answer to the question of this torment. To speak here of a God who could not suffer would make God a demon. To speak here of an absolute God would make God an annihilating nothingness. To speak here of an indifferent God would condemn men to indifference."[22]

Wiesel's work is complex; he declares his fury at God in one moment and prays to that same God for strength the next. Moltmann, however, is quick to turn Wiesel's struggle into a vehicle through which to proclaim the proper "Christian" response to suffering.[23] Wiesel's image of the death of his faith (however ambivalent he may be about that death) becomes, for Moltmann, neither more nor less than a pure affirmation of what he terms the *theologia crucis*, in which God, through Christ, "humbles himself and takes upon himself the eternal death of the godless and godforsaken, so that all the godless and godforsaken can experience communion with him."[24] The death of Jews on the gallows at Auschwitz is, for Moltmann, merely an echo, or a subtype, of the death of a Jew on a cross at Calvary; the lesson of the latter applies to the former, as well. Dorothee Soelle also reads the exact same passage from Wiesel, with similar results, although she goes on to note the potential danger of such an interpretation, to which Moltmann remains oblivious, noting that "To be sure, one must ask the effect of such an interpretation, which connects Christ with those gassed in Auschwitz and those burned with napalm in Vietnam. Wherever one compares the incomparable—for instance, the Romans' judicial murder of a first-century religious leader and the fascist genocide in the twentieth century—there, in a sublime manner, the issue is robbed of clarity, indeed the modern horror is justified."[25] Moltmann's Jews function much like the soldiers of the First World War, pointing the way towards human participation in Christ's

21. Wiesel, *Night*, 77.
22. Moltmann, *Crucified God*, 274.
23. Wiesel does come to the image of God suffering alongside Israel—particularly in *All Rivers Run to the Sea*; it is a concept with strong roots in the Rabbinic tradition. That Wiesel later adapted this vocabulary for his own in no way excuses Moltmann from his misreading of his much earlier work, *Night*, where the predominant attributes of God are absence, silence, and indifference.
24. Moltmann, *Crucified God*, 276.
25. Soelle, *Suffering*, 146.

sacrifice, though without the theological danger that they might be mistaken for Christ himself.[26]

Of the works that do attempt to address the Holocaust as though it makes a claim for the alteration of Christianity's religious imagination, many are cosmetic, not to mention circular, in nature, focused on the issue of Christian antisemitism as something which must be addressed because its consequences have proven to be undesirable, out of an impulse of charity towards other peoples, rather than because it is theologically flawed in its own right.[27] Such critiques involve three distinctive themes, although any one work of "Christian response to the Holocaust" is likely to combine several of these. There is (1) a very simple critique of the language of Christian Scripture and its use in preaching, in which Israel or "the Jew" is figured as an agent of active opposition to the Christian message.[28] This is

---

26. If I appear too hard on Moltmann, he finds a ready defender in Haynes, *Prospects*, esp. 114–22. Haynes wishes to give Moltmann credit for the depth of his engagement with Jewish sources—not just Wiesel, but also with elements of the rabbinic tradition—and search for a re-orientation of the relation between Judaism and Christianity, especially in light of the personal horror he experienced upon learning of the events of the Holocaust while interned as a German prisoner of war in Scotland. Haynes has persuaded me to acknowledge the probability of Moltmann's good intentions. However, this does not render what he has actually written in this passage any less problematic. See also Echardt, "Jürgen Moltmann."

27. See, for example, Cargas, *Shadows of Auschwitz*; Davies, *Anti-Semitism and the Christian Mind*; Fasching, *Narrative Theology*; Haynes, *Reluctant Witness*; Littell, *The Crucifixion of the Jews*; see also the essays collected in Fasching, *Jewish People*; Rittner and Roth, *"Good News" After Auschwitz?*

28. The work of Davies, Haynes, and Fasching falls mainly into this and the following category, as does Gregory Baum's early work, *Jews and Gospel*, as well as a number of official publications by church groups, such as *Nostra Aetate* or the various statements collected in Brockway, *Theology of the Churches*.

Michael B. McGarry notes that, while *Nostra Aetate* "committed the Church to a posture of dialogue with no mention about missions to the Jews," in the other Vatican documents, "where reference is made to the Jewish people, Christ is presented as the fulfillment of Israel's hopes"; in other words, the correction of what is presented in *Nostra Aetate* as a cosmetic flaw, a slight error of language, goes no further than that document itself—either the flaw is too slight to merit correction elsewhere (in which case why was *Nostra Aetate* necessary?), or else it is not really cosmetic at all, and changing the language of the other documents would have imperiled their message. See McGarry, "Path to a Journey," 152. The 2000 Declaration of the Congregation for the Doctrine of the Faith, *Dominus Iesus*, while acknowledging the ongoing import of inter-religious dialogue proposed by *Nostra Aetate*, seeks to re-establish the supremacy of the revelation through Christ *for all people*, warning against pluralism and relativism within inter-religious dialogue—suggesting that the correction of language put forth in *Nostra Aetate* should be read as the barest cosmetic concession possible. For a brief gloss on the controversy

often accompanied by (2) a broader critique of the doctrine of supersessionism, which transforms Judaism into an outmoded belief system and Jews into subjects for conversion.[29] Finally, a number of writers engage in (3) an historical critique of Christianity's complicity in, or failure to protest against, the Holocaust.[30]

I do not mean here to downplay the degree to which antisemitism has been entwined with Christianity for much of the latter's history, nor to suggest, contrary to my argument elsewhere, that what is said and done in liturgy is separable from doctrine, is vestigial to "real" theology. However, a critique of what German, or even European, churches did or failed to do in the 1930s and 1940s reveals flaws in those churches at that time; it does not necessarily undermine the Christian message as a whole.[31] Moreover, a critique of antisemitic *language*, regardless of the circumstances in which that language occurs, critiques the symptoms and ignores the underlying cause, the aspects of the belief system which requires such language to validate itself.[32] This is the point made by Rosemary Radford Ruether, in her seminal 1974 work *Faith and Fratricide: The Theological Roots of Anti-Semitism*.[33]

Rosemary Radford Ruether's Fractured Christology

Ruether distinguishes between anti-Judaism, which she treats as a purely theological position, and anti-Semitism, which she treats as the (undesirable) social outgrowth of that theological position. She argues that

---

surrounding *Dominus Iesus*, see the introduction to Rittner and Roth, *"Good News" After Auschwitz*, ix–x.

29. See especially the discussion of Barth, Moltmann, and van Buren in Haynes, *Prospects*.

30. The work of Cargas and the essays in Rittner and Roth are fairly representative of this position. See also Ericksen and Heschel, *Betrayal*, and especially Brumlik, "Post-Holocaust Theology."

31. This is not to dismiss the body of historical work that has revealed a global system of indifference which contributed to the severity of the Holocaust—for example, see Barnett, *Bystanders*; Goldhagen, *Hitler's Willing Executioners*; Levin, *His Majesty's Enemies*; Ritter and Roth's introduction to *"Good News" After Auschwitz?*—however, that historical work seldom crosses over into theological critique except in the most roundabout fashion.

32. My critique of this body of Christian post-Holocaust theology is similar to Judith Plaskow's critique of the male-dominated Jewish tradition in *Standing Again at Sinai*, 121–69.

33. The impact Ruether's work has had on later Biblical scholars is traced in Smiga, *Pain and Polemic*.

Worship in the Ruins

anti-Judaism was a necessary position in Christianity's early self-definition, calling it "the left hand of Christology."[34] It is this link between antisemitism and Christology, between an undesirable social outcome and a core theological principal, which distinguishes Ruether's work from the critiques I outlined above. Although Ruether's own critique is based in a critique of language, she acknowledges that language itself is only a symptom of a deeper issue in Christian theology, and that to eliminate antisemitism requires a re-thinking of the entire theological system, not simply a change in vocabulary:

> To reaffirm Jesus' hope in his name, then, is not to be able to claim that in Jesus this hope has already happened, albeit in invisible form. Nor does it mean that it is now only in his name that this hope can be proclaimed. It is simply to say that, for those who were caught up with him in that lively expectation, it is now in his memory that they reaffirm his hope. They are sure that his death was not in vain. Ultimately, God will vindicate his hope, by revealing that victory over all the oppressive forces of evil for which he lived and died. It is now in his name that *we* (those who inherit the memories of this first community of Jesus' companions) reaffirm this hope, and it is in his name that this victory will be finally manifest for us. [. . .] This is the theological content behind the proclamation of Jesus' resurrection. [. . .] In this proleptic experiencing of the final future of mankind in advance, we reaffirm Jesus' hope in his name. He becomes the mediator of this hope to us and to our descendants. But this hope was not finally fulfilled either in his lifetime or in his death. The Resurrection reaffirms his hope, in the teeth of historical disappointment, that evil will be overcome and God's will be done on earth. The messianic meaning of Jesus' life, then, is paradigmatic and proleptic in nature, not final and fulfilled.[35]

This is a rather radical position, and were I a Christian I suspect I would be deeply dissatisfied with Ruether's revised Christology.[36] The transformation

---

34. This phrase is used by Gregory Baum in his introduction to the book; it is otherwise a frequently-bandied shorthand for Ruether's argument, although it does not, so far as my reading has uncovered, actually appear in Ruether's text itself.

35. Ruether, *Faith and Fratricide*, 149.

36. Ruether's conclusions in *Faith and Fratricide* have certainly not gone uncriticized; for a summary of reactions to her work, see Gager, *Origins of Anti-Semitism*, 24–34; also Dietrich, *God and Humanity*, 24–26; Idinopulos, *Betrayal of spirit*, 55–71; Taylor, *Anti-Judaism and Early Christian Identity*, 130–31. For a broader critique of Ruether (more focused on her feminist theology), see also Hampson, *Theology and Feminism*, 35,

of Jesus from the son of God, the "true God from true God" of the Nicene creed, who died to cleanse humanity from its oppression by the forces of evil, and into a man who died *in the hope* that God will someday cleanse humanity from its oppression by the forces of evil certainly makes him a far less ambivalent figure for Judaism (and for Jews) than he has been for the past two thousand years. In fact, it makes him almost indistinguishable from any other person who has ever died in the hope that God will someday cleanse humanity from its oppression by the forces of evil: a noble figure, but not quite worth founding a religion on. Ruether herself seems rather hard pressed to argue for faith in this drastically reduced Christ; she writes that his death and resurrection "is a paradigm for those for whom it has become a paradigm."[37] While Ruether does begin from a charitable impulse, from the assumption that antisemitism has been shown to have undesirable results, and therefore doctrine which leads to antisemitism must be incorrect, the degree of the upheaval evident in her Christology is indicative of the depths to which she finds antisemitism entwined with the Christian tradition, contrary to the historically contextualized, Jewish Jesus that she reads between the lines of the Gospels.

Moreover, the distinction with which she begins her argument is already flawed. Admittedly, it has become popular for Christian theologians to draw a distinction between anti-Judaism and anti-Semitism, between objecting to the Jewish faith as incapable of providing redemption, and objecting to Jews as people incapable of being redeemed. However, while the latter leads to Auschwitz, where Jews are permitted their Jewishness—and, indeed, many from assimilated families, whose parents or grandparents may have converted to Christianity, have Jewishness forced, or reinforced,

---

158; Sawyer, "Gender" 472. Motyer, "Bridging the Gap," 148, is also highly relevant here, although his focus is not on Ruether but on Tina Pippin, who has drawn conclusions similar to Ruether's. Discussion of Ruether's Christology typically focuses upon her innovations in feminist theology, which also centers on a Christological question, the now famous query "Can a male savior save women?" See, for example, Greene-McCreight, *Feminist Reconstructions*, 78–80. For a connection between Ruether's work with Christian anti-Semitism and feminist Christology, see Isherwood, *Introducing Feminist Christologies*, 33–37. There are, however, a (relatively small) number of Christian theologians who have found Ruether's conclusions in *Faith and Fratricide* compelling—for example, Hall, *Professing the Faith*, 90. Wesley J. Wildman uses Ruether as an example of what he terms a "Modest Christology," a non-absolutist, non-universalizing doctrine; in this, he sees similarities between her position and that of Ernst Troeltsch, James M. Gustafson, and Tom Driver (see *Fidelity with Plausibility*, 270). See also Clark M. Williamson, *Guest in the House of Israel*, 167.

37. Ruether, *Faith and Fratricide*, 250.

upon them—but can do nothing to save their own bodies, the former leads just as surely to the Inquisition, in which Jews are able, and indeed compelled, to save their bodies at the cost of their souls, through conversion and assimilation. What Ruether and others who make this distinction and treat anti-Judaism as the lesser of two evils (though still evil) fail to grasp is that both anti-Judaism and anti-Semitism attack Jews at the very core of their being, and aim to rob them of a vital component of selfhood. The distinction to be drawn, then, is not between what each does, that one is more damaging or less escapable than the other, but rather the way that each does it.

John Roth's Fractured Theodicy

The fracture in Ruether's Christology is deep, but she maintains an ultimately hopeful outlook. Jesus died in the hope of a final redemption; his memory conveys that hope to the community of believers who have allowed themselves to be caught up in his story. While it has not happened yet, God *will* heal the brokenness of the world. There is, however, another movement in Christian theology which sees in the Holocaust a proof against precisely this hope, undermining belief not in the divinity of Christ or the finality of the redemption offered by his sacrificial death, but in the ultimate goodness of God's own self. This strand of thought is typified by John Roth, who coined the term "Protest Theodicy" as the title of his essay in *Encountering Evil: Live Options in Theodicy*.[38] Roth argues that the event of the Holocaust necessitates a reconsideration of traditionally held assumptions about God's ability to ultimately redeem the world. Roth criticizes God as "wasteful," and protests against attempts to justify this wastefulness as somehow necessary in the larger scheme of creation.[39] In his view, to take seriously God's sovereignty and omnipotence leads necessarily to the conclusion that God has been, and continues to be, capable of preventing, and therefore responsible for, the enormous loss of human life that has characterized the past century of human history. In light of this, he ultimately concludes that while God may be good, God cannot reasonably be considered to be perfectly good.[40] As the critical responses to his essay indicate, this position is a sharp departure from the traditional Christian view. In fact, Roth, in

---

38. Not to be confused with Protest *Theology*, coined by David Blumenthal, which will be discussed later on in this chapter.

39. Davis et al., *Encountering Evil*, 4.

40. Ibid., 34.

PART THREE: Absent Mourners

his attempt to take seriously what he sees as the radical evil manifest in the Holocaust, arrives at a theological position quite similar—and sympathetic—to the Jewish sources he draws upon.

The respondents to Roth's essay, a group of his colleagues from the Claremont Schools in California, represent "virtually all the available Christian options on the Theodicy problem" according to the book's editor, Stephen T. Davis. Thus, an examination of their critiques of Roth is helpful in illuminating exactly where Roth's theological response to the Holocaust stands *vis à vis* the Christian tradition. D. Z. Phillips, whose own contribution to the volume argues (in a vein similar to Roth's) that theodic language ought to be rejected, as it forces its proponents into untenable positions, makes the claim (correctly refuted by Roth as "weak"—both in terms of the God it presents and the argumentative strength of the claim itself) that Roth fails to "consider the possibility that God's only sovereignty is the sovereignty of love."[41] Phillips posits a divine withdrawal (a hypothesis that would be familiar to a Kabbalist, though neither he nor Roth makes this connection) to create space for humanity's freedom as the ultimate act of God's love—but in so doing fails to address the extent to which a truly sovereign God must still be held to account for the consequences of such a withdrawal.[42]

John Hick, who later on characterizes his own position as "An Irenaean Theodicy,"[43] objects that "If Roth were to give serious attention to the eschatological dimension of the religions, he would see options other than the unattractive idea of heavenly compensation for the ills of earth. The alternative is the ultimate fulfillment of human potential through a long and often painful process of moral and spiritual growth in a universe that is, in Bonheoffer's phrase, '*etsi deus non daretur*' ('as if there were no God')."[44] Note that in critiquing Roth here, Hick also falls back on the hypothesis of a divine withdrawal. His larger point, however, consistent with his self-professed Irenaean position, is that the evils of this world are justified through the "moral and spiritual growth" that results from them (and that they are the result of), and that this justification can only be understood in

---

41. Ibid., 24.

42. Ibid., 145–64. Roth's critique of Phillips charges that he "has not rejected theodicy but disguised it," noting that to define God—as Phillips does—as simply excluding any negative capacity ("divine withdrawal" is, according to Phillips, "an act of love") is "to enforce silence that gives evil privileges it does not deserve." See ibid., 170–74.

43. Ibid., 38–52.

44. Ibid., 30.

eschatological terms. It is the issue of eschatology (or, rather, its absence) that Hicks finds most problematic about the position Roth expresses in his essay.[45]

This objection is shared by Stephen T. Davis, who concludes that "real solidarity with the victims and sufferers is telling them the truth. And the truth is that the Christian message of hope through the love of God as expressed pre-eminently in Christ is good news for all people, even those who suffered and died unjustly, maybe *especially* for them. Part of that truth is that 'the sufferings of this present time are not worth comparing with the glory about to be revealed to us' (Rom. 8:18)."[46] Roth correctly characterizes this notion as "obscene," stating that it "may get high marks as religious hyperbole, but it scarcely seems like solidarity with the victims."[47] I myself am disinclined even to give it credit as religious hyperbole; it seems, instead, a complete—and completely irresponsible—retreat from the reality of suffering in this world. I find this assessment confirmed when the same unfortunate claim is repeated in Davis's own contribution to the volume, "Free Will and Evil," which otherwise embraces a roughly Augustinian position in order to place the fault of evil squarely on human shoulders (much in the way that Phillips does, though without the explicit assumption of a divine withdrawal).[48] In his own essay, however, he uses as the example of suffering fading into insignificance not the Holocaust, but an episode from his own life when, in the ninth grade, he suffered severe embarrassment after his mother sent him to school wearing an unfashionable pair of trousers.[49] "That episode," he writes, "is now more amusing than painful," and so, he suggests, will all earthly pain be, at the end of time, when "the vision of the face of God that we will then experience will make all previous suffering such that the pain will no longer matter."[50] Such a blithely narcis-

---

45. Roth contends in his rejoinder that his essay addresses eschatological issues "by implication"; he agrees with Hicks that an eschatological view is "crucial, because without it, history's slaughter-bench debris accumulates without redemption" (ibid., 31). Roth, as I read him, admits the possibility of, and continues to hope for, an eschatological redemption; he simply discounts total certainty in such a redemption, or the expression thereof, as an ethically valid theological strategy at the present time.

46. Ibid., 23.

47. Ibid., 33.

48. Ibid., 85.

49. Ibid., 84–85.

50. Ibid., 85. A similar hypothesis is put forth by Miroslav Volf, in *The End of Memory*—the major difference being that Volf, having personal experience of suffering beyond mere embarrassment, does not move so quickly to such an easy dismissal of

PART THREE: Absent Mourners

sistic equation of the suffering endured by the victims of the Holocaust with the embarrassment endured by a schoolboy wearing unfashionable trousers seriously undermines Davis's claim to take seriously, or to be taken seriously regarding the theological problems posed by evil and suffering.

The more reasonable objection to Roth's position posed by Davis is that the God Roth posits, lacking the characteristic of *complete* moral goodness, is not worthy of worship.[51] This objection is also put forth by Hick (who writes that "if Roth really believes that the situation is as bad as he depicts it, then the God he still seems to believe in is the Devil!"),[52] and the final contributor to the volume, the process theologian David Ray Griffin. Griffin especially objects to Roth's assertion that "God must be a mixture of good and evil," stating that

> I see no basis for hope that a partly evil deity could be led to repent. The moral defect in God is presumably eternal, and many philosophers, from Aristotle to Hartshorne, have held that the eternal and the necessary are identical. In the first edition of this book, Roth replied to this point by saying: "If God's power is bound only by his own unnecessitated will . . ., then God can change his ways." However, the traditional doctrine that God's will is not necessitated by anything outside of God did not entail that God's basic character or will could change. [. . .] It seems a rather desperate hope that, assuming that God has had a mean streak for not only the past 15 billion years but from all eternity, our protests in the next century or so will bring about a change.[53]

Griffin's own essay posits a relatively weak God, creating the universe from pre-existing chaos, and therefore never fully accountable for the result.[54] Given the emphasis he places upon divine power as "shared power," on God's creation as always an act of compromise and co-creation, it is curious that he cannot imagine the possibility that God may choose to change, or

---

pain. Rather, he acknowledges and wrestles with the difficulties posed to eschatological "forgetting" by issues such as the continuity of personal identity (recall my discussion of Locke from chapter one). In the end, I do not find Volf convincing—though this is largely because I do not share his religious presuppositions. Neither, however, do I find him as easy to dismiss out of hand as Davis.

51. Davis et al., *Encountering Evil*, 22.

52. Ibid., 29.

53. Ibid., 26. Griffin's assumption that the only point of protest against God is to "bring about a change" is problematic. As I shall argue later, there are other valid reasons for protest—not the least of which is to avoid complicity.

54. Ibid., 108–25.

that human protest may bring about such change.⁵⁵ Indeed, Griffin's objection here seems less a general failure of imagination, and more a specific inability to reconcile the process deity that he envisions with the sovereign deity presumed by Roth.

The problem of worship brought up by Roth's critics presupposes that God is, by definition, that which must be worshipped—and, conversely, a being that they cannot bring themselves to worship cannot be God. By positing a God who lacks—or must be assumed to lack—the attribute of perfect goodness, Roth has departed from what his interlocutors recognize as theological speculation and into a position from which they find his continued profession of faith barely tenable; he has, from their vantage point, ceased to believe in God.⁵⁶ That Roth himself continues to find worship not only possible but necessary seems to fall outside the boundaries of what is possible within the Christian tradition; his theology has fractured past recognizability.

WORSHIP IN A FRACTURED SPACE

Entering into the sanctuary of the Kaiser-Wilhelm-Gedächtniskirche is like entering another world. Stepping from the sunny plaza through a pair of large, bronze doors, the visitor passes through a small, dark vestibule before emerging into a chamber of light. The noise of the streets outside vanishes completely. The blue glow that characterizes the exterior of the building at night pales in comparison to the submarine hue that pulses from the tall interior walls. The space is dominated by blue—and by the large, gold, risen Christ suspended over the altar, designed by Karl Hemmeter, which "gives the church its optical focus and at the same time expresses who should be at the center of every service."⁵⁷

The visitor, too, is suspended, attention temporarily arrested upon entering the space; it takes a moment for the eyes to adjust to the new environment. It takes several moments of careful study to begin to discern the points of continuity between the interior and the exterior—the small, multicolored ceramic floor tiles echoing the larger concrete circles of the

---

55. Ibid., 122.

56. Hick makes this criticism explicitly, though gently; the others hedge it off with protestations about their personal knowledge of Roth's character and religious commitment, leaving only implicit the suggestion that if they did not know him so well, their response to his stated position may not be so charitable.

57. KWG (MH).

PART THREE: Absent Mourners

plaza outside; and the joins in the stained glass echoing the cracks in the old tower.[58] It takes much longer to notice, if one ever does, the space's optical illusions: the pattern of the interior glass does not match the exterior; the number of chambers in the concrete panels also differs between the outside and the inside—and the strength of the light emanating from the walls never varies, or betrays a hint of the weather outdoors. The sanctuary is actually constructed out of two sets of stained glass walls; the light pours through the glass from the space in between them (which also serves to dampen sound).[59]

The arrangement of furnishings within the church is absolutely typical of other Protestant churches in the area, with the altar and font at the front, directly across from the entrance, and rows of chairs facing all in the same direction.[60] The strongest reminder of the church's history is a wall to the visitor's right as they enter the space, on which is displayed a bronze plaque with the inscription "Den Evangelischen Martyren Der Jare 1933–1945" ("The Protestant Martyrs of the years 1933–1945"), alongside a crucifix and a quote from 1 John 5:4. A piece of paper clipped to the rail in front of the plaque explains to German-speaking visitors that the cross, from thirteenth-century Spain, was a gift from Dr. Dibelius, the former Bishop of Berlin, on 20 July 1964—the twentieth anniversary of the most famous plot to assassinate Hitler. The paper further informs the visitor that this display is meant to echo similar ones at the KWG's Catholic sister-church, Maria Regina Martyrum, and at Plötzensee.[61] Immediately to the right of the plaque is a charcoal drawing of a mother and child: the Madonna of Stalingrad, drawn by Lieutenant Kurt Reuber, a Protestant pastor and a physician in the German army, during the Battle of Stalingrad in 1942, and presented to the KWG in 1983.[62] Joseph Perry has noted that this image by itself carries strong resonances with the collective memory of the victimization of ordinary Germans—and especially German Christians—at

---

58. The stained glass was designed by Gabriel Loire. See Gerlach, *Berlin*, 6.

59. Gerlach, *Berlin*, 6.

60. Mr. Wegener attested that, while the chairs are moveable, he cannot recall them having ever been shifted from the configuration in which they are set. Additionally, the font is, while not attached to the floor, so heavy as to render it practically immobile.

61. For a discussion of the Plötzensee memorial, see Koshar, *From Monuments to Traces*, 183–87.

62. See Perry, "The Madonna of Stalingrad."

Worship in the Ruins

the hands of the Nazi regime, and that its placement directly beside the "Martyr's Tablet" serves to reinforce these resonances.[63]

Such resonances also carry over to the copy of the image on display in the Millennium Chapel at Coventry Cathedral, described in the Cathedral's online literature as "a special place to pray for prisoners of conscience, those who have been imprisoned because of their faith or political views."[64] This is not the only point of similarity between the two churches; Coventry Cathedral was also destroyed in a bombing raid during the Second World War, on the night of 14 November 1940.[65] When it was rebuilt, the ruins of the old cathedral also were incorporated into the site of the new construction, and the new construction at Coventry is also, in its own way, a showpiece of modernist architecture.[66]

The ruins of Coventry Cathedral are still treated as active sacred space; scattered notices posted around the old sanctuary entreat visitors to respect it as a house of prayer. This is a sharp contrast to the KWG, the ruined tower of which has been converted into something akin to a museum—although the opening of the display asks visitors "to remember that the former vestibule of the old church is *not a museum*, but a place of remembrance, contemplation and exhortation" (emphasis added). It is difficult, however, to reconcile this request with the very museum-like display that clutters the place of contemplation—and a "place of remembrance, contemplation and exhortation" is still rather different from a place of worship.

In spite of the differences in the way each site is presented to the public, both spaces do still host liturgy—and, in fact, they host the same liturgy. Every Friday, at noon (local time), a small crowd gathers to recite the Litany of the Cross of Nails. This practice originated at Coventry Cathedral, in the aftermath of the bombing. The Provost of the Cathedral had the words "Father Forgive" carved into the wall behind where the altar used to stand, and three of the nails that once held the beams of the collapsed roof were bound together to form a cross.[67] These two motifs became the centerpieces of the Community of the Cross of Nails. After the war, the Cathedral sent

---

63. Perry, "The Madonna of Stalingrad," 11.
64. School Visits Team, "Coventry Cathedral."
65. Herbert, "Bad Faith at Coventry," 536.
66. For details of the competition process leading to the design of the new Coventry Cathedral, and especially the impact of modernist architecture on such, see Campbell, "Towards a New Cathedral."
67. Community of the Cross of Nails, "Overview."

PART THREE: Absent Mourners

crosses as gestures of reconciliation to churches at Kiel, Dresden, and Berlin (the last of which is still on display in the ruined tower of the KWG); since then, 156 Centers have been added to the community, each "working for peace and reconciliation within their own communities and countries."[68] Every Friday, at noon (local time), the Litany of Reconciliation is recited in the ruins[69] of the KWG and of Coventry Cathedral. This litany reflects the Community of the Cross of Nails's broad approach to reconciliation; while the impetus for the Community came from a very particular historical event, its focus is less on mending specific political rifts, and more on correcting systemic (or "original") sin—what Judaism refers to as *tikkun olam*, the mending of a fractured world. The combination of the litany and the surrounding ruins sends a powerful message: the world, like the worship space, is not yet whole.

But if this is the message of worship in the ruins, what is one to make of the spatial logic that, at both sites, compels the visitor to turn their back on the ruins in order to enter the space of everyday worship? The new sanctuaries at both Coventry and the KWG are constructed so that the old building is difficult (in the former case) or impossible (in the latter) to see from within the new, and during worship only the minister—and the large golden Christ that hangs in the KWG—looks towards it. Thus, during the most important moments of Christian liturgy, the only people who are fully present in the ruins, fully aware of the brokenness they signify, are those who stand outside the sanctuary.

---

68. Community of the Cross of Nails, "Overview." Note that not all Cross of Nails Centres are churches; they may also be "reconciliation centres, prisons, NGOs, and schools."

69. At Coventry Cathedral, the litany is recited at noon on every weekday, but Monday to Thursday it is in the new building.

SIX

Outside the Sanctuary

I watch Michaela bake a pie. She smiles and tells me that her mother used to roll the pastry this way. Unknowingly, her hands carry my memories. I remember my mother teaching Bella in the kitchen. Michaela says: "My mother used to cut the dough this way, which she learned from her aunt, you know, the one who married the man who had a brother in New York . . ." On and on, casually, offhand, Michaela's mother's stories of relatives from the next town, from across the ocean, unroll like the crust. The bold dress cousin Pashka wore to her niece's wedding. The cousin who met and married a girl in America but she came from his own home town, can you believe it, he had to travel halfway around the world just to meet the neighbor's daughter. . . . I remember my mother urging Bella not to reveal the secret ingredients of her honey cake—the envy of Mrs. Alperstein—not ever, except to her own daughter, God willing. A few tablespoons of porridge so it will be smooth and moist as cream, and honey from acacias so the cake will come out golden . . .

—ANNE MICHAELS, *FUGITIVE PIECES*, 192–93.

The Great War remains an important touchstone of Canadian cultural memory, filtered through the redemptive metanarrative of Western Christianity. It is therefore of interest to both theologians and scholars of religion and nationalism to carefully observe the manner in which that memory is either supported or challenged by the memory of the Holocaust, which, in spite of academic protestations about Roma and Sinti and homosexuals and political prisoners, is generally treated as a particularly Jewish tragedy. The gap between the memorialization of the two events is the gap between Christians and Jews, between the Greeks and the Bible, between

PART THREE: Absent Mourners

those who stand secure within the rebuilt sanctuary and those who work to redeem the world outside of it; it is a measure of the extent to which the catastrophic rupture has been, if not mended, then at least rendered mendable.

In 2010, the doctrine committee of The Presbyterian Church in Canada delivered to the General Assembly a report on supersessionism and a proposed statement on the relationship between Canadian Presbyterians and the Jewish people.[1] The report relies heavily on Ruether's idea of a distinction between anti-Judaism and anti-Semitism, decrying the latter, while still insisting that a proper Christian relationship to Judaism necessarily involves the former; the "Canadian Presbyterian Statement on Our Relationship with the Jewish People" speaks in glowing terms of specific efforts to evangelize Jews, such as the Christian Synagogue in Toronto.[2] The statement declares gratitude "for the establishment of a homeland for the Jewish people", while both the statement and the report consistently refer to "Jews in Canada"—and never to Canadian Jews.

Of course, this is just one report, one statement, in one denomination, in one country; nevertheless, it is a potent indicator of how wide the fractures between Jews and Christians remain. The drafters of the report are hardly unique in assuming that "the establishment of a homeland for the Jewish people" has shifted all the work of relating to the religious Other into the realm of international relations. They are not alone in their seeming inability to imagine or respond to Canadian Jews, individuals whose identities are formed and informed both by the national mythos, with all of its deeply Christian influences, and by the cultural inheritance of Judaism. Speaking coherently from, and of, the dual cultural inheritance is just as much a problem for Jewish theology as it is for Christians.

In this chapter, alongside Jewish post-Holocaust theologies, I will read two very recent novels by Canadian Jewish authors, Anne Michaels and Edeet Ravel. These books bring issues of Holocaust memory and Canadian national identity into direct conversation with each other, and offer constructive interruptions into both discourses. Instead of the predictable and instantly recognizable Eastern European Orthodox women that anchor the

---

1. A&P (2010), 291–355.
2. I say "near-total" first because the report does manage to cite David Novak in support of its embrace of supersessionism, but moreso because the section dealing specifically with the Hebrew Bible is, in fact, quite well-informed and so carefully written that a casual reader may be forgiven for initially mistaking it for part of another document entirely. For a more complete critique of the report, see Godin, "Interfaith Monologue."

theology of Melissa Raphael (discussed below), Michaels and Ravel give us bad Jews: assimilated Jews, atheist Jews, intermarried Jews, unmarried Jews, gay Jews, Jews who don't know how to pray, Jews who know how to pray but don't, Jews who eat pepperoni pizza, Jews for whom Jewishness exists more as an interruption to their ability to be uncomplicatedly Canadian than as an identity in its own right. And instead of the entwinement of national and familial loyalties, bundled neatly together and always on a steady path towards "happily ever after" found by Anne Shirley, Rilla Blythe, or Klara Becker, Michaels and Ravel depict isolation, dysfunction, dislocation, children whose families are dead and families whose children wish they were dead, characters who move through the world as confused about their point of origin as they are about their destination. It is these stories, and others like them, that best showcase the diversity, the complexity and the messiness of the world with which theology now contends.

Both of these works are complex literary constructions; *Fugitive Pieces* is less a novel than it is a very long prose poem, and *Your Sad Eyes* is dense with intertextual references—for example, the protagonist, Maya, is a modern, Jewish, lesbian re-visioning of Anne of Green Gables, with an "overly long, freckled body," "Pre-Raphaelite red hair," and grey eyes.[3] Both of these works focus, in whole (Ravel) or in part (Michaels) on the children of holocaust survivors, who "internalize the unresolved traumatic memories of their parents and thus suffer similar anxieties."[4] Both texts, then, portray the Holocaust as already part of inherited collective memory, what Marianne Hirsch has termed "postmemory," rather than as an immediate experience (even the Holocaust survivor featured in the first part of *Fugitive Pieces* is a child escapee; later in life he seeks to partake of cultural memory as a way of sharing in the experience the rest of his family underwent).[5] The Holocaust is a trace, haunting the edges of the narrators' lives, present in the *lacunae* that open up between them and their parents, their homes and

---

3. YSE, 7, 84. Maya's romance with the Diana Barry-esque Rosie ("Two black braids, large dark eyes, black eyebrows, heartbreaking mouth. Skin that glowed like the skin of red-cheeked children in coloured frontspiece illustrations;" see YSE, 54) is more overtly sexual than Anne and Diana's, and after Rosie meets her "Fred Wright," a boy named Glenn, Maya does not enter into what Montgomery might have presented as an adult sexual relationship with a man, but becomes a fixed part of Montreal's lesbian bar scene—an option that was not available to Anne (or Montgomery)—see YSE, 2.

4. Goertz, "Transgenerational Representations," 35.

5. Hirsch, *Family Frames*, 22–23; see also Hirsch, "Generation of Postmemory," 103–28.

other homes, their interior existence and the wider world. It is in these gaps that liturgical mending becomes possible.

JEWISH POST-HOLOCAUST THEOLOGY: PROTEST AND COVENANT

While it is true that, as the selections in the recent anthology of Jewish Holocaust Theology, *Wrestling With God*, make clear, the most Orthodox expressions of Jewish theology remained more or less unchanged and unchallenged by the events of the Holocaust, it is also true that these are the exception rather than the rule—especially in North America and Europe. Traditional doctrines which place the responsibility for suffering upon its victims (either as punishment for corporate sin—*mi-penei hata'einu*—or as a test of faith, carrying biblical resonances with the book of Job, or the *Akedah*), or suggest that Jewish victimhood is cosmically necessary to correct the balance of the world (ideas of the scapegoat, or the ten righteous men) seem deeply unsatisfactory in light of the tremendous suffering visited largely upon observant, Orthodox, Eastern-European Jews.[6] Absent a convincing explanation for the events of the Holocaust, critical Jewish concepts such as chosenness and covenant became open to critique.

One of the earliest and sharpest of such critiques came from Richard Rubenstein, in his 1966 book, *After Auschwitz*. Rubenstein, much like Roth (with whom he has collaborated on several volumes), is driven by his horror at the events of the Holocaust—and the degree to which he perceives traditional Jewish theology to have contributed to those events—to formulate a theological position that is difficult to recognize as a normative expression of his religion.[7] Rubenstein is often treated as the Jewish arm of the Christian "Death of God" theological movement and, while he has acknowledged the similarities between his own work and that movement, it is perhaps more accurate to characterize his central theological concern as the *silence* of God—or, even more accurately, the non-intervention of God

---

6. This is an extremely brief gloss of material that has been covered extensively elsewhere, especially in Katz et al., *Wrestling With God*; Katz, *Post-Holocaust Dialogues*; the essays collected in Katz, *Impact of the Holocaust*; as well as the introductions to countless other books on "Post-Holocaust Theology."

7. Roth and Rubenstein have co-authored *Approaches to Auschwitz*, as well as *Politics of Latin American Liberation Theology*. For a summary of criticism leveled against Rubenstein's relationship to Judaism, see Braiterman, *(God) After Auschwitz*, 87–89.

into history.[8] Rubenstein's theological project is predicated on a wholesale rejection of the idea of any "special status"—a unique covenant with God—being afforded to Jews; this stems largely from a conviction that the assumption of such a status led to, and helped to justify, the Holocaust.[9] In place of the God of the covenant, doubly discredited through the complicity of the covenant in promoting persecution and through the failure of God to protect the Jewish people from that persecution, Rubenstein advocates a return to the *After Auschwitz* "God of Nature," a neo-paganism, although, as Zachary Braiterman has been at pains to point out, a neo-paganism tempered with a strong Jewish flavor, not least of which is its finding its centre in the modern-day land of Israel.[10]

Scandalous as Rubenstein's theology was, it is easy to read later Jewish Post-Holocaust theologians as his respondents, attempting to rescue God and covenant from the void to which Rubenstein had consigned them, and surveys of post-Holocaust theology tend to support this approach, placing Rubenstein at the beginning and arranging others (always Emil Fackenheim, and some assortment of others including Eliezer Berkovits, Ignaz Maybaum, Irving Greenberg, and Arthur Cohen) afterwards.[11] While this is generally correct, except for the case of Maybaum, whose book *The Face of God after Auschwitz* was published the year prior to Rubenstein's *After Auschwitz*, such a reading undermines the extent to which each thinker

---

8. Rubenstein employs the "Death of God" metaphor from the first chapter of *After Auschwitz*, in which he describes it as a goal "at the heart of the Nazi program" (Rubenstein, *After Auschwitz*, 35). He discusses the connections between his work and the Christian movement in a later chapter in that same volume, "Death of God Theology and Judaism" (243–64). The major point of contrast, as Rubenstein himself points out, is that the Christian Death of God theologians take the metaphor as generally positive, while for Rubenstein it is a tragedy and a theological scandal.

9. See especially "The Dean and the Chosen People," in Rubenstein, *After Auschwitz*, 47-60.

10. See especially "The Meaning of Torah in Contemporary Jewish Theology: An Existentialist Philosophy of Judaism," in Rubenstein, *After Auschwitz*, 113–29; and Braiterman, *(God) After Auschwitz*, 94–100.

11. See, again, Braiterman, *(God) After Auschwitz*; Katz, *Post-Holocaust Dialogues*; Morgan, *Beyond Auschwitz*; Cohn-Sherbok, *Holocaust Theology*. This arrangement is departed from in Katz et al., *Wrestling With God*, which follows a strict chronological order, placing the more traditionally-minded Ignaz Maybaum's "suffering servant" theology prior to Rubenstein (along with contributions from Martin Buber, Abraham Joshua Heschel, Joseph Soloveitchik, and Zvi Koitz, all of whom are usually left out of post-Holocaust surveys, although the first three of these are included in Braiterman's general discussion of modern Jewish theodicies).

PART THREE: Absent Mourners

directly engages first and foremost with the Holocaust and Jewish tradition. Emil Fackenheim, for example, does cite Rubenstein in his 1970 work, *God's Presence in History* (and in a number of his later works), but only as a preliminary gesture towards what Fackenheim characterizes as a spurious argument, before he arrives at the real business of God-wrestling which occupies him for the duration of that work.[12]

Fackenheim also offers a revision of the notion of covenant, through his famous proposal of the 614th commandment:

> Jews are forbidden to hand Hitler posthumous victories. They are commanded to survive as Jews, lest the Jewish people perish. They are commanded to remember the victims of Auschwitz lest their memory perish. They are forbidden to despair of man [sic] and his world, and to escape into either cynicism or otherworldliness, lest they cooperate in delivering the world over to the forces of Auschwitz. Finally, they are forbidden to despair of the God of Israel, lest Judaism perish.[13]

As Steven Katz has pointed out, the addition to the traditional 613 commandments contained in the revelation at Sinai constitutes a major upheaval of previous understandings of the covenant between God and Israel.[14] The "614th commandment" was not spoken by God, was not transmitted in Torah, does not constitute revelation in the normative sense. Moreover, as Michael Wyschogrod has noted, that the source of this commandment is "The Commanding Voice of Auschwitz" creates the problematic situation of divine commandment arising from and being transmitted through radical evil.[15] To these critiques I would add a third, related point: the covenant at Sinai was a mutual covenant, which placed obligations on both Israel and God. It was also freely entered into by the Israelites who had travelled to that place willingly. Fackenheim's 614th commandment, by contrast, was given to a quite literally captive audience, unable to either accept or reject it (in the legalized language associated with sexual assault, 'incapable of

---

12. Fackenheim, *God's Presence in History*, 30–31. Of course, Fackenheim's title itself constitutes an argument against Rubenstein's denial of God's presence in history, though there I am aware of no direct evidence that he intended it as such.

13. Emil L. Fackenheim, *Quest for Past and Future*, 20; also quoted in *God's Presence in History*, 84. Fackenheim, *To Mend the World*, xix, dates the original formulation of this commandment to 1967, with no reference made to Rubenstein at all.

14. Katz, *Post-Holocaust Dialogues*, 218–19.

15. Michael Wyschogrod, "Faith and the Holocaust," cited in Braiterman, *(God) After Auschwitz*, 135.

consent'), and thus does not, cannot, have the same weight of obligation upon the people to whom it was given. It also neatly sidesteps any issue of God's responsibilities or obligations.

Zachary Braiterman has argued that the "614th commandment" "was just a trope (in and of itself barely adequate) that stood for the far more critical motif of supernatural revelation"; both Braiterman and Katz conclude that, contrary to Fackenheim's rhetoric, the "Commanding Voice of Auschwitz" "does not constitute a divine imperative, but only a human response."[16] However, even granting Braiterman's contention that the 614th commandment is a case of overblown rhetoric attached to Fackenheim's lifelong fascination with revelation, I still find Fackenheim's understanding of covenant and commandment problematic, insofar as that understanding (in general) may be reflected in what he has written about this particular case. Fackenheim does not dispense with the God of the covenant, with the God of history, but at moments he does risk transforming that God into precisely the sort of arbitrary tyrant that Rubenstein protested against.

DAVID BLUMENTHAL: FACING THE ABUSING GOD

Richard Rubenstein grounded *After Auschwitz* in psychoanalytic theory, using Freudian analysis to account for the depravities of the Nazi regime. David Blumenthal's work also borrows liberally from psychology, but rather than attempting to account for the Holocaust, his focus is on attempting to heal the trauma that it caused. Blumenthal is remarkably uninterested in defending God's actions, or lack thereof, but neither is he willing to abandon either God or the covenant. Instead, he seeks to find some way to mend the relationship between God and Israel. To this end, he turns to testimony and strategies of child abuse survivors.[17] In Blumenthal's theology, God is figured as a parent who has betrayed the fundamental trust of his children.[18] The relationship of trust and dependence between parent

---

16. Braiterman, *(God) After Auschwitz*, 135, 149; see also Katz, *Post-Holocaust Dialogues*, 218.

17. Blumenthal, *Facing the Abusing God*, xvii.

18. Blumenthal occasionally—especially when composing prayers—departs from gender-neutral language and employs the male pronoun out of considered and deliberate deference to his own male religious imagination (*Facing the Abusing God*, 284); contrary to my usual practice I maintain the gendering of Blumenthal's God—and, in the next section, the opposite gendering of Melissa Raphael's God—out of deference to the particularly *human* characteristics of that God.

PART THREE: Absent Mourners

and child intensifies the damage done by the betrayal. His conclusion is a synthesis between classical Jewish understanding of God's attributes and contemporary abuse counseling techniques:

> we will point the finger, we will identify the Abuser, we will tell this ugly truth. We will not keep silent, neither out of fear nor out of love [. . .] We will cling tenaciously to our rage, and we will speak [. . .] We will say, "The fault is not ours. You are the Abuser. The fault was yours. You repent. You return to us."
>
> [. . .] we will not deny our own spirituality [. . .] we will affirm the reality of God's presence, God's power, and even God's love [. . .] ours will be an acknowledgment of the Other Who is present to us in fear *and* in kinship, in terror *and* in presence.[19]

Blumenthal is unwilling to abandon God, so much so that his theology of protest becomes, at its heart, a mode of liturgical expression, a means by which to address God. Blumenthal is unwilling to abandon the covenant, so much so that his protests against God's abuse are grounded in the language of Jewish liturgy. The longest section of the book, "Text-ing," consists of four Psalms (128, 44, 109, and 27) laid out with commentary surrounding their verses, in the distinctive style of Jewish textual scholarship.[20] The final thirty pages of the book contain psalms selected presumably for their thematic and emotional resonances, and retranslated to intensify those resonances—a protest hallel—and prayers from the traditional liturgy, slightly rewritten to call God to account for God's abuse, while at the same time acknowledging God's sovereignty.

Blumenthal's approach is sensitive and nuanced, but it is not beyond criticism. One reviewer has complained that his analogy between the Holocaust and child abuse is never fully unpacked, relying instead on a surface understanding of what abuse and recovery actually entails.[21] A perusal of Blumenthal's bibliography reveals a far wider reading in the texts of the Jewish tradition than in psychology.[22] Of the psychological sources he

---

19. Blumenthal, *Facing the Abusing God*, 266–67.

20. The practice of surrounding a core text with multiple commentaries seems to have its roots in the Talmud, but has evolved into a reasonably common method of textual interpretation—compare, for example, the series edited by Hoffman, *My People's Prayerbook*.

21. Jennifer L. Rike, Review of *Facing the Abusing God*, 206–9.

22. "Translations," "Commentaries," and "Classic Jewish Texts" each are given their own bibliographic heading, while psychology texts are lumped together along with contemporary critical theory, student papers, Hebrew grammar, and a significant number of Blumenthal's own works under a catch-all heading labeled "Studies."

does utilize, he leans most heavily on the work of Alice Miller, the author of several popular books on child psychology, and Eliana Gil. Gil's book, *Treatment of Adult Survivors of Childhood Abuse*, is a fairly standard clinical manual, from which Blumenthal's five-step program appears to be derived.[23] However, he engages with these sources primarily in "Text-ing," placing their words alongside the Psalms under study; he does not appear to read them critically, nor does he explicitly carry forward insight from these readings into the next section, "Re-Sponse," which consists of dialogues with an adult survivor of child abuse (Diane) and a systematic theologian (Wendy), as well as an essay written by a rape survivor (Beth, one of Blumenthal's students).[24] Indeed, he completely avoids responding to Diane's charge that he is "far too strongly influenced by Miller," who "does not understand the physically and sexually abused child who has grown to be an adult."[25] His posture in this section is, instead, one of listening, letting the voices he invites into his world of dialogue speak for themselves.

This listening stance is both difficult to argue against and, at the same time, deeply unsatisfactory. I take it to stem from Blumenthal's conviction that speech is central to both liturgy and to the healing process, and, therefore, from a desire to guard the sanctity and autonomy of each individual's act of self-narration. In this regard, Blumenthal's refusal to interject, to impose his own academic narrative on the personal testimonies he incorporates into his scheme is admirable. However, by incorporating the personal testimonies of others with minimal comment, Blumenthal enacts a more subtle appropriation, advancing his own argument via the experience of others, letting those other voices speak for him—and, in some cases, pre-empting the reader's own response. This is most deeply problematic with regard to the essay written by Beth, which is presented with only the barest of introduction. The dialogues with Diane and Wendy do include responses from Blumenthal himself—though, as mentioned above, he avoids addressing specific criticisms, in favor of making more general statements about God and relationship.

His conversation with Wendy involves a greater degree of academic rigor than the exchange with Diane, though again, Wendy does most of the talking. This is not to say that the exchange with Diane lackes intellectual

---

23. See Blumenthal, *Facing the Abusing God*, 167–69, "Con-Verses."
24. Ibid., xx.
25. Ibid., 196. He similarly ignores another protest from Diane regarding his use of Gil; see ibid., 207–9.

PART THREE: Absent Mourners

weight or interest, but Blumenthal seems more willing to engage and respond to the specific points Wendy raises. This contributes to a disturbing pattern of power and value hierarchies in this section. While both Diane and Wendy are known in their correspondence with Blumenthal only through their first names, and the introduction to "Re-sponse" identifies them both as professors, the acknowledgements identify Wendy Farley by her full name, bringing her professional credentials into the world of the text; the presence of her book in the bibliography does just as much to assure the reader that she is being taken seriously by Blumenthal as a conversation partner as his own response to her critique does. Diane does not have a surname; this is an understandable method of protecting her privacy, but it also removes her academic credentials and credibility from view, and Blumenthal's failure to engage with or respond to her specific criticisms about his use of texts further diminishes those credentials, so that her identity is, in the end, reduced in complexity; she is simply a survivor of child abuse (and, one senses, her function is to speak on behalf of all survivors of child abuse, rather than as a full person in her own right). Finally, Beth, the rape survivor, is not named at all in the acknowledgements, nor does Blumenthal validate her voice through any sort of introduction or response; the only context the reader is given is that she is a student, that she was raped, and that she wrote about it. This follows the structure of the first part of the book, in which Blumenthal closed every chapter with a disruption, a counter-text; but it also opens some troubling questions about power dynamics. If Beth is one of Blumenthal's students, if this reflection was produced in the context of a class, what power dynamics were involved in obtaining her consent to publish it? Where is the line between making space for other voices to be heard and appropriating those voices—and is the position of that line altered when issues of authority are introduced? Would any of these issues provoke as much discomfort without the additional problem that it is a male author who uses women's voices in this way? Blumenthal does not even begin to ask these questions in the text itself.

Wendy Farley's chapter ends with her delivering a critique similar to my own, that Blumenthal "just lay[s] [texts] side by side," that his "multivalency—perhaps esotericism—has become an excuse for not taking [his] work seriously."[26] To this, Blumenthal responds that "[u]pon reflection, I do not think my taking this side-by-side position is lack of courage or intellect;

---

26. Ibid., 224.

Outside the Sanctuary

I have proved myself in many situations in these matters."[27] Exactly how, or in what situations, Blumenthal has proved himself is never elaborated upon; we are privy to Wendy's reflection on what Blumenthal has said, but must take Blumenthal's word for the existence of his own reflective process—we are only permitted to know the results of that reflection, not its content. Moreover, Wendy's voicing and Blumenthal's dismissal of this critique serves also to dismiss in advance any similar objections that might be raised by the reader. By incorporating criticism of his text into the text itself, Blumenthal insulates it from outside critique; in his attempt to maintain a position of openness to other voices, Blumenthal actually risks cutting off dialogue.

While these difficulties ought not be overlooked, they negate neither the deep commitments with which Blumenthal writes, nor the contribution which Blumenthal makes to Jewish Post-Holocaust Theology. This contribution is twofold. First, he borrows from his Christian colleagues the concept of a systematic theology, which permits him to engage first with fundamental Jewish principles regarding the attributes of God.[28] Beginning from what my Protestant colleagues would characterize as the Doctrine of God, rather than from the reaction to historical events which served as the point of departure for previous post-Holocaust theologians, permits Blumenthal to place at the centre of his discourse the issue of relationship that has haunted the edges of much other work in this area. Discourse about God's presence in history is a thinly-masked discourse about the validity of the covenant between God and Israel: does history demonstrate that God has kept God's promises? The mutuality of the covenant, the fact that it makes demands on both Israel and God, points to the fact that what the covenant is actually doing is providing a formal structure for the dialogical relationship between God and Israel. Attempts to argue for the continued validity of the covenant, for the continued presence of God in history, over and against the apparent witness of the death camps, are attempts, however halting and abstract, to find some way to continue to remain in relationship with God.

Second, Blumenthal realizes that relationship cannot be worked out in the abstract, that "[t]heology is not real unless one can pray it."[29] This is an extension of the therapeutic focus of Blumenthal's project, which

27. Ibid., 225.
28. Ibid., 5.
29. Ibid., 284.

PART THREE: Absent Mourners

places speech at the centre, but it is also, again, a direct statement of a notion that has haunted previous work. Roth's critics rejected his God as one they could not worship, rather than one in whom they could not believe; Blumenthal acknowledges the correctness of this position and, at the same time, recognizes that one possible key to release theology (Jewish theology in particular, although I suspect this insight applies at least to Christianity as well) from the trap of the theodical dilemma is to correct notions of what worship entails, rather than attempting to minimize the reality of suffering or God's apparent responsibility for it.

FUGITIVE PIECES

Fugitive Pieces is divided into two parts. The first takes the form of the memoirs of the fictional poet Jakob Beer, composed in the last months of his life, before he is struck by an automobile and killed at the age of sixty.[30] It begins with an account of his escape from the site of his parents' murder at the hands of Nazi soldiers, and his eventual rescue by Athos, a Greek geologist working on an excavation at the nearby iron-age settlement of Biskupin. Jakob's recounting of this trauma is fragmentary, and scattered throughout the narrative; it rises to the surface periodically and interrupts his adult existence. In the interest of clarity, as both of the novels I discuss in this chapter feature memoirs, older documents re-read during the "present" of the novels themselves, I have departed from the customary use of the present tense when describing actions that form part of what the novel characterizes as "past"—Jakob's memoirs and Maya's journals.

After the war's end, Athos removed Jakob from the political instability of the Greek Civil War and moves them to Toronto, where Athos obtained a university post.[31] But Athos, in spite of his best efforts, could not protect Jakob from a confrontation with history. Although Jakob "tried to bury images, to cover them over with Greek and English words, with Athos's stories, with all the geologic eras," at night, his dead family "simply rose, shook the earth from their clothes, and waited."[32] When Athos died, Jakob was left to re-assemble not only his own life, but Athos's final project, *Bearing False Witness*, a book on the SS-Ahnenerbe, the Nazi unit devoted to ancient history and archaeology. "The night I finished the work of my koumbaros,"

---

30. This information is conveyed in the frontspiece to the book.
31. FP, 79
32. FP, 93.

Jakob says, "I wept with emptiness as I typed his dedication, for his colleagues at Biskupin: 'Murder steals from a man his future. It steals from him his own death. But it must not steal from him his life.'"[33] The theme of service rendered by the living to the dead runs throughout the book.

Jakob was haunted by the memory—or, more accurately, absence—of his sister, Bella.[34] Besides his book, Athos left behind another unfinished task. In a drawer that otherwise contained mementos of Athos's long-dead wife, Jakob found "a thick folder containing faint blue carbons and newspaper cuttings," evidence that Athos had, up until the end of his life, continued to search for Bella.[35] Athos had begun this search almost immediately after the war, before he and Jakob left Greece for Canada. When Jakob first mentioned it, he presented it as a hopeless task.[36] But from the time that Jakob and Athos moved to Toronto, Bella's silence became an increasingly central focus of Jakob's life.

Jakob met and married Alex, the daughter of a British doctor whose slang-filled speech and leftist politics appear as much a rebellion against her upper-class background as Jakob's desire for her reads as an effort at escape from his own past.[37] Throughout the marriage, however, Jakob continued to be haunted by the uncertainty of Bella's fate.[38] He became increasingly obsessed with survivor testimonies and documentation relating to the death camps, and the strain of this obsession, his survivor guilt, eventually caused his marriage to fail.[39] Some years later, after Jakob became successful at transmuting his unresolved past into poetry, he met Michaela, a museum curator of mixed Russian and Spanish descent.[40] In spite of a considerable age difference between the two (Michaela is twenty-five years younger), they were capable, in a way that Jakob and Alex were not, of sharing their past with one another.[41] This mutual recognition led to a second marriage,

---

33. FP, 120
34. FP, 10.
35. FP, 117.
36. FP, 59.
37. See FP, 127–36.
38. FP, 136–41.
39. See Garwood, "Holocaust and the Power of Powerlessness."
40. FP, 178–79.
41. See especially FP, 182, where Michaela weeps for Bella, and Jakob experiences "The joy of being recognized and the stabbing loss: recognized for the first time."

PART THREE: Absent Mourners

and Jakob's memoirs end with a letter to the child that he hopes to conceive with Michaela:

> Child I long for: if we conceive you, if you are born, if you reach the age I am now, sixty, I say this to you: Light the lamps but do not look for us. [. . .] Light the lamp, cut a long wick. One day when you've almost forgotten, I pray you'll let us return. That through an open window, even in the middle of a city, the sea air of our marriage will find you. I pray that one day in a room lit only by night snow, you will suddenly know how miraculous is your parents' love for each other.
> My son, my daughter: May you never be deaf to love.
> Bela, Bella: Once I was lost in a forest. I was so afraid. My blood pounded in my chest and I knew my heart's strength would soon be exhausted. I saved myself without thinking. I grasped the two syllables closest to me, and replaced my heartbeat with your name.[42]

This is not the end of the book, however. In the second part, the narrative is picked up by Ben, a student of the man who introduced Jakob and Michaela, who is sent to Idhra to recover Jakob's journals. Ben is the child of Holocaust survivors, and his portion of the book is primarily devoted to the excavation of his own past, with his search for (and reflection upon) Jakob's journals lending structure to his reminiscences.[43]

Like Jakob, Ben is accompanied by family ghosts, by his memories of his dead parents and his estranged wife, Naomi; like Jakob, he is haunted by silence. But in Ben's narrative, the silence comes from the living, not the dead. He recalls the silence that pervaded his childhood home, the things that his parents would not speak of—or that his mother spoke only in a whisper, outside his father's hearing.[44] He recalls the "generous" silences of Naomi, "who rarely clamps her jaw with frustration or anger (those usually come out in tears); her silence is usually wise."[45] It is the combination of these two silences that caused the rupture in Ben's marriage to Naomi:

---

42. FP, 194–95.

43. My colleague, Mark Godin, has argued that Ben attempts to use Jakob's life-writing as an interpretative tool for his own life, deliberately re-casting events from his own experience as echoes of Jakob's narrative—but that, in so doing, Ben frequently misreads or misunderstands Jakob's lessons. See Godin, *Discerning the Body*, 203–8.

44. FP, 122–23. Ben is, in many ways, an archetypical representation of the Survivor's Child—see Kertzer, "Listening as a Holocaust Survivor's Child."

45. FP, 208.

Ben's mother confided to Naomi that she had had two children before Ben, before the war, a secret which Naomi unwittingly kept until after the deaths of Ben's parents, when Ben discovered a picture of the pre-war family.[46] It was Naomi who explained to Ben that his parents "hoped that if they did not name me, the angel of death might pass by. Ben, not from Benjamin, but merely 'ben'—the Hebrew word for son."[47]

Unable to forgive Naomi's complicity in the silences that damaged his childhood, Ben embarks upon an affair with a younger American woman named Petra, which terminates abruptly upon the discovery of Jakob's journals.[48] After reading them, he chooses to return home to Naomi—although whether they reconcile as husband and wife is left an open question at the book's end.[49]

MELISSA RAPHAEL: SEEKING THE FACE OF GOD

Important as Blumenthal's insights are, he is by no means the last word in Jewish engagement with or response to the Holocaust. Melissa Raphael, writing some ten years later and with a vastly different set of methodological preoccupations, also has made a significant contribution to the pool of potential imaginative strategies from which Jewish theological memory can draw in its response to the Holocaust. In *The Female Face of God in Auschwitz*, Raphael begins from her commitment as a feminist to let the voices of women be heard at the centre of Jewish experience, rather than on its margins. In applying this commitment to the Holocaust, she not only improves historical scholarship and extends the reach of feminist Jewish scholarship, she also offers a unique understanding of the way that the relationship between God and Israel is worked out in history.

Raphael, like Blumenthal, places the theology of Image at the centre of her investigation. This is a distinctively Jewish doctrine, originating in the text of Parshat Beresheit, Genesis 1:27. The notion that humanity bears the Image of God means that humanity becomes a source of theological understanding: the attributes of God are reflected in humanity; a statement that can be made about humanity also applies to God. Blumenthal began by dividing God's Image into the two essential attributes of "holiness" and

46. FP, 252–53.
47. FP, 253.
48. FP, 281.
49. FP, 284–94.

PART THREE: Absent Mourners

"personality"; while his study focuses more on the latter, and tends to reach for an understanding of God couched in human terms, it is quite significant that he also admits that holiness is part of the theology of Image—humans partake of, and are able to understand themselves through, Godliness.[50] This move also has scriptural roots, of course—for example, the commandments in Leviticus that Israel is to be holy as God is holy.[51] But the theology of Image in Blumenthal's (and Raphael's) formulation is not simply a Jewish gloss on Platonism; humanity is not a pale copy of God. Rather, "[h]umanity, in its individual and collective existence, is created in God's image and hence struggles, together with God, to live the depth of that image."[52] The theology of Image reveals God and humanity locked in mutual regard, each learning how to be themselves through encounter with the other.[53]

For Raphael, the theology of Image is expressed most fully in the face to face encounter between human beings—particularly Jews, and more particularly Jewish women.[54] The core of her study is a lengthy examination of the way that such face-to-face encounters functioned to conceal and reveal the presence of God in the concentration camps: the dehumanizing filth of the camps effecting *hester panim*, the hiding of God's face, and small acts of defiance—cleanliness, recognition of humanity—serving to reveal the face of God in the face of the camp inmates. In this way, Raphael not only suggests that God was present to victims of the Holocaust, she also suggests that God suffered with the victims, rather than being implicated as a cause of their suffering.

The problematic nature of Raphael's theology should, by this point, be clear: she neglects God's sovereignty in favor of God's immanence. Her abused, rather than abusing, God comes close to acting as an echo of

---

50. Blumenthal, *Facing the Abusing God*, 6–8.
51. E.g., Lev 19:2 and 11:44.
52. Blumenthal, *Facing the Abusing God*, 8.
53. This reading of the Theology of Image owes a great deal to Miles, *God: A Biography*.
54. In her emphasis upon the face, Raphael is, of course, drawing on the thought of Martin Buber and Emanuel Levinas. She discusses these influences explicitly in *Female Face of God*, 100–106. It should also be noted that Raphael differentiates between covenantal theology and theology of Image, arguing that "[c]ovenental relationship is [. . .] a witness to the theology of image that posits a relation of recursive presence between God and persons" (*Female Face of God*, 88). One could, then, argue that Raphael's work, in focusing on theology of Image, does little to rescue the idea of covenant. However, in her later chapters especially, Raphael invokes the figure of the Shekhinah following Israel, in particular, into exile; the particular bond implied by this image is a form of covenantal theology.

Moltmann's *theologia crucis*, albeit recast in a Jewish, feminist key.[55] God is to be pitied, rather than brought to account; however great the sufferings of the human victims of the Holocaust, God's suffering must be infinitely greater, as God partook in the suffering of each victim. However, such a critique neglects the Kabbalistic roots of Raphael's thought, the acknowledgement of fracture at the heart of creation. The *Shekhinah* she posits is God in exile from God's own self; a fragmentary part of God, but not the entirety of Divine Being.[56] Thus, Raphael's work is best read as a corrective to previous post-Holocaust theologies, all of which focus on the classically omnipotent God of the covenant, rather than the weakly immanent *Shekhinah*. What Raphael says of the latter does not necessarily invalidate what other theologians have said of the former. It is possible—and, perhaps, necessary—to both acknowledge God's suffering presence within the Holocaust and to seek redress from God for permitting the Holocaust to happen.

"THIS DIARY OF A YOUNG GIRL NOT IN HIDING, NOT HEROIC":[57] *YOUR SAD EYES AND UNFORGETTABLE MOUTH*

Your Sad Eyes and Unforgettable Mouth is a frame story, which follows Maya Levitsky, who in 2008 is an art historian at a Montréal CEGEP, as she re-reads (and re-writes) her adolescent journals, from the years 1968 to 1973.[58] These journals record her coming-of-age in the Montréal Jewish community, which at the time was home to the world's third largest population of Holocaust survivors.[59] Most of the adults whom Maya encounters are survivors; most of her peers are, like herself, children of survivors.

---

55. See above, note 20.
56. See Raphael, *Female Face of God*, 133.
57. YSE, 2.
58. A CEGEP—*Collège d'enseignement général et professionnel*—is a two- to three-year postsecondary program which is mandatory for students from Québec secondary schools (which end a year earlier than schools in the rest of Canada or the United States) who wish to enter university, and also provides vocational training for students who do not wish to continue on a university track. Teachers at CEGEP are required to have a Master's degree (in academic fields) or significant professional experience (in vocational fields).
59. This is a frequently cited figure, even today—it is still, for example, featured prominently in the literature on the web site of The Montreal Holocaust Memorial Centre. However, a wave of emigration following the 1981 referendum has depleted the overall Jewish population of Montréal, leaving Toronto as the home of the largest survivor

PART THREE: Absent Mourners

At the beginning of Maya's revisiting (and, possibly, although the text itself is unclear on this point, revisioning) of her past, in 1968, she was twelve years old and living in Côte des Neiges with her grandmother and mother: "Bubby Miriam, Fanya, Maya. Three mad women. Mad, mad, mad."[60] She attended a state school run by the Protestant school board;[61] she had no friends, "Not real friends—not friends you met outside of school. Fanya would never let me visit just anyone; she'd insist on coming with me, inspecting the premises, meeting the parents. And what would they make of her garbled snippets of horror-history, her prophetic alarms?"[62] The distance that Fanya's post-traumatic speech patterns and protective parenting imposed between Maya and her classmates began to dissolve when Maya spent a summer at Camp Bakunin.[63] This brought Maya her introduction to the community of Jewish youth in which she eventually made her home—and her first contact with Anthony, a charming (though slightly erratic) camp counselor.[64]

After that summer, Maya met Rosie Michaeli. In part because Rosie's own parents were Holocaust survivors, she accepted Maya's home life without the embarrassment or judgment that Maya feared from her classmates. In a scene reminiscent of the first meeting between Anne Shirley and Diana Barry in L. M. Montgomery's *Anne of Green Gables*, the two girls pledged firm friendship with one another. As a mark of her devotion to Rosie, Maya spent the rest of the summer learning Hebrew in order to pass the admission

---

population in Canada (see Torczyner and Brotman, "The Jews of Canada," 228–29, 240. For a general overview of Holocaust survivor populations in Canada, see Bialystok, *Delayed Impact*, 73–74.

60. YSE, 9.

61. Since 1925 there have been two school boards in Montréal: the Catholic school board, which historically has operated primarily French-language schools, and the Protestant school board, which historically has operated primarily English-language schools. Since 1965, the "Protestant" school board has included members of the Jewish community, and been charged with supplying education to Jewish pupils (although privately run Hebrew schools continue to exist); the real distinction between the two school boards has more to do with the language of instruction which they oversee than with religious adherence. See Sancton, *Governing the Island of Montreal*, 48–49. However, from Maya's general ignorance of Judaism prior to meeting Rosie—she does not, for example, understand what the word "kosher" means (see YSE, 36–37)—it appears that Maya was one of only a few Jewish children at her school.

62. YSE, 14–15.

63. YSE, 20.

64. YSE, 28. Maya's introduction to her own Jewishness is faintly reminiscent of a similar transition undergone by the protagonist of Chaim Potok's *Davita's Harp*.

test for Eden, the Jewish school which Rosie and the rest of the children from Camp Bakunin attended. Maya's circle of friendship grows, including Patrick, the spoiled, moody son of Vera Moore a child psychologist who once, briefly treated Maya—and also, we eventually discover, Anthony's brother. Vera herself, both in name and physical description, appears to be an echo of the self-sacrificing Leslie Moore from L. M. Montgomery's *Anne's House of Dreams*.

At the moment of this revelation, the workings of the story resolve into clarity: Maya, the narrator, is really a spectator, peering in from the outside on the Moore's family drama. This is confirmed in the novel's final pages, when Maya's narrative is replaced by several pages of free verse titled "Eikah" ("Lamentations"), which read as an excerpt from the story Vera told to Gerald, Anthony and Patrick's father, on their first night together. This narrative's appearance at the end of the book has the character of the curtain being drawn aside at the end of a puppet-show, finally revealing what has been in the background all along, manipulating the action on stage. But this is not quite true: Heisenberg's uncertainty principle applies to narrative as well as to particle physics, and so Maya observes, but also cannot avoid participating in, and therefore changing, Vera's story and the impact its echo has on her children.

All the divergent strands of narrative, the characters who drifted in and out of the story without apparent rhyme or reason, converge in the book's climax. Maya, Rosie, and Patrick celebrated their graduation from secondary school with a trip to the Moore's holiday cottage. Their idyll was interrupted by Anthony's sudden reappearance. He and Maya engaged in an abortive attempt at intimacy, in which she found herself unable to touch him sexually. The following morning, the residents of the cottage experienced a second unexpected interruption in the arrival of a group of local youth, including a boy named Glenn, with whom Rosie fell instantly in love. As Maya gazed at Rosie, recognizing the depth of feeling she had desired in their relationship directed at another, Anthony gazed at Maya (gazing at Rosie)—and then, unnoticed by either girl, he walked into the woods and shot himself.

Maya, Rosie, and Patrick agreed to bury Anthony, to spare his mother the pain of knowing that he had shot himself. Instead, Patrick resolved to forge letters from his brother, perpetuating the illusion that he had travelled in his father's footsteps to pursue a monastic existence in India.[65] The three

---

65. YSE, 237.

PART THREE: Absent Mourners

vowed never to disclose the secret, and then went their separate ways—though the "cab money" Patrick left the girls was sufficient for Maya to move out of her mother's home and attend Cégep.[66] She began "a new life," a life without Rosie, without "the appalling muddle that intimacy turned out to be."[67]

Maya's new life without intimacy is, in the end, as illusive as Ben's new life on Idhra; thirty-five years after Anthony's death, the end of her narrative finds her reflecting again on the event that prompted her trip into the past: dinner with Patrick after his mother's funeral. She sees that, over the years, his "self-protective irony had strayed into the arena of offhand nastiness. He had become cruel."[68] There is no explicit parallel drawn between Patrick and Maya's attempts at self-isolation, but immediately after recounting Patrick's unfeeling behavior towards his wife, Maya sets about re-establishing contact with Rosie, who is now married to Glenn. The final scene in Maya's narrative is of her departing, at Glenn's request, to visit Rosie who has been suffering from severe depression:

> We think we aren't important; we tell ourselves that because we were helpless and ineffectual once, this is who we are, and our exits don't matter—no one will miss us. I told myself that Rosie had Glenn. My desertion was a way of mourning through imitation, a way we have of re-enacting the worst traits of whoever it is we've lost. For those tangled reasons, and others, I did to Rosie what Anthony did to me.
>
> Of course, I don't know why she's in trouble. I only know I haven't been there to help out. And I also know something else that doesn't occur to us when we're young, and when what we have in common with our fellow-travellers is being young, and it seems as if it's easy to find friends. It only dawns on us later, as people drift away, that friends are in fact hard to come by, hard to replace.
>
> I've already bought my plane ticket and arranged for a dog sitter. I leave tomorrow morning. The past is irretrievable. I will never be in Eden again, trailing after Rosie, helping her gather up her books. I'm waiting, as Anthony did not, to see what comes next.[69]

---

66. YSE, 243–44.
67. YSE, 244, 245.
68. YSE, 257.
69. YSE, 260.

LITURGY AND THE THEOLOGY OF IMAGE: SPEAKING GOD'S FACE

Raphael's intervention into post-Holocaust theology is essential, but incomplete. She provides a much-needed framework for understanding God's action—or part of God's action—in the Holocaust (and, in theory, all other instances of radical suffering throughout history), and therefore a foundation upon which continued relationship between God and Israel may be built; she does not provide a terribly detailed vision of how that relationship ought to be enacted, liturgically. She does not immediately appear to answer Blumenthal's dictum that "[t]heology is not real unless one can pray it"; moreover, she seems to break with the previous tradition of feminist Jewish theological intervention, which has tended to both begin from and end with practical concerns about the inclusion of women in Jewish life, Jewish law, and, especially, Jewish liturgy.[70]

However, a closer reading of Raphael's text reveals a strong suggestion of precisely such practical concerns, although their application to the present day is left as an exercise for the reader. The significance of Raphael's argument that, in Auschwitz, God was revealed in and through the face-to-face encounter between Jewish women, through the recognition and recovery of mutual humanity, extends far beyond Auschwitz. The process of *tikkun*, the reconciliation of "the exiled God to God," begun in the camps must, if it is to be a meaningful reconciliation, continue into the present day.[71] Raphael's enumeration of the acts which help to accomplish that reconciliation broadens and challenges existing concepts of liturgy: needlework, washing, touch, feeding, dressing, collecting, carrying; the bending of one body towards another.[72] In saying that these acts did constitute *tikkun*, encounter, prayer, Raphael is also saying that they still do constitute such in the present, and will continue to do so for the foreseeable future; the sacred and quotidian meet and merge, finding one another in the same sort of mutual regard that characterizes the human/Divine relationship described by the theology of Image.

This is still not a fully satisfactory response; a theology drawn from the particularities of predominantly Eastern European Orthodox women is

---

70. Blumenthal, *Facing the Abusing God*, 284. For examples of earlier works of Jewish Feminist Theology, see Adler, *Engendering Judaism*; Plaskow, *Standing Again at Sinai*; see also the essays collected in Heschel, *On Being a Jewish Feminist*.

71. Raphael, *Female Face of God*, 133.

72. E.g., ibid., 154.

not a universal cure for Holocaust-induced religious anxiety—there is no universal cure, and attempts to invent one risk falling into the same trap as First World War memorialization, in which individual lives are collapsed together into the collective Glorious Dead.[73] This collapsing is a diminishment of both humanity and God's Image in humanity. It is also inescapable; the enormity of loss in the Holocaust (or the First World War, or, for that matter, any other war, genocide, or natural disaster) is too great to approach in its entirety without losing sight of individual lives and experiences. Theology is conducted in the tense space in between individual and universal concerns, and thus is, at its best and most honest, always inadequate, never stable or complete. This is where an element of protest or reproach, such as Roth and Blumenthal endorse, becomes a necessary corrective—not as a repudiation of God, but as an acknowledgement of incompleteness, a refusal to subscribe to a tidy—and misleading—universal narrative.

But just as Raphael's theology supplements and corrects, rather than substitutes for, the patriarchal tradition of Judaism, so do the liturgical acts she describes supplement, rather than supplant, the previous liturgical innovations carried out by other Jewish feminists. To point, as Raphael does, to the liturgical significance of the routines and rituals of a Jewish home, traditionally the domain of women, is not to suggest that a Jewish woman's space of worship should be limited to the home—or, in fact, that a man is only capable of encountering God within the walls of a synagogue. God, with and through encounter with humanity, must be praised, reproached, and helped to mend; I suspect that we will learn that the spaces and languages which permit this are far more numerous than have yet been imagined.

---

73. Raphael notes this limitation in her study, but maintains that "[r]eligious feminists who wish to affirm female difference rather than erasing it in the name of equality with the male norm (the historic tendency of Reform Judaism) must take seriously the Orthodox contention that women have [...] the priestly power to mediate the presence of God" (*Female Face of God*, 77). While Raphael is correct that such a contention, when it is taken seriously and not merely deployed in order to keep women in the kitchen and out of the synagogue, is an important step forward for Jewish feminism, it is at the same time deeply dependent on binary gender identification, leaving little room for intersex or transgendered spirituality to arise.

BEN AND MAYA: "I MUST GIVE WHAT I MOST NEED"[74]

Ben and Maya's stories have a similar trajectory. Both cut off with the narrator on their way to, but not yet arrived at, a reunion—but both intended reunions follow separations caused mainly by a failure to recognize the personhood of, and, therefore, the Image of God in, others. Both, in other words, have experienced the failure or absence of quotidian liturgical moments. These failures point both towards the continued fracture in the world and towards the possibility of mending, the existence of opportunities for healing encounters (even if those opportunities are mostly missed opportunities). Focusing on failure also leaves room to acknowledge the brokenness of the world, and a movement towards confronting and correcting it, rather than wallowing in illusions of perfection and happy endings.

Both Ben and Maya's encounter with the world began with parents whose lives were marked by their experiences in the Holocaust, and both are, in turn, marked by their parents' experiences. As has already been mentioned, Maya's mother initially stood between Maya and any potential friendships she might have formed, though this was mitigated later on when Maya met other children of Holocaust survivors, who were able to understand and accept as normal the eccentricities of a parent who had spent time "*there*."[75] Ben also "learned not to bring school friends home," also found himself embarrassed to admit outside observers into his home life, but his understanding of his parents' pasts is more painfully immediate than Maya's vague comprehension of what happened *there*.[76] Maya's mother is a mostly comic character, who causes Maya embarrassment, but no real harm; Ben's recollection of his father, by contrast, interweaves scenes of them listening to classical music together, "[h]is absent fingers combing through my short hair," with a painful scene involving an apple:[77]

> My father found the apple in the garbage. It was rotten and I'd thrown it out—I was eight or nine. He fished it from the bin, sought me in my room, grabbed me tight by the shoulder, and pushed the apple to my face.
> "What is this? What is it?"

---

74. FP, 294.

75. "*There*" is the oblique reference to the camps used by the characters in YSE; see, for example, 95, 121, 231. For both Maya and Ben, the Holocaust takes on a distance, a tinge of unreality, like a fairy tale; cf. Brauner, "Breaking the Silences," 30.

76. FP, 229.

77. FP, 217.

PART THREE: Absent Mourners

> "An apple—"[78]
> "Is an apple food?"
> "Yes."
> "And you throw away food? You—my son—you throw away food?"
> "It's rotten—"
> "Eat it . . . Eat it!"
> "Pa, it's rotten—I won't—"
> He pushed it into my teeth until I opened my jaw. Struggling, sobbing, I ate. Its brown taste, oversweetness, tears.[79]

Food is a thematic element in both books, which reveals a great deal about relationships between characters; this is consistent with research findings that show Holocaust survivors experience lasting psychological effects of food deprivation in the ghettos and camps.[80] Maya's mother obsessively monitored her daughter's food consumption, serving her elaborate meals while refusing any assistance in their preparation, and not partaking of them herself.[81] Rosie's father "recoiled from money" and spent it "as quickly as possible" on, among other things, large restaurant dinners for his family, during which "he himself drank only coffee."[82] Of all the adult survivors in Ravel's novel, Vera Moore is the only one who appears to take pleasure in food for its own sake, employing a personal chef.[83] The final section of the book portrays her on the road to Prague, in the back of a truck driven by Russian soldiers, meditating on the pleasure of fresh eggs:

> *eggs were part of my future*
> *if I found Katya I would eat two lightly salted poached eggs on buttered toast*[84]

The precision with which Vera imagined her eggs—lightly salted, on buttered toast—is a sharp contrast to Ben's father eating "dutifully, methodically, tears streaming down his face, animal and spirit in such raw evidence,

---

78. FP, 213–14.

79. FP, 218.

80. See Sinder et al., "Holocaust Survivors Report." Ben's father's hoarding behavior is far more in line with these findings than Maya's mother's compulsive feeding.

81. YSE, 11.

82. YSE, 110.

83. YSE, 131, 174, 215–16.

84. YSE, 263.

knowing he was degrading both."⁸⁵ But Vera's eating was, like her other domestic behaviors, an attempt at substitution for, or mimicry of, a lifestyle predicated on familial relationships that she herself lacked. Where Maya and Rosie accepted the food that their parents pressed upon them out of affection for those parents, Patrick rejected what his mother offered for reasons that none of the characters even pretend have to do with the food itself.⁸⁶

Vera is an inversion of the other two parents in the book (and of Ben's father), who feed their children but are themselves incapable of enjoying food; she takes great pleasure in her food, but cannot share that pleasure with her children. In none of these cases, however, is the encounter between parent and child one of mutual recognition: the parents use their children in an attempt to restore what they themselves were deprived of (and are now incapable of possessing for themselves);⁸⁷ the children accept or reject what is offered, either ignorant or resentful of the parental need which prompts the offering. The Image of God is visible in these scenes only as a trace, a fragment.

The apparent exception to this lack of mutuality is Ben's early relationship with his mother, who "was determined to impress upon me the absolute, inviolate necessity of pleasure," her "painful love for the world."⁸⁸ Ben became, for a time, his mother's confidante, the vessel into which she poured the memories that his father could no longer bear to contemplate.⁸⁹ But Ben was an imperfect vessel: he heard his mother's stories, but did not understand the grip they held on her life; he did not, perhaps could not, cling to the world with the same mix of fear and wonder as she did. Like Maya (and Patrick and Anthony), he grew ashamed and resentful of his parents, seeking to "free" himself from their constraints, realizing only later that he "created a deeper harm. She was afraid. I believe that for moments my mother actually distrusted me. [. . .] This happened even more frequently once Naomi entered our lives."⁹⁰ Whether Naomi's encounter

---

85. FP, 214.

86. See, for example, YSE, 134.

87. This is made explicit in a conversation between Maya and Sheila, one of the Camp Bakunin girls, in which Sheila points out that Maya's mother "lost everything, she wants to make up for it by giving you everything," and Maya complains that "It just makes me feel guilty" (YSE, 151).

88. FP, 223.

89. FP, 222–29.

90. FP, 231.

PART THREE: Absent Mourners

with Ben's parents was more properly liturgical, a space of encounter in which the Image of God became clearly visible to all concerned, is unclear; the text is written from Ben's point of view. What is quite clear is that the closeness between Naomi and Ben's mother led directly to the fracturing of Naomi and Ben's relationship, as discussed above.

What all these relationships have in common is a strange choreography of projection and attachment: one person reaches for the other in an attempt to hold them close and transform them into what that person most needs. Maya and Ben's mothers poured their loss into their children, seeking some sort of vicarious compensation. Rosie pours all of her energy into pleasing her parents, hoping to infuse her father with a will to live that he lacks for himself.[91] Ben's father attempted to mold his son in his own image, and Ben in turn transfers his resentment from his dead father to the dead poet whose life he seeks to imitate, and from his dead mother to the wife whom he sees as the final living reminder of that mother's betrayal. Anthony desired not Maya as the reader knows her, but as the nickname/persona he gave her at camp, "Joan of Arc," able to see past his defensive pretense and straight into his soul;[92] Maya desired Rosie, untroubled by the latter's casual liaisons with boys, spinning out elaborate fantasies in which Rosie featured as a passive object in need of rescue that only she could provide—and abandoned Rosie when another rescuer appeared on the scene.[93] And Vera, whose family life was troubled from its beginning by the past that she had meant to leave behind, insulated herself behind a thin veneer of domestic comfort; her children resented and eventually fled their roles in the family charade—Anthony went so far as to shoot himself. The memory of the Holocaust, both immediate and inherited/constructed, seeps from person to person, marring their connection with others.

The failure of the relationships that drive both novels is important, but it is not the whole story, or even the most important part of the story; God's seeming abandonment of covenant, and the Christian churches' seeming complicity in the mass death of the two World Wars is not the only lesson to be read from the constructed memory of the last century, or even the most important lesson. The important gesture in all of this is not the missed connection, but the stretching of one hand towards another; not the failure of relationship, but the attempt at any relationship at all.

91. YSE, 182.
92. See, especially, YSE, 38 and 221–25.
93. YSE, 79.

CONCLUSION

After Jakob Beer's obsession with the past drove away his first wife, he returned to Greece, to his guardian Athos's old family home on the island of Idhra. There, he found his prayer shawl, "a gift from Athos after the war, never worn, folded carefully and still stored in its cardboard box."[94] He found a slim volume of Psalms that Athos once retrieved from a rubbish bin. Immersing himself in the book, he permitted himself be flooded by the voices of the past that, during his years in Canada, he had tried to keep at bay.[95] In the dark night, with his never-worn prayer shawl and book of Psalms fished from the trash, Jakob imagined, in painful detail, what happened to his sister, Bella:

> We know they cried out. Each mouth, Bella's mouth, strained for its miracle. They were heard from the other side of the thick walls. It is impossible to imagine those sounds.
>
> At that moment of utmost degradation, in that twisted reef, is the most obscene testament of grace. For can anyone tell with absolute certainty the difference between the sounds of those who are in despair and the sounds of those who want desperately to believe? The moment when our faith in man is forced to change, anatomically—mercilessly—into faith.[96]

At the end of this vigil, Jakob concluded that "*To remain with the dead is to abandon them. All the years I felt Bella entreating me, filled with her loneliness, I was mistaken. I have misunderstood her signals. Like other ghosts, she whispers; not for me to join her, but so that, when I'm close enough, she can push me back into the world.*"[97] Prompted, in part, by obtaining tangible relics of his past, Jakob abandoned his futile quest for communion with "ghosts" and returned to Canada, where he met and married Michaela; they lived happily together until they were struck by a car, and died within two days of each other. This is not a happy ending, but it does have a sense of fulfillment which some critics have found problematic, on the grounds that it minimizes the horrors of the Holocaust in favor of a narrative in which "love conquers all."[98] This is doubly troubling, as Jakob's story becomes the

94. FP, 156
95. See FP, 139.
96. FP, 168.
97. FP, 170.
98. See, for example, Kertzer, "Listening as a Holocaust Survivor's Child"; King, *Memory, Narrative, Identity*, 121–47; Bentley, "Anne Michaels' *Fugitive Pieces*"; Cook, "At the Membrane of Language and Silence"; Annick Hillger, "Afterbirth of Earth."

PART THREE: Absent Mourners

lens through which we read Ben's; it is easy to assume that Ben's own departure from Idhra heralds a return to Naomi and happily-ever-after, although the relics Ben carries are of Jakob's past, not his own, and his narrative ends still up in the air, both literally and figuratively: on a plane over the Atlantic, unresolved. And it is easy, too, to read Maya as an extension of Jakob and Ben, last seen on her way back to Rosie and the resumption of the eternal friendship pledged by Anne Shirley and Diana Barry. But these readings are mis-readings. Jakob is an inversion of Ben and Maya: he grapples with his own past, and makes a new life for himself; they grapple with the memories bequeathed to them by the previous generation, and attempt to reconstruct relationships that they had previously damaged and abandoned.

Ben sits in the air and imagines his reunion with Naomi, interweaving it with memories of his parents, newly reconsidered in light of Jakob's journals: "But now, from thousands of feet in the air, I see something else. My mother stands behind my father and his head leans against her. As he eats, she strokes his hair. Like a miraculous circuit, each draws strength from the other. I see that I must give what I most need."[99] But the reunion exists only in Ben's imagination—and so, for all we know, does the memory. As far as Ben's resolve to give what he most needs, while it is a powerful closing sentence, Ben has not proven adept at determining his needs at any other point in his narrative—why should we assume that he has suddenly grown wise (especially as he also imagines that he "will stop myself from confessing I was on Idhra with a woman"—in spite of his anger over what he perceived as Naomi's deception, it would appear that honesty is not something Ben feels that he has much need of).[100] And Maya, in her rush to return to Rosie in her hour of need, never spares a thought for Tyen, the current (potential) lover who haunts the edges of her narrative in the present.[101] None of these endings is perfect, complete, or even final. What resolution may be had from them exists only in the mind of the reader. We may guess, or imagine, but never know for sure whether Ben finds himself forgiven, whether Maya's presence proves as healing to Rosie as Glenn hopes. The only certainty we have is that both Ben and Maya have made the attempt: they stretch their hands out towards another, in the hope that this time there will be contact, encounter. They wait to see what comes next.

---

99. FP, 294.
100. FP, 294.
101. See YSE, 40–43, 251.

This is not, by itself, redemption.

At most, it is a gesture in that direction:
halting, flawed, doomed (or so it seems) to failure.

But it is the best we have.

Coda

This conclusion is not simple or satisfactory. It may seem to be barely a conclusion at all; this book, much like the two novels discussed in this chapter, may appear to terminate abruptly, *en route* to a destination but never actually arriving. Unsatisfactory as it may be, however, I remain convinced that this suspension is the most appropriate response to the material addressed in this book.

The preceding pages have explored a number of strategies for reconciling the promises of theology with the messy realities of history: the encounter between Israel and Amalek passed into Scripture and became a model by which subsequent conflicts have been understood; the commandment to remember has resonated through the centuries. But the forms of memorialization that were adequate prior to 1914 were destabilized by the First World War; while theological narratives dominated by a sacrificial *ethos* still provided a framework for public memorialization, social and liturgical commemorative practice had to shift slightly to accommodate the disruptions of the war. These slight adjustments, in turn, proved completely inadequate to the task of addressing the Holocaust. In total, the events of the twentieth century constitute a thorough assault on traditional forms of memorialization, the end result of which is that no more simple adjustments to existing social or theological narratives are possible. Instead, the complex phenomenon of remembrance must be addressed by an equally complex and profound cultural, aesthetic, and theological shift.

Early in my research, it became apparent that up through the First World War, memorials functioned as temporal boundary markers, attesting to the completion of a phase in history: there was a war, it ended, we built a statue to remind us what it was all about. This sense of finality is among the characteristics of memorials that have been unsettled by the Holocaust; simple statues are replaced by entire museums, and even these fail to convey a solid sense of "what it was all about." I have attempted, instead, a sort of theological realism: to honor the complexity of the material in the form of this book, as well as to resist the urge for a conclusion that is neat, simple, easily optimistic—and ultimately dishonest.

Fin.

Bibliography

NOVELS AND PLAYS

Anouilh, Jean. *Antigone*. Paris : La Table Ronde, 1947.
———. "Antigone" (1944). In *Antigone and Eurydice: Two Plays by Jean Anouilh*. Translated by Lewis Galantière. London: Methuen, 1951.
Boyden, Joseph. *Three Day Road*. New York: Penguin, 2005.
Hodgkins, Jack. *Broken Ground*. Toronto: McClelland & Stewart, 1999.
McCrae, John. "In Flanders Fields." *Punch*, 6 December 1915.
Michaels, Anne. *Fugitive Pieces*. 1996. Reprint, London: Bloomsbury, 1998.
Montgomery, L. M. *Anne of Avonlea*. Boston: L. C. Page, 1909. Reprint. London: Puffin, 1982.
———. *Anne of Green Gables*. Boston: L. C. Page, 1908. Reprint. London: Puffin, 1994.
———. *Anne's House of Dreams*. Toronto: McClelland, Goodchild and Stewart; New York: Stokes, 1917. Reprint. London: Puffin, 1981.
———. *Anne of the Island*. Boston: L. C. Page, 1915. Reprint. London: Puffin, 1981.
———. *The Blue Castle*. Toronto: McClelland and Stewart; New York: Stokes, 1926.
———. *The Blythes are Quoted*. Edited by Benjamin Lefebvre. Toronto: Penguin, 2009.
———. *Emily Climbs*. Toronto: McClelland and Stewart; New York: Stokes, 1925.
———. *Emily of New Moon*. Toronto: McClelland and Stewart; New York: Stokes, 1923.
———. *Emily's Quest*. Toronto: McClelland and Stewart; New York: Stokes, 1927.
———. *Rainbow Valley*. Toronto: McClelland and Stewart; New York: Stokes, 1921. Reprint. Toronto: McClelland and Stewart, 1987.
———. *Rilla of Ingleside*. Toronto: McClelland and Stewart; New York: Stokes, 1921. Reprint. New York: Bantam, 1992.
———. *A Tangled Web*. Toronto: McClelland and Stewart, 1931.
Ondaatje, Michael. *Anil's Ghost*. London: Picador, 2000.
Potok, Chaim. *Davita's Harp*. New York: Ballantine, 1996.
Ravel, Edeet. *Your Sad Eyes and Unforgettable Mouth*. Toronto: Viking, 2008.
Sophocles. *Antigone*. In *Sophocles* vol. II, Loeb Classical Library, edited and translated by Hugh Lloyd-Jones. Cambridge: Harvard University Press, 1994.
Urquhart, Jane. *The Stone Carvers*. London: Bloomsbury, 2002.
Wiesel, Eli. *Night*. Translated by Stella Rodway. London: Penguin, 1981.

Bibliography

ARCHIVES AND MUSEUMS

Kaiser-Wilhelm-Gedächtniskirche. Memorial Hall, permanent exhibit. Visited 5 August 2008.

Queen's University, Kingston, ON. Walter S. Allward Collection.

Veterans Affairs Canada. "The Monument-Design Competition." Online: http://www.vac-acc.gc.ca/remembers/sub.cfm?source=memorials/ww1mem/vimy/sg/04_monument/01_competition. Accessed 20 January 2010.

LITURGICAL SOURCES

Jewish

Gubkin, Liora. *You Shall Tell Your Children: Holocaust Memory in American Passover Ritual*. Picastaway, NJ: Rutgers University Press, 2007.

Hammer, Reuven. *Entering the High Holy Days: A Complete Guide to the History, Prayers, and Themes*. Philadelphia: Jewish Publication Society, 2005.

Hoffman, Lawrence A. *Beyond the Text: A Holistic Approach to Liturgy*. Bloomington, IN: Indiana University Press, 1987.

———, editor. *My People's Prayerbook: Traditional Prayers, Modern Commentaries*. 10 vols. Woodstock, VT: Jewish Lights, 1997–2007.

Christian

The Church of Scotland. *A Book of Common Order: Being Forms of Prayer and Administration of the Sacraments, and Other Ordinances of the Church*. 5th ed. Edinburgh: Blackwood and Sons, 1884.

———. *A Book of Common Order: Being Forms of Prayer and Administration of the Sacraments, and Other Ordinances of the Church*. 12th ed. Edinburgh: Blackwood and Sons, 1929.

Ferguson, James. *Prayers for Common Worship: Morning and Evening Every Lord's Day throughout the Course of the Christian Year*. London: Allenson , 1936.

Free Church of Scotland. *A New Directory for the Public Worship of God: Founded on the Book of Common Order (1560–64) and the Westminster Directory (1643–45) and Prepared by the Public Worship Association in connection with the Free Church of Scotland*. 2nd ed. Edinburgh: MacNiven & Wallace, 1898.

The Presbyterian Church in Canada. *The Book of Family Devotion*. Toronto: Oxford University Press, 1919.

———. *Book of Common Order for Use in Church Services and Offices*. Toronto: Oxford University Press, 1922.

———. "A Liturgy for Remembrance Day." Online: http://www.presbyterian.ca/webfm_send/269. Accessed 11 August 2009.

———. "A Remembrance Day Service for November 11, 2007, Theme: The Way to Peace." Online: http://www.presbyterian.ca/webfm_send/899. Accessed 11 August 2009.

Bibliography

SCRIPTURAL AND LEGAL COMMENTARY

Black, Matthew, and H. H. Rowley, editors. *Peake's Commentary on the Bible*. London: Routledge, 1962.

Buttrick, George Arthur, editor. *The Interpreter's Bible*. Volumes I and II. New York: Abingdon, 1953.

Childs, Brevard. *Exodus: A Commentary*. London: SCM, 1974.

———. *Memory and Tradition in Israel*. London: SCM, 1972.

Craigie, Peter C. *The Book of Deuteronomy*. Grand Rapids: Eerdmans, 1976.

Driver. S. R. *Critical and Exegetical Commentary on Deuteronomy*. Edinburgh: T. & T. Clark, 1973.

Dunn, James D. G., and John W. Rogerson, editors. *Eerdmans Commentary on the Bible*. Grand Rapids: Eerdmans, 2003.

Eslinger, Lyle. "More Drafting Techniques in Deuteronomic Laws." *Vetus Testamentum* 34.2 (1984) 221–26.

Fackenheim, Emil. *The Jewish Bible after the Holocaust: A Re-reading*. Bloomington, IN: Indiana University Press, 1990.

Fox, Everett. *The Five Books of Moses: Genesis, Exodus, Leviticus, Numbers and Deuteronomy: A New Translation with Introductions, Commentary and Notes*. New York: Schocken, 1995.

Ginzberg, Louis. *Legends of the Jews: Volumes III and IV*. Charleston, SC: Forgotten, 2008.

Hendel, Ronald. *Remembering Abraham: Culture, Memory and History in the Hebrew Bible*. Oxford: Oxford University Press, 2005.

Hershman, Abraham, translator. *The Code of Maimonides: Book Fourteen, the Book of Judges*. New Haven: Yale University Press, 1949.

Hirsch, Samson Raphael. *The Pentateuch (translated and explained)*. Translated by Isaac Levy. Volume V: *Deuteronomy*. 2nd ed. Gateshead, UK: Judaica, 1989.

Meyers, Carol. *Exodus*. The New Cambridge Bible Commentary. Cambridge: Cambridge University Press, 2005.

Miles, Jack. *God: A Biography*. New York: Vintage, 1996.

Nahmanides. *Commentary on the Torah*. Translated by Charles B. Chavel. New York: Shilo, 1973.

Nelson, Richard D. *Deuteronomy: A Commentary*. Lousiville, KY: Westminster John Knox, 2002.

Niditch, Susan. *War in the Hebrew Bible: A Study in the Ethics of Violence*. Oxford: Oxford University Press, 1993.

Propp, William H. *Exodus 1–18: A New Translation with Introduction and Commentary*. The Anchor Bible. New York: Doubleday, 1999.

Sagi, Avi. "The Punishment of Amalek in Jewish Tradition: Coping with the Moral Problem." *Harvard Theological Review* 87.3 (1994) 323–46.

Shapira, Kalonymos Kalmish. *Sacred Fire: Torah from the Years of Fury 1939–1942*. Translated by J. Hershy Worch. Northvale, NJ: Aronson, 2002.

Weinfeld, Moshe. *Deuteronomy and the Deuteronimic School*. Oxford: Clarendon, 1972.

ET CETERA

Aciman, André. "In a Double Exile." In *False Papers: Essays on Exile and Memory*, 107–10. New York: Farrar, Strauss, and Giroux, 2000.

Bibliography

Adler, Rachel. *Engendering Judaism: An Inclusive Theology and Ethics*. Boston: Beacon, 1998.
Albinus, Lars. *The House of Hades: Studies in Ancient Greek Eschatology*. Aarhus, Denmark: Aarhus University Press, 2000.
Alles, Gregory. "Exchange." In *Guide to the Study of Religion*, edited by Willi Braun and Russel T. McCutcheon, 110-24. New York: Academic, 1980.
Anderson, Benedict. *Imagined Communities*. Rev. ed. London: Verso, 1991.
Anderson, Greg. *The Athenian Experiment: Building an Imagined Political Community in Ancient Attica, 508-490 BCE*. Ann Arbor, MI: University of Michigan Press, 2003.
Arendt, Hannah. *Eichmann in Jerusalem: A Report on the Banality of Evil*. New York: Penguin, 1963.
―――. "Personal Responsibility under Dictatorship" [1964]. In *Responsibility and Judgment*, 17-48. New York: Schocken, 2003.
Assman, Jan. "Collective Memory and Cultural Identity." Translated by John Czaplicka. *New German Critique* 65 (1995) 125-33.
Atwood, Margaret. *Survival: A Thematic Guide to Canadian Literature*. Toronto: Anansi, 1972.
Barnett, Victoria. *Bystanders: Conscience and Complicity during the Holocaust*. Westport, CT: Praeger, 1999.
―――. *For the Soul of the People: Protestant Protest against Hitler*. Oxford: Oxford University Press, 1998.
Baum, Gregory. *The Jews and the Gospel: A Re-examination of the New Testament*. London: Bloomsbury, 1961.
Benjamin, Walter. "Theses on the Philosophy of History." In *Illuminations*, translated by Harry Zorn, 245-55. London: Pimlico, 1999.
Bentley, D. M. R. "Anne Michaels' *Fugitive Pieces*." *Canadian Poetry* 41 (1997) 5-20.
Berliner, David C. "The Abuses of Memory: Reflections on the Memory Boom in Anthropology." *Anthropological Quarterly* 78.1 (2005) 197-211.
Berry, Edmund G. "Antigone and the French Resistance." *The Classical Journal* 42.1 (1946) 17-18.
Berton, Pierre. *Marching as to War*. Toronto: Doubleday Canada, 2001.
Bethge, Eberhard, and Victoria Barnett. *Dietrich Bonhoeffer: A Biography*. Minneapolis: Fortress, 2000.
Bialystok, Franklin. *Delayed Impact: The Holocaust and the Canadian Jewish Community*. Montréal: McGill-Queen's University Press, 2000.
Blumenthal, David R. *Facing the Abusing God: A Theology of Protest*. Louisville: Westminster/John Knox, 1993.
Bradshaw, Paul F., and Lawrence A. Hoffman, editors. *The Making of Jewish and Christian Worship*. Notre Dame, IN: University of Notre Dame Press, 1991.
Braiterman, Zachary. *(God) After Auschwitz: Tradition and Change in Post-Holocaust Jewish Thought*. Princeton: Princeton University Press, 1998.
Bramall, Rebecca. Review of *Theories of Memory: A Reader*, edited by Michael Rossington and Anne Whitehead. *Memory Studies* 1 (2008) 341-43.
Branach-Kallas, Anna. "Carving the Names of 'Not-Persons': Ex-centric Perspectives on Community In Jane Urquhart's *The Stone Carvers*." *Central European Journal of Canadian Studies/Revue d'Études Canadiennes en Europe Centrale* 3 (2003) 65-74.

———. "Exploring the Dark Tunnels of Memory." In *Place and Memory in Canada: Global Perspectives*, edited by Magdalena Paluszkiewicz-Misiaczek et al., 59–68. Krakow: Polska Academia Umiejetnosci, 2005.

Brandon, Laura. *Art or Memorial? The Forgotten History of Canada's War Art*. Calgary: University of Calgary Press, 2006.

Brauner, David. "Breaking the Silences: Jewish-American Women Writing the Holocaust." *The Yearbook of English Studies* 31 (2001) 24–38.

Brockway, Allan, Paul van Buren, Rolf Rendtorff, and Simon Schoon, editors. *The Theology of the Churches and the Jewish People: Statements by the World Council of Churches and Its Member Churches*. Geneva: WCC, 1988.

Brown, Robert Craig, and Donald Loveridge. "Unrequited Faith: Recruiting the CEF 1914–1918." *Revue internationale d'histoire militaire* 54 (1982) 53–79.

Brumlik, Micha. "Post-Holocaust Theology: German Theological Responses since 1945." In *Betrayal*, edited by Ericksen and Heschel, 169–88. Minneapolis: Augsburg Fortress, 1999.

Burkert, Walter. *Homo Necans: The Anthropology of Ancient Greek Sacrificial Ritual and Myth*. Translated by Peter Bing. Berkeley: University of California Press, 1982.

Bushnell, Horace. *The Vicarious Sacrifice, Grounded in Principles Interpreted by Human Analogies*. Volume 1. New York: Scribner, Armstrong, & Co., 1877.

Butler, Judith. *Antigone's Claim: Kinship between Life & Death*. New York: Columbia University Press, 2000.

Campbell, Louise. "Towards a New Cathedral: The Competition for Coventry Cathedral 1950–51." *Architectural History* 35 (1992) 208–34.

Canadian Battlefields Memorials Commission. *Canadian Battlefield Memorials*. Ottawa: King's Printer, 1929.

Cargas, Harry James. *Shadows of Auschwitz: A Christian Response to the Holocaust*. Chestnut Ridge, NY: Crossroad, 1990.

Castelli, Elizabeth A. *Martyrdom and Memory: Early Christian Culture Making*. New York: Columbia University Press, 2004.

Cecil, Lamar. *Wilhelm II: Emperor and Exile, 1900–1941*. Chapel Hill, NC: University of North Carolina Press, 1996.

Chodoff, Paul. "The Holocaust and its Effects on Survivors: An Overview." *Political Psychology* 18.1 (1997) 146–57.

Clairmont, Christoph W. *Patrios Nomos: Public Burial in Athens during the Fifth and Fourth Centuries B.C.: The Archaeological, Epigraphic-literary and Historical Evidence*. Oxford: B.A.R., 1983.

Clark, Elizabeth A. *History, Theory, Text: Historians and the Linguistic Turn*. Cambridge: Harvard University Press, 2004.

Clark, Joseph. "The 'Sacred Names' of the Nation's Dead: War and Remembrance in Revolutionary France." In *Memory, Mourning, and Landscape*, edited by Elizabeth Anderson et al., 21–42. Amsterdam: Rodopi, 2010.

Closterman, Wendy E. "Family Members and Citizens: Athenian Identity and the Peribolos Tomb Setting." *Helios* 33S (2006) 49–78.

Cohn-Sherbok, Dan, editor. *Holocaust Theology: A Reader*. Exeter, UK: University of Exeter Press, 2002.

Collins Gallery. "Tim Davies: Cadet 31 March–5 May." Press release. Glasgow: 2006.

Commonwealth War Graves Commission. "The Structural Maintenance of the Commission's Cemeteries and Memorials." Maidenhead, UK: pamphlet, n.p., n.d.

Bibliography

Community of the Cross of Nails. "An Overview." Coventry Cathedral, Online: http://www.crossofnails.org/about/. Accessed 31 August 2009.

———. "Litany of Reconciliation." Coventry Cathedral, Online: http://www.crossofnails.org/litany/. Accessed 31 August 2009.

Connerton, Paul. *How Societies Remember*. Cambridge: Cambridge University Press, 1989.

Cook, Méira. "At the Membrane of Language and Silence: Metaphor and Memory in *Fugitive Pieces*." *Canadian Literature* 164 (2000) 12–33.

Coser, Lewis A. "The Revival of the Sociology of Culture: The Case of Collective Memory." *Sociological Forum* 7.2 (1992) 365–73.

Crane, Susan A. "Writing the Individual Back into Collective Memory." *The American Historical Review* 102.5 (1997) 1372–85.

Cremer, Douglas J. "Protestant Theology in Early Weimar Germany: Barth, Tillich, and Bultmann." *Journal of the History of Ideas* 56.2 (1995) 289–307.

Curl, James Stevens. *A Celebration of Death: An Introduction to Some of the Buildings, Monuments, and Settings of Funerary Architecture in the Western European Tradition*. London: Constable, 1980.

Davies, Alan T. *Anti-Semitism and the Christian Mind: The Crisis of Conscience after Auschwitz*. New York: Herder and Herder, 1969.

Davis, Stephen T. et al. *Encountering Evil: Live Options in Theodicy*. Edited by Stephen T. Davis. 2nd ed. Louisville: Westminster John Knox, 2001.

de Certeau, Michael. *The Writing of History*. Translated by Tom Conley. New York: Columbia University Press, 1988.

DeLaura, David J. "Anouilh's Other 'Antigone.'" *The French Review* 35.1 (1961) 36–41.

Derderian, Katherine. *Leaving Words to Remember: Greek Mourning and the Advent of Literacy*. Leiden: Brill, 2001.

Deutsch, Rosamund E. "Anouilh's Antigone." *The Classical Journal* 42.1 (1946) 14–17.

Diefendorf, Jeffrey M. *In the Wake of War: The Reconstruction of German Cities after World War II*. Oxford: Oxford University Press, 1993.

Dietrich, Donald J. *God and Humanity in Auschwitz: Christian-Jewish Relations and Sanctioned Murder*. New Brunswick, NJ: Transaction, 1995.

"Dominus Iesus." On the Unicity and Salvific Universality of Jesus Christ and the Church. Congregation for the Doctrine of the Faith, 6 August 2000. Online: http://www.vatican.va/roman_curia/congregations/cfaith/documents/rc_con_cfaith_doc_20000806_dominus-iesus_en.html.

Drain, Susan. "Community and the Individual in *Anne of Green Gables*: The Meaning of Belonging." *Children's Literature Association Quarterly* 11.1 (1986) 15–19.

Durflinger, Serge. "Safeguarding Sanctity: Canada and the Vimy Memorial during the Second World War." In *Vimy Ridge: A Canadian Reassessment*, edited by Geoffrey Hayes, Andrew Iarocci, and Mike Bechthold, 291–312. Waterloo, ON: Wilfrid Laurier University Press, 2007.

Durkheim, Émile. *The Elementary Forms of Religious Life*. 1915. Translated by J. W. Swain. New York: Free, 1965.

Echardt, A. Roy. "Jürgen Moltmann, the Jewish People, and the Holocaust." *Journal of the American Academy of Religion* 44.4 (1976) 675–91.

Edwards, Owen Dudley, and Jennifer H. Litster. "The End of Canadian Innocence: L. M. Montgomery and the First World War." In *L. M. Montgomery and Canadian Culture*, edited by Irene Gammel and Elizabeth Epperly, 31–48. Toronto: University of Toronto Press, 1999.

Eisen, Arnold M. *Galut: Modern Jewish Reflection on Homelessness and Homecoming.* Bloomington, IN: Indiana University Press, 1986.

Eisenman, Peter. "Memorial to the Murdered Jews of Europe." In *Materials on The Memorial to the Murdered Jews of Europe*, published by The Foundation for the Memorial to the Murdered Jews of Europe, 10–12. Berlin: Nicolai, 2005.

Eksteins, Modris. *Rites of Spring: The Great War and the Birth of the Modern Age.* Rev. ed. Boston: Mifflin, 2000.

Epperly, Elizabeth. *The Fragrance of Sweet Grass: L. M. Montgomery's Heroines and the Pursuit of Romance.* Toronto: University of Toronto Press, 1992.

Ericksen, Robert P., and Susannah Heschel, editors. *Betrayal: German Churches and the Holocaust.* Minneapolis: Fortress, 1999.

Evans, Suzanne. *Mothers of Heroes, Mothers of Martyrs: World War I and the Politics of Grief.* Montreal: McGill-Queen's University Press, 2007.

Ezrahi, Sidra DeKoven. *Booking Passage: Exile and Homecoming in the Modern Jewish Imagination.* Berkeley: University of California Press, 2000.

Fackenheim, Emil. *God's Presence in History: Jewish Affirmations and Philosophical Reflections.* New York: New York University Press, 1970.

———. *Quest for Past and Future: Essays in Jewish Theology.* Westport, CT: Greenwood, 1968.

———. *To Mend the World: Foundations of Post-Holocaust Jewish Thought.* 2nd ed. Bloomington: Indiana University Press, 1994.

Fasching, Darrell J., editor. *The Jewish People in Christian Preaching.* Lewiston, NY: Mellen, 1984

———. *Narrative Theology After Auschwitz: From Alienation to Ethics.* Minneapolis: Augsburg Fortress, 1992.

Ferrario, Sarah Brown. "Replaying *Antigone*: Changing patterns of Public and Private Commemoration at Athens c. 440–350." *Helios* 33S (2006) 79–117.

Filipczak, Dorota, editor. *Bringing Landscape Home in the Writings of Jane Urquhart.* Łodz, Poland: University of Łodz Press, 2009.

Fischer, Heidi. "Matthäuskirche (Church of St. Matthew), Pforzheim, 1951–53." In *Eiermann (1904–1970) Architect and Designer: The Continuity of Modernism*, edited by Annemarie Jaeggi, 156–59. Ostfildern, Germany: Hatje Cantz, 2004.

Foley, Barbara. "Fact, Fiction, Fascism: Testimony and Mimesis in Holocaust Narratives." *Comparative Literature* 34.4 (1982) 330–60.

Freud, Sigmund. *Moses and Monotheism.* Translated by Katherine Jones. London: Hogarth, 1939. Reprint. New York: Random House, 1996.

Fulbrook, Mary, and Martin Swales. *Representing the German Nation.* Manchester: Manchester University Press, 2000.

Fussell, Paul. *The Great War and Modern Memory.* Reprint. Oxford: Oxford University Press, 2000.

Gager, John G. *The Origins of Anti-Semitism: Attitudes towards Judaism in Pagan and Christian Antiquity.* Oxford: Oxford University Press, 1983.

Gammel, Irene. "Life Writing as Masquerade: The Many Faces of L. M. Montgomery." In *The Intimate Life of L. M. Montgomery*, edited by Irene Gammel, 3–15. Toronto: University of Toronto Press, 2005.

Bibliography

———. *Looking for Anne of Green Gables: The Story of L. M. Montgomery and Her Literary Classic*. New York: St. Martin's, 2008.

Garwood, Alfred. "The Holocaust and the Power of Powerlessness: Survivor Guilt in an Unhealed Wound." *British Journal of Psychotherapy* 13.2 (2007) 243–58.

Geertz, Clifford. *The Interpretation of Culture*. New York: Basic, 1973.

Gerlach, Erwin. *Berlin: Kaiser-Wilhelm-Gedachtnis-Kirche*. Translated by Katherine Vanovitch. Schnell Art Guide No. 2313. 5th ed. Regensburg, Germany: Schnell & Steiner, 2007.

Girard, René. *Violence and the Sacred*. Translated by Patrick Gregory. Baltimore: Johns Hopkins University Press, 1972.

Godin, Mark. *Discerning the Body: A Sacramental Hermeneutic in Literature and Liturgy*. Unpublished PhD thesis, University of Glasgow, 2009.

———. "Interfaith Monologue: The Presbyterian Church in Canada's Statement of Relationship with the Jewish People." In *Do I Know You? Religious Stereotyping and Interreligious Relations*, edited by Jesper Svartvik and Jakob Wiren. New York: Palgrave, forthcoming 2013.

Goertz, Karein. "Transgenerational Representations of the Holocaust: From Memory to 'Post-Memory.'" *World Literature Today* 72.1 (1998) 33–38.

Goldhagen, Daniel. *Hitler's Willing Executioners: Ordinary Germans and the Holocaust*. New York: Vintage, 1997.

Goldhill, Simon. "Civic Ideology and the Problem of Difference: The Politics of Aeschylean Tragedy, Once Again." *The Journal of Hellenic Studies* 120 (2000) 34–56.

———. *The Orestia*. Cambridge: Cambridge University Press, 2004.

Goldy, Robert G. *The Emergence of Jewish Theology in America*. Bloomington, IN: Indiana University Press, 1990.

Granatstein, J. L., and J. M. Hitsman. *Broken Promises: A History of Conscription in Canada*. Toronto: Oxford University Press, 1977.

Green, Arthur. *These are the Words: A Vocabulary of Jewish Spiritual Life*. Woodstock, VT: Jewish Lights, 1999.

Greene-McCreight, Kathryn. *Feminist Reconstructions of Christian Doctrine: Narrative Analysis and Appraisal*. Oxford: Oxford University Press, 2000.

Griffith, Mark. "Introduction" and "Commentary." In *Antigone*, by Sophocles, edited by Mark Griffith, 1–69, 119–355. Cambridge: Cambridge University Press, 1999.

Hake, Sabine. *Topographies of Class: Modern Architecture and Mass Society in Weimar Berlin*. Ann Arbor, MI: University of Michigan Press, 2008.

Halbwachs, Maurice. *The Collective Memory*. Translated by Mary Douglas. New York: Harper & Row, 1980.

———. *On Collective Memory*. Edited and translated by Lewis A. Coser. Chicago: University of Chicago Press, 1992.

———. "Individual Consciousness and Collective Mind." *The American Journal of Sociology* 44.6 (1930) 812–22.

———. "Individual Psychology and Collective Psychology." *American Sociological Review* 3.5 (1938) 615–23.

Hall, Douglas John. *Professing the Faith: Christian Theology in a North American Context*. Minneapolis; Fortress, 1993.

———. *Thinking the Faith: Christian Theology in a North American Context*. Minneapolis: Fortress, 1991.

Hampson, Margaret Daphne. *Theology and Feminism*. Oxford: Blackwell, 1990.

Hauerwas, Stanley. "Christianity: It's Not a Religion: It's an Adventure (1991)." In *The Hauerwas Reader*, edited by John Berkman and Michael Cartwright, 522–35. Durham, NC: Duke University Press, 2001.

Hayes, Geoffrey, Andrew Iarocci, Mike Bechthold, editors. *Vimy Ridge: A Canadian Reassessment*. Waterloo, ON: Wilfrid Laurier University Press, 2007.

Haynes, Stephen R. *Prospects for Post-Holocaust Theology*. Atlanta: Scholars, 1991.

———. *Reluctant Witness: Jews and the Christian Imagination*. Louisville, KY: Westminster John Knox, 1995.

Heiney, Donald. "Jean Anouilh: The Revival of Tragedy." *College English* 16.6 (1955) 331–35.

Held, George F. "Antigone's Dual Motivation for the Double Burial." *Hermes* 111.2 (1983) 190–201.

Herbert, James D. "Bad Faith at Coventry: Spence's Cathedral and Britten's *War Requiem*." *Critical Inquiry* 25.3 (1999) 535–65.

Hervieu-Léger, Danièle. *Religion as a Chain of Memory*. Translated by Simon Lee. Cambridge: Polity, 2000.

Heschel, Susannah, editor. *On Being a Jewish Feminist*. Rev. ed. New York: Schocken, 1995.

Hillger, Annick. "'Afterbirth of Earth': Messianic Materialism in Anne Michaels' *Fugitive Pieces*." *Canadian Literature* 160 (1999) 28–45.

Hirsch, Marianne. *Family Frames: Photography, Narrative and Postmemory*. Cambridge: Harvard University Press, 1997.

———. "The Generation of Postmemory." *Poetics Today* 29.1 (2008) 103–28.

Hirst, William, and David Manier. "Towards a Psychology of Collective Memory." *Memory* 16.3 (2008) 183–200.

Hockenos, Matthew D. *A Church Divided: German Protestants Confront the Nazi Past*. Bloomington, IN: Indiana University Press, 2004.

Holst-Warhaft, Gail. *Dangerous Voices: Women's Laments and Greek Literature*. London: Routledge, 1992.

Holt, Philip. "Polis and Tragedy in the 'Antigone.'" *Mnemosyne* 52.6 (1999) 658–90.

Horowitz, Elliott. *Reckless Rites: Purim and the Legacy of Jewish Violence*. Princeton, NJ: Princeton University Press, 2006.

Hucker, Jacqueline. "'After the Agony in Stony Places': The Meaning and Significance of the Vimy Monument." In *Vimy Ridge: A Canadian Reassessment*, edited by Geoffrey Hayes, Andrew Iarocci, and Mike Bechthold, 279–90. Waterloo, ON: Wilfrid Laurier University Press, 2007.

Hurst, John E. "John McCrae's Wars." In *Canada and the Great War: Western Front Association Papers*, edited by Briton C. Busch, 66–77. Montreal: McGill-Queen's University Press, 2003.

Hutton, Patrick H. "Recent Scholarship on Memory and History." *The History Teacher* 33.4 (2000) 533–48.

———. "Sigmund Freud and Maurice Halbwachs: The Problem of Memory in Historical Psychology." *The History Teacher* 27.2 (1994) 145–58.

Hynes, Samuel. *A War Imagined: The First World War and English Culture*. New York: Atheneum, 1991.

Idelsohn, A. Z. *Jewish Liturgy and its Development*. New York: Holt, 1932.

Idinopulos, Thomas A. *Betrayal of Spirit: Jew-hatred, the Holocaust, and Christianity*. Aurora, CO: The Davies Group, 2007.

Isherwood, Lisa. *Introducing Feminist Christologies*. London: Continuum, 2007.

Bibliography

Jacobs, Louis. *Judaism and Theology: Essays on the Jewish Religion*. London: Mitchell, 2005.

Jaeggi, Annemari. "Chancery of the German Embassy, Washington, D.C., 1958–64." In *Eiermann (1904–1970) Architect and Designer: The Continuity of Modernism*, edited by Annemari Jaeggi, 186–87. Ostfildern, Germany: Hatje Cantz, 2004.

———, editor. *Egon Eiermann (1904–1970) Architect and Designer: The Continuity of Modernism*. Ostfildern, Germany: Hatje Cantz, 2004.

Joseph, Gerhard. "The Antigone as Cultural Touchstone: Matthew Arnold, Hegel, George Eliot, Virginia Woolf, and Margaret Drabble." *Proceedings of the Modern Language Association* 96.1 (1981) 22–35.

Kabierske, Gerhard. "(Kaiser Wilhelm Memorial Church) Berlin, 1956–63." In *Eiermann (1904–1970) Architect and Designer: The Continuity of Modernism*, edited by Annemarie Jaeggi, 172–77. Ostfildern, Germany: Hatje Cantz, 2004.

Katz, Steven T., editor. *The Impact of the Holocaust on Jewish Theology*. New York: New York University Press, 2005.

———. *Post-Holocaust Dialogues: Critical Studies in Modern Jewish Thought*. New York: New York University Press, 1983.

Katz, Steven T., Shlomo Biderman, and Gershon Greenberg, editors. *Wrestling with God: Jewish Theological Responses during and after the Holocaust*. Oxford: Oxford University Press, 2007.

Kelly, Geffrey B., and F. Burton Nelson. *The Cost of Moral Leadership: The Spirituality of Dietrich Bonhoeffer*. Grand Rapids: Eerdmans, 2002.

Kennedy, Rebecca Futo. *Athena's Justice: Athena, Athens, and the Concept of Justice in Greek Tragedy*. Bern: Lang, 2009.

Kertzer, Adrienne. "*Fugitive Pieces*: Listening as a Holocaust Survivor's Child." *English Studies in Canada* 26.2 (2000) 193–217.

Kieser, Clemens. "Hardenberg Private Residence, Baden-Baden, 1958–60." In *Eiermann (1904–1970) Architect and Designer: The Continuity of Modernism*, edited by Annemarie Jaeggi, 178–81. Ostfildern, Germany: Hatje Cantz, 2004.

Kilian, Crawford. *The Great War and the Canadian Novel, 1915–1926*. MA Thesis, Simon Fraser University, 1972.

King, Nicola. *Memory, Narrative, Identity: Remembering the Self*. Edinburgh: Edinburgh University Press, 2000.

Kluckhohn, Clyde. "Myth and Rituals: A General Theory." *Harvard Theological Review* 35 (1942). Reprinted as a booklet. Indianapolis: Bobbs-Merril, 1962.

Koshar, Rudy. *From Monuments to Traces: Artifacts of German Memory, 1870–1990*. Berkeley: University of California Press, 2000.

Kübler-Ross, Elisabeth. *On Death and Dying*. London: Tavistock, 1973.

Kurts, Donna C., and John Boardman. *Greek Burial Customs*. Ithaca, NY: Cornell University Press, 1971.

Ladd, Brian. *The Ghosts of Berlin: Confronting German History in the Urban Landscape*. Chicago: University of Chicago Press, 1997.

Lang, Kurt. "Review: How the Past Lives On." *Contemporary Sociology* 22.4 (1993) 596–600.

Langston, Scott M. *Exodus through the Centuries*. Oxford: Wiley-Blackwell, 2006.

Laytner, Anson. *Arguing with God: A Jewish Tradition*. Lanham, MI: Rowman & Littlefield, 1990.

Levin, Itamar. *His Majesty's Enemies: Great Britain's War against Holocaust Victims and Survivors.* Translated by Natasha Dornberg and Judith Yalon-Fortus. Westport, CT: Greenwood, 2001.
Levinas, Emmanuel. *In the Time of the Nations.* Translated by Michael B. Smith. Bloomington, IN: Indiana University Press, 1994.
Levitt, Laura. *American Jewish Loss after the Holocaust.* New York: New York University Press, 2007.
Link, Arthur S. Review of *The Papers of Woodrow Wilson: Volume 35: October 1, 1915–January 27, 1916. The Journal of Southern History* 49.2 (1983) 318–19.
Littell, Franklin. *The Crucifixion of the Jews: The Failure of Christians to Understand the Jewish Experience.* New York: Harper & Row, 1975.
Locke, John. *An Essay Concerning Human Understanding.* Edited and abridged by John W. Yolton. London: Everyman, 1993.
Longworth, Philip. *The Unending Vigil: A History of the Commonwealth War Graves Commission 1917–1984.* London: Cooper, 1985.
Loraux, Nicole. *The Invention of Athens.* Translated by Alan Sheridan. Cambridge: Harvard University Press, 1986.
Maciejewski, Paul K., Baohui Zhang, Susan D. Block, and Holly G. Prigerson. "An Empirical Examination of the Stage Theory of Grief." *Journal of the American Medical Association* 297.7 (2007) 716–23.
MacKay, L. A. "Antigone, Coriolanus, and Hegel." *Transactions and Proceedings of the American Philological Association* 93 (1962) 166–74.
Marteinson, John. *We Stand on Guard: An Illustrated History of the Canadian Army.* Montreal: Ovale, 1992.
Marx, Karl. *The Eighteenth Brumaire of Louis Bonaparte.* New York: 1852 (original German language publication). Translator unknown. New York: International, 1963.
Maus, Marcel. *The Gift: Forms and Functions of Exchange in Arabic Societies.* Translated by Ian Cunnison. New York: Norton, 1967.
Mayer, Arno J. *The Persistence of the Old Regime: Europe to the Great War.* London: Croom Helm, 1981.
McClymond, Kathryn. *Beyond Sacred Violence: A Comparative Study of Sacrifice.* Baltimore: The Johns Hopkins University Press 2008.
McGarry, Michael B. "The Path to a Journey." In *Faith Transformed: Christian Encounters with Jews and Judaism,* edited by John C. Merkle and Walter J. Harrelson, 144–61. Collegeville, MN: Liturgical, 2003.
Migliore, Daniel. *Faith Seeking Understanding: An Introduction to Christian Theology.* Grand Rapids: Eerdmans, 1991.
Misztal, Barbara A. *Theories of Social Remembering.* Maidenhead, UK: Open University Press, 2003.
Mitchell, Bruce, and Fred C. Robinson. *A Guide to Old English.* 5th ed. Oxford: Blackwell, 1992.
Moltmann, Jürgen. *The Crucified God: The Cross of Christ as the Foundation and Criticism of Christian Theology.* Translated by R. A. Wilson and John Bowden. Minneapolis: Fortress, 1993.
Montgomery, L. M. *The Alpine Path: The Story of My Career.* 1917. Reprint. Markham, ON: Fitzhenry & Whiteside, 1997.
———. *The Selected Journals of L. M. Montgomery, Volume II: 1910–1921.* Edited by Mary Rubio, and Elizabeth Waterston. Toronto: Oxford University Press, 1987.

Bibliography

The Montreal Holocaust Memorial Centre. <http://www.mhmc.ca/en> Accessed 25 November 2009.

Morgan, Michael L. *Beyond Auschwitz: Post-Holocaust Jewish Thought in America*. Oxford: Oxford University Press 2001.

Morton, Desmond. *Marching to Armageddon*. Toronto: Lester & Orpen, 1989.

———. *When Your Number's Up: The Canadian Soldier in the First World War*. Toronto: Random House, 1994.

Motyer, Stephen. "Bridging the Gap: How Might the Fourth Gospel Help Us Cope with the Legacy of Christianity's Exclusive Claim over against Judaism?" In *The Gospel of John and Christian Theology*, edited by Richard Bauckham and Carl Mosser, 143–67. Grand Rapids: Eerdmans, 2008.

Nagy, Gregory. *The Best of the Achaeans: Concepts of the Hero in Archaic Greek Poetry*. Baltimore: The Johns Hopkins University Press, 1979.

Nelson, F. Burton. "The Life of Dietrich Bonhoeffer." In *The Cambridge Companion to Dietrich Bonhoeffer*, edited by John W. deGruchy, 22–49. Cambridge: Cambridge University Press, 1999.

Niebuhr, H. Richard. *Christ and Culture*. 1951. 2nd ed. San Francisco: HarperSanFrancisco, 2001.

Nietzsche, Friedrich. "On the Uses and Disadvantages of History for Life" [1874]. Translated by R. J. Hollingdale. In *Untimely Meditations*, edited by Daniel Breazale, 57–124. Cambridge: Cambridge University Press, 1997.

Nora, Pierre. "Between Memory and History: Les Lieux de Mémoire." Translated by Marc Roudebush. *Representations* 26 (1989) 7–24.

———, editor. *Les Lieux de Mémoire*. Volume 1 of 3. Paris : Gallimard, 1984.

———, editor. *Realms of Memory: Rethinking the French Past*. Volume 1 of 3. Edited by Lawrence D. Kritzman. Translated by Arthur Goldhammer. New York : Columbia University Press, 1996.

Nostra Aetate: Declaration of the Relation of the Church to Non-Christian Religions. Vatican II, 28 October 1965.

O'Brien, Joan V. *Guide to Sophocles' Antigone: A Student Edition with Commentary, Grammatical Notes, & Vocabulary*. Carbondale, IL: Southern Illinois University Press, 1978.

Olick, Jeffrey K. *The Politics of Regret: On Collective Memory and Historical Responsibility*. New York: Routledge, 2007.

Pächter, Henry Maximilian. *Weimar etudes*. New York: Columbia University Press, 1982.

Page, Max. "The Life and Death of a Document: Lessons from the Strange Career of *The Diary of Anne Frank*." *The Public Historian* 21.1 (1999) 87–97.

Parfit, Derek. *Reasons and Persons*. Oxford: Clarendon, 1984.

Patterson, Cynthia B. "The Place and Practice of Burial in Sophocles' Athens." *Helios* 33S (2006) 9–48.

Perry, Joseph B. "The Madonna of Stalingrad: Mastering the (Christmas) Past and West German National Identity after World War II." *Radical History Review* 83 (2007) 7–27.

Pieren, Kathrin. "'Being Jewish is More than the Holocaust Experience': What Visitors See at the Jewish Museum Berlin." *Social History in Museums* 29 (2004) 79–85.

Plaskow, Judith. *Standing Again at Sinai: Judaism from a Feminist Perspective*. New York: HarperCollins, 1991.

Bibliography

The Presbyterian Church in Canada. *The Acts and Proceedings of the 40th General Assembly of The Presbyterian Church in Canada*. Toronto, 1914.

———. *The Acts and Proceedings of the 41st General Assembly of The Presbyterian Church in Canada*. Toronto, 1915.

Pritchett, W. Kendrick. *The Greek State at War*, Part IV. Berkeley: University of California Press, 1985.

Raphael, Melissa. *The Female Face of God in Auschwitz: A Jewish Feminist Theology of the Holocaust*. London: Routledge, 2003.

Rehm, Rush. *Marriage to Death: The Conflation of Wedding and Funeral Rituals in Greek Tragedy*. Princeton, NJ: Princeton University Press, 1994.

Reichberg, Gregory M., Henrik Syse, and Endre Begby, editors. *The Ethics of War: Classic and Contemporary Readings*. Oxford: Blackwell, 2006.

Retallack, James N. *Imperial Germany 1871–1918*. Oxford: Oxford University Press, 2008.

Rickards, Maurice, and Michael Moody. *The First World War: Ephemera, Mementos, Documents*. London: Jupiter, 1975.

Ricoeur, Paul. "Life in Quest of Narrative." Translated by David Wood. In *On Paul Ricoeur: Narrative and Interpretation*, edited by David Wood, 20–33. London: Routledge, 1991.

———. *Memory, History, Forgetting*. Translated by Kathleen Blamey and David Pellauer. Chicago: University of Chicago Press, 2004.

———. "Narrative Identity." Translated by David Wood. In *On Paul Ricoeur: Narrative and Interpretation*, edited by David Wood, 188–99. London: Routledge, 1991.

Rike, Jennifer L. Review of *Facing the Abusing God: A Theology of Protest* by David R. Blumenthal. *Journal of the American Academy of Religion* 65.1 (1997) 206–9.

Rittner, Carol, and John K. Roth, editors. *"Good News" After Auschwitz? Christian Faith within a Post-Holocaust World*. Macon, GA: Mercer University Press, 2001.

Rosenfeld, Alvin H. *The Writer Uprooted: Contemporary Jewish Exile Literature*. Bloomington, IN: Indiana University Press, 2008.

Rosenfeld, David G. "A Flawed Prophecy? Zakhor, the Memory Boom, and the Holocaust." *Jewish Quarterly Review* 97.4 (2007) 508–20.

Rossington, Michael, and Anne Whitehead, editors. *Theories of Memory: A Reader*. Edinburgh: Edinburgh University Press, 2007.

Roth, John K., and Richard Rubenstein. *Approaches to Auschwitz: The Holocaust and its Legacy*. Louisville: Westminster John Knox, 2003.

———. *The Politics of Latin American Liberation Theology: The Challenge to U.S. Public Policy*. Washington, DC: Washington Institute Press, 1988.

Rubenstein, Richard, *After Auschwitz: Radical Theology and Contemporary Judaism*. Indianapolis, IN: Bobbs-Merrill, 1966.

Ruether, Rosemary Radford. *Faith and Fratricide: The Theological Roots of Anti-Semitism*. New York: Seabury, 1974.

Sancton, Andrew. *Governing the Island of Montreal: Language Differences and Metropolitan Politics*. Berkley: University of California Press, 1985.

Sawyer, Deborah F. "Gender." In *The Blackwell Companion to the Bible and Culture*, edited by John F. A. Sawyer, 464–79. Oxford: Wiley-Blackwell, 2006.

Scarry, Elaine. *The Body in Pain: The Making and Unmaking of the World*. New York: Oxford University Press, 1985.

Schechtman, Marya. *The Constitution of Selves*. Ithaca, NY: Cornell University Press, 1996.

Schlesinger, Alfred C. "Anouilh's Antigone Again." *The Classical Journal* 42.4 (1947) 207–9.

Bibliography

Schneider, Rolf. *The Jewish Museum, Berlin*. Die Neuen Architekutführer 2. 1999. Reprint. Berlin: Stadtwandel, 2002.
School Visits Team, Coventry Cathedral. "Coventry Cathedral Virtual Tour: Millennium Chapel." Online: http://coventrycathedraltour.org.uk/node.php?n=millennium_chapel#. Accessed 29 August 2009.
Schwartz, Bill. "Memory." In *New Keywords: A Revised Vocabulary of Culture and Society*, edited by Tony Bennett, Lawrence Grossberg, and Meghan Morris, 214–17. Oxford: Blackwell, 2005.
Service Personell & Veterans Agency (An Executive Agency of the Ministry of Defense, UK). Biography of Major General Sir Fabian Ware. Online: http://www.veterans-uk.info/remembrance/ware.html. Accessed 3 July 2009.
Shipley, Robert. *To Mark Our Place: A History of Canadian War Memorials*. Toronto: NC Press, 1987.
Sieverts, Thomas. *Cities Without Cities: Between Place and World, Space and Time, Town and Country*. Translated by Daniel de Lough. London: Routledge, 2003.
Signer, Michael A., editor. *Memory and History in Christianity and Judaism*. Notre Dame, IN: University of Notre Dame Press, 2001.
Sinder, Amy J., Nancy S. Wellman, and Oren Baruch Stier. "Holocaust Survivors Report Long-Term Effects on Attitudes towards Food." *Journal of Nutrition Education and Behaviour* 36.4 (2004) 189–200.
Smiga, George M. *Pain and Polemic: Anti-Judaism in the Gospels*. Mahwah, NJ: Paulist, 1992.
Soelle, Dorothee. *Suffering*. Translated by Everett Kalin. Minneapolis: Fortress, 1975.
Sourvinou-Inwood, Christiane. "Assumptions and the Creation of Meaning: Reading Sophocles' Antigone." *The Journal of Hellenic Studies* 109 (1989) 134–48.
Stallings, Douglas, editor. *Fodor's Eastern and Central Europe*, 21st ed. New York: Fodor's, 2008
Steiner, George. *Antigones: The Antigone Myth in Western Literature, Art and Thought*. Oxford: Oxford University Press, 1984.
Stiftung Denkmal für die ermordeten Juden Europas. "The Design Concept for the Information Centre." No pages. Online: <http://www.denkmal-fuer-die-ermordeten-juden-europas.org/en/thememorial/informationcentre/design>. Accessed 16 October 2009.
Swift, Louis J. *The Early Fathers on War and Military Service*. Wilmington, DE: Glazier, 1983.
Tanner, Kathryn. *Theories of Culture: A New Agenda for Theology*. Minneapolis: Fortress, 1997.
Taylor, Miriam S. *Anti-Judaism and Early Christian Identity: A Critique of the Scholarly Consensus*. Leiden: Brill, 1994.
Thucydides. *History of the Peloponnesian War*. In *Thucydides* vol. I, Loeb Classical Library. Edited and translated by Charles Forster Smith. London: Heinemann, 1928.
Tickle, Phyllis. *God-Talk in America*. New York: Crossroad, 1998.
Tippett, Maria. *Art at the Service of War: Canada, Art, and the Great War*. Toronto: University of Toronto Press, 1984.
Toher, Mark. "On 'Thucydides' Blunder': 2.34.5." *Hermes* 127.4 (1999) 497–501.
Torczyner, Jim L., and Shary L. Brotman. "The Jews of Canada: A Profile from the Census." American Jewish Committee, 1995. Online: http://www.bjpa.org/Publications/downloadPublication.cfm?PublicationID=3179. Accessed 25 November 2009.

Bibliography

Turner, Victor. *The Ritual Process: Structure and Anti-Structure.* Ithaca, NY: Cornell University Press, 1969.

Tyler, Edward B. *Primitive Culture: Research into the Development of Mythology, Philosophy, Religion, Language, Art, and Custom.* Volume 1. 2nd ed. London: Murray, 1873.

Tyrrell, Wm. Blake, and Larry J. Bennett. *Recapturing Sophocles' Antigone.* Lanham, MD: Rowman & Littlefield, 1998.

Urquhart, Jane. Interview by Linda Richards. *January Magazine* (June 2001). Online: http://januarymagazine.com/profiles/urquhart.html. Accessed 22 August 2009.

Vance, Jonathan F. *Death So Noble: Memory, Meaning, and the First World War.* Vancouver: UBC, 1997.

Vincent, Alana. "Seder and Imagined Landscape." In *Memory, Mourning and Landscape*, edited by Elizabeth Anderson et al., 147–63. Amsterdam: Rodopi, 2010.

Vitoria, Francisco. *Political Writings.* Edited and translated by Anthony Pagden and Jeremy Lawrence. Cambridge: Cambridge University Press, 1991.

Volf, Miroslav. *The End of Memory: Remembering Rightly in a Violent World.* Grand Rapids: Eerdmans, 2006.

Verdery, Katherine. *The Political Lives of Dead Bodies: Reburial and Postsocialist Change.* New York: Columbia University Press, 1999.

Walzer, Michael. *Exodus and Revolution.* New York: Basic, 1985.

Ward, Janet. *Weimar Surfaces: Urban Visual Culture in 1920s Germany.* Berkeley: University of California Press, 2001.

Ware, Fabian. "Introduction." In *The Silent Cities*, by Sidney C. Hurst. London: Methuen 1929.

Watson, Janet S. K. *Fighting Different Wars: Experience, Memory, and the First World War in Britain.* Cambridge: Cambridge University Press, 2004.

Wheeler, Michael. *Death and the Future Life in Victorian Literature and Theology.* Cambridge: Cambridge University Press, 1990.

Wiesel, Eli. *All Rivers Run to the Sea: Memoirs.* New York: Schocken, 1995.

Wildman, Wesley J. *Fidelity with Plausibility: Modest Christologies in the Twentieth Century.* Albany, NY: SUNY, 1998.

Wilkinson, Alan. *The Church of England and the First World War.* London: SPCK, 1978.

Williams, Raymond. *Keywords: A Vocabulary of Culture and Society.* New York: Oxford University Press, 1983.

Williamson, Clark M. *A Guest in the House of Israel: Post-Holocaust Church Theology.* Louisville, KY: Westminster John Knox, 1993.

Winter, Jay. *Remembering War: The Great War between Memory and History in the Twentieth Century.* New Haven, CT: Yale University Press, 2006.

Winter, Jay, and Emmanuel Sivan. *War and Remembrance in the Twentieth Century.* Cambridge: Cambridge University Press, 1999.

Wyschogrod, Michael. "Faith and the Holocaust." *Judaism* 20.3 (1971) 286–94.

Yates, Nigel. *Liturgical Space: Christian Worship and Church Buildings in Western Europe 1500–2000.* Aldershot, UK: Ashgate, 2008.

Yerushalmi, Yosef Hayim. *Zakhor: Jewish History and Jewish Memory.* Seattle: University of Washington Press, 1982.

Index

Aaron (biblical character), 16
Aciman, André, vi
Adler, Rachel, 161n70
Aeschlyus, 33n2
Agag (biblical character), 5, 12n5
Albinus, Lars, 42n36
Allward, Hugh, 85n8
Allward, Walter, 7, 83–87, 89,
    90n22, 98–104, 111, 113–14,
    126n17, 127
Amalek, ix, 4–6, 11–32, 111, 171
Anacharsis (character), 32, 38n26
Anderson, Benedict, 2n4
Anderson, Elizabeth, 64n47
Anderson, Greg, 34n8
Anouilh, Jean, ix, 33, 38n26, 41–43
Antigone (character), 4, 6, 32–33,
    34n10, 35, 37–44, 74n85, 75,
    104, 105n47, 109
Aristotle, 20, 136
Athos (character), 152–53, 167
Augustine of Hippo, 135

Balaam (biblical character), 12n5
Barnett, Victoria, 125n13
Barth, Karl, 130n29
Barthélémy, Jacques, 32, 38n26
Baum, Gregory, 129n28, 131n34
Becker, Klara (character), 44, 74n85,
    100–109, 143
Becker, Tilman (character),
    100–101, 108n55

Beer, Bella (character), 141, 153–54,
    167
Beer, Jakob (character), 152–54,
    167–68
Beer, Michaela (character), 141,
    153–54, 167
Ben (character), 154–55, 160,
    163–66, 168
Benjamin, Walter, 21, 31
Bennett, Larry J., 34n6, 35–36,
    37n20, 38n24, 39n28, 40n31,
    43n38
Bentley, D. M. R., 167n98
Bergson, Henri, 21
Berkovits, Eliezer, 145
Berliner, David C., 29n58
Berry, Edmund G., 41n34
Berton, Pierre, 83n3
Bethge, Eberhard, 125n13
Bialystok, Franklin, 158n59
Bloch, Marc, 27
Blumenthal, David, 8, 133n38,
    147–52, 155–56, 161–62
Blumenthal, W. Michael, 119n2
Blythe, Anne [née Shirley] (character), 54–64, 67, 70, 73–75, 80,
    101n30, 143, 158, 168
Blythe, Gilbert (character), 53,
    59–61, 63, 101n30
Blythe, Jem, 71, 80
Blythe, Rilla (character), 63–64,
    66–74, 105n47, 143

Index

Blythe, Walter (character), 64–67, 69–74, 80, 83, 105b
Boardman, John, 42n36
Bonaparte, Louis, 22
Bonhoeffer, Dietrich, 125
Bordon, Robert, 88
Boyden, Joseph, 102n34
Braiterman, Zachary, 144–47
Bramall, Rebecca, 20n29
Branach-Kallas, Anna, 100n28, 101n33, 109n56
Brandon, Laura, 83n4, 86n10, 90n21, 99n26
Brauner, David, 163n75
Brockway, Allan, 129
Brooke, Rupert, 64
Brotman, Shary L., 158n59
Brown, Robert Craig, 57n23, 88n18
Brumlik, Micha, 130n30
Buber, Martin, 145n11, 156n54
Buren, Paul van, 130n29
Bushnell, Horace, 68–69
Butler, Judith, 34n10, 37n21, 39n28

Campbell, Louise, 139n66
Cargas, Harry James, 129n27, 130n30
Castelli, Elizabeth A., 25n47, 26n48, 27n53
Cecil, Lamar, 125n11
Chaucer, 23n36
Childs, Brevard, 4n15, 13n7, 14–15, 27
Cicero, 20
Clairmont, Christoph, 34
Clark, Elizabeth A., 30n64
Closterman, Wendy E., 36n18
Cohen, Arthur, 145
Cohn-Sherbok, Dan, 145n11
Connerton, Paul, 24–31
Cook, Méira, 167n98
Coser, Lewis A., 24, 26n48
Craigie, Peter C., 13n7, 16n18
Crane, Susan A., 23n37, 26n48

Cremer, Douglas J., 49n5
Creon (character), 33, 35, 37–43, 104
Curl, James Steven, 74n87
Cuthbert, Marilla (character), 54–56
Cuthbert, Matthew (character), 53–56, 60–62, 67, 73–75

Davies, Alan T., 129n28
Davies, G. Henton, 13n7
Davies, Tim, 114–15
Davis, Stephen T., 133n39, 134–36
de Certeau, Michael, 30n64
Derderian, Katherine, 35n14
Descartes, René, 21
Deutsch, Rosamund E., 41n33
Dibelius, 138
Diefendorf, Jeffrey M., 126n18
Dietrich, Donald J., 131n36
Driver, S. R., 12n7
Driver, Tom, 132n36
Durflinger, Serge, 113n1
Durkheim, Emilé, 24

Echardt, A. Roy, 129n26
Edwards, Owen Dudley, 52n6, 57n22, 58n28, 64n45
Eiermann, Egon, 126–27
Eisenman, Peter, 123
Eksteins, Modris, 125n11
Epperly, Elizabeth, 63n44, 70n66
Ericksen, Robert P., 130n30
Eslinger, Lyle, 14n8
Eteocles (character), 37–38, 42–43
Evans, Suzanne, 69n63, 70, 85n9, 90n22
Ezrahi, Sidra, 2

Fackenheim, Emil, 30n65, 145–46
Farley, Wendy, 149–51
Fasching, Darrell J., 129n27
Ferguson, James, 78n102
Ferrario, Sarah Brown, 35n14, 36n16, 37n20

Index

Ford, Kenneth (character), 63–64, 70
Fox, Everett, 4n15
Freud, Sigmund, 21, 24
Fulbrook, Mary, 125n12
Fussell, Paul, 60n36, 65

Gager, John G., 131n36
Galantière, Lewis, 41, 42n35, 43n37
Gammel, Irene, 52n6, 54, 55n12, 67
Garwood, Alfred, 153
Gerlach, Erwin, 138n59
Gil, Eliana, 149
Gillis, Ruby (character), 53, 57–61, 73
Ginzberg, Louis, 16–17
Godin, Mark, 142n2, 154n43
Goebbels, Joseph, 126
Goertz, Karein, 143n4
Goldhagen, Daniel, 130n31
Goldhill, Simon, 32, 33n2, 37n20
Granatstein, J. L., 70n69, 87n15, 88n17, 89n20
Greenberg, Irving, 145
Greene-McCreight, Kathryn, 132n36
Griffin, David Ray, 136–37
Griffith, Mark, 34n10, 35n14, 38n25, 40n30
Gustafson, James M., 132n36

Haemon (character), 32, 39n26, 43
Hake, Sabine, 125n12
Halbwachs, Maurice, 24–31
Hall, Douglas John, 132n36
Haman (biblical character), 5, 12n5, 15n13, 30n65
Hammer, Reuven, 3n12
Hampson, Daphne, 131n36
Hartshorne, Charles, 136
Hauerwas, Stanley, 3n10
Hayes, Geoffrey, 83n3, 88n19
Haynes, Stephen R., 129n28, 130n29
Hegel, 20, 34n

Hegel, 34n10
Heiney, Donald, 43n39
Hemingway, Ernest, 53n7
Hemmeter, Karl, 137
Hendel, Ronald, 12n4
Herbert, James D., 139n65
Hershman, Abraham, 12n6, 74n87
Hervieu-Léger, Danièle, 25n47
Heschel, Abraham Joshua, 145n11
Heschel, Susannah, 130n30, 161n70
Hick, John, 134–37
Hillger, Annick, 167n98
Hirsch, Marianne, 31, 143
Hirsch, Samson Raphael, 16, 17n22
Hirst, William, 26n48
Hitler, Adolf, 30n65, 126, 138, 146
Hitsman, J. M., 70n69, 87n15, 88n17, 89n20
Hockenos, Matthew D., 126
Hodgkins, Jack, 102n34
Hoffman, Lawrence A., 3n9, 148n20
Holst-Warhaft, Gail, 35n13
Holt, Philip, 40n32
Horowitz, Elliott, 12n5, 18n23, 19n26
Hucker, Jacqueline, 99n26
Hume, David, 20
Hurst, John E., 65n51
Hutton, Patrick H., 24n40, 26n48
Hynes, Samuel, 53n7, 74n87, 85n9

Idinopulos, Thomas, 131n36
Irenaeus, 134
Irigaray, Luce, 34n10
Ismene (character), 37, 39

Jacobi, Gerhard, 125
Jacobs, Louis, 106n48
Johnstone, William D., 12n7
Joshua (biblical character), 16, 27

Kabierske, Gerhard, 126n, 127n19
Kadishman, Menashe, 121–22
Katz, Steven T., 144–47

191

Index

Kelly, Geffrey B., 125n13
Kennedy, Rebecca Futo, 33n4
Kertzer, Adrienne, 154, 167
Kilian, Crawford, 53n7
King, Nicola, 1n1, 109, 167n98
Koitz, Zvi, 145n11
Koshar, Rudy, 125n10, 126n15, 138n61
Kurts, Donna C., 42n36

Lacan, Jacques, 34n10
Ladd, Brian, 126n18
Lang, Kurt, 26n48
Langston, Scott M., 125n13
Levin, Itamar, 130n31
Levinas, Emmanuel, 4, 156n54
Levitsky, Maya (character), 143, 152, 157–60, 163–66, 168
Levitt, Laura, 31, 124n8
Libeskind, Daniel, 119, 121, 123
Litster, Jennifer H., 52n6, 57n22, 58n28, 64n45
Littell, Franklin, 129n27
Locke, John, 20, 136n50
Loire, Gabriel, 138n58
Longworth, Philip, 47, 48n1, 74n88, 76n94
Loraux, Nicole, 37n19
Loveridge, Donald, 57n23, 88n18
Luria, Isaac, 17
Lynde, Rachel (character), 54–57, 61
Lynde, Thomas (character), 53, 55–56, 60–61

Macaulay, Thomas, 23
MacKay, M. A., 41n32
Maimonides, 12n6, 74n87
Manier, David, 26n48
Marteinson, John, 83n3
Marx, Karl, 21–24, 27
Maus, Marcel, 67n57
Maybaum, Ignaz, 145
Mayer, Arno J., 125n11
McClymond, Kathryn, 67n57

McCrae, John, 65–66, 69n62, 98
McGarry, Michael B., 129n28
Meyers, Carol, 4n15, 13n7
Michaeli, Rosie (character), 143n3, 158–60, 164–66, 168
Michaels, Anne, vi, 141–43, 152–55, 163–65, 167–68
Miles, Jack, 156n53
Miller, Alice, 149
Misztal, Barbara A., 25n47
Mitchell, Bruce, 23n36
Moltmann, Jürgen, 127–29, 130n29, 157
Montgomery, L. M. (Lucy Maud), 7, 49, 52–76, 80, 82–83, 85n8, 87, 88n17, 101n30, 143n3, 158–59
Moore, Anthony (character), 158–60, 165–66
Moore, Leslie (character), 63–64, 159
Moore, Patrick (character), 159–60, 165
Moore, Vera (character), 159, 164–66
Morgan, Michael L., 145n11
Morton, Desmond, 70n69, 88n18, 101n30
Moses (biblical character), 12, 24n40, 27
Motyer, Stephen, 132n36

Nagy, Gregory, 14n9, 19n28
Nahmanides, 15n14
Naomi (character), 154–55, 165–66, 168
Napoleon, 22–23
Nelson, F. Burton, 125n13
Nelson, Richard D., 4n15, 13n7
Niditch, Susan, 4–6
Nietzsche, Friedrich, 21–23, 27
Nora, Pierre, 28–30
Novak, David, 142n2

Index

O'Brien, Joan V., 36, 38
O'Sullivan, Eamon, 100–109
Olick, Jeffrey K., 25n47
Osborne, H. C., 87n13, 99n27

Pächter, Henry Maximilian, 125n12
Parfit, Derek, 20n32
Park, J. Edgar, 13n7
Parker, Pierson, 13n7
Patterson, Cynthia B., 33n3, 35–36, 39n28, 40n32
Pericles, 36n16
Perry, Joseph, 138, 139n63
Phillips, D. Z., 134–35
Pieren, Kathrin, 119n2, 120n4
Pippin, Tina, 132n36
Plaskow, Judith, 19n28, 130n32, 161n70
Plato, 19–20
Polynices (character), ix, 7, 33, 35n14, 37–43, 75
Potok, Chaim, 158n64
Pritchett, W. Kendrick, 34n7
Propp, William H., 13n7

Raphael, Melissa, 8, 143, 147n18, 155–57, 161–62
Rashi, 14n8, 17, 18n23, 19
Ravel, Edeet, 142–43, 157–60, 163–66, 168–69
Rehm, Rush, 38n24
Retallack, James N., 125n9
Reuber, Kurt, 138–39
Ricoeur, Paul, 2–3, 20n32, 28–29
Rike, Jennifer L., 148n21
Rittner, Carol, 129n27, 130n28
Robinson, Fred C., 23n36
Rodin, 90n22
Rogerson, John W., 12n7
Roos, Lena, 15n13
Rosenfeld, David G., 29n58
Rossington, Michael, 20–23
Roth, John K., 129n27, 130n28, 133–37, 144, 152, 162

Rubenstein, Richard, 144–47
Ruether, Rosemary Radford, 130–33, 142
Rylaarsdam, J. Coert, 13n7

Sagi, Avi, 17
Sancton, Andrew, 158n61
Saul (biblical character), 5, 12n5
Sawyer, Deborah F., 132n36
Scarry, Elaine, 5–6, 36n17, 43
Schechter, Franz, 125
Schechtman, Marya, 2n2, 20–21
Schlesinger, Alfred C., 41n33
Schneider, Rolf, 119n1, 121n5
Schwartz, Bill, 23–24
Shapira, Kalonymos Kalmish, 17–18, 30
Shipley, Robert, 90n22
Shires, Henry H., 13n7
Sieverts, Thomas, 126n18, 127n19
Sinder, Amy, 164n80
Smiga, George M., 130n33
Soelle, Dorothee, 128,
Soloveitchik, Joseph, 145n11
Sophocles, ix, 32–43, 100, 104
Sourvinou-Inwood, Christiane, 105n47
Stalker, David, 13n7
Stead, J. C., 53n7
Steiner, George, 32, 35n14, 38n25, 39n26, 40n31
Swales, Martin, 125n12

Tanner, Kathryn, 19n27
Taylor, Miriam S., 131n36
Thucydides, 34, 36n16
Tippett, Maria, 85n9
Toher, Mark, 34n7
Torczyner, Jim L., 158n59
Troeltsch, Ernst, 132n36
Tyrrell, William Blake, 34n6, 35–36, 37n20, 38n24, 39n28, 40n31, 43n38

Index

Urquhart, Jane, 7, 32, 47, 49, 82, 100–109, 111–14

Vance, Jonathan F., 51–52, 60n36, 62–64, 66n56, 69, 71n73, 72, 73n82, 75, 76n96, 78n104, 83–84, 85n9, 86n11
Ventre, André, 83, 84n6, 85–86, 87n13
Volf, Miroslav, 25n47, 29n58, 135n50, 136n50

Walzer, Michael, 7n24
Ward, Janet, 126n15
Ware, Fabian, 48–49, 51, 52n4, 74–76
Watson, Janet S. K., 53n7, 87
Wegener, Gerrit, 127n19, 138n60
Wheeler, Michael, 51n2, 52, 62
Whitehead, Anne, 20–23
Wiesel, Eli, 127–28, 129n26
Wildman, Wesley J., 132n36
Wilhelm I, 125
Wilhem II, 125
Wilkinson, Alan, 51–52, 55, 62, 76, 78n102
Williamson, Clark M., 132n36
Wilson, Woodrow, 65
Winter, Jay, 29n58
Wright, Diana [née Barry] (character), 143n3, 158, 168
Wright, G. Ernest, 4n15
Wyschogrod, Michael, 146

Yates, Frances, 20
Yates, Nigel, 77n99
Yerushalmi, Yosef Hayim, 19n28, 29–30

www.ingramcontent.com/pod-product-compliance
Lightning Source LLC
Chambersburg PA
CBHW051738230426
43670CB00012B/2065